Merrill

Physics

*Principles
and Problems*

AUTHOR

Craig Kramer
Physics Teacher
Bexley High School
Bexley, Ohio

GLENCOE
McGraw-Hill

New York, New York   Columbus, Ohio   Mission Hills, California   Peoria, Illinois

A Glencoe/McGraw-Hill Program

Merrill Physics: Principles & Problems

Student Edition
Teacher Wraparound Edition
Problems and Solutions Manual
Teacher Resource Package
Transparency Package
Laboratory Manual:
  Student and Teacher Editions

Study Guide, Student Edition
Lesson Plan Booklet
English/Spanish Glossary
Computer Test Bank

Contents

ISBN 0-02-826725-7

Send all inquiries to: **GLENCOE DIVISION, Macmillan/McGraw-Hill**
936 Eastwind Drive
Westerville, Ohio 43081

Printed in the United States of America.

3 4 5 6 7 8 9 10 11 12   POH   05 04 03 02 01 00 99 98 97 96

To the Teacher

The *Laboratory Manual* presents a learner-centered, classroom-tested, flexible laboratory program that emphasizes the processes of science, the concepts of physics, and the attitudinal objectives of students. Students experience the principles of physics in action using the laboratory as the setting. The experiments are designed to promote enthusiasm for science via laboratory activities from which learners gain successful and observable results. The *Laboratory Manual* involves the non-science-oriented student and helps this student build a wide range of skills and favorable attitudes toward science. Students work in a cooperative learning situation as a lab team to collect data and discuss observations for analysis.

The skills of communicating experimental results to others through a laboratory report are developed as the student uses the report sheets that accompany each experiment. All experiments give definite results if the student uses reasonable care. The student is expected to achieve only the precision that the equipment and methods dictate. That is, the student is not expected to achieve precise solutions to difficult laboratory problems. Simple apparatus required for experiments is common to nearly all school physics laboratories. A list of the equipment and materials needed for 24 students for a full year is included below.

Teacher notes are printed in the front of the teacher's edition of the *Laboratory Manual* for easy reference. These include science process skills, alternative materials, teaching suggestions, troubleshooting, and sample observations and data. Suggestions for modification of apparatus to suit individual laboratory situations are provided in many investigations. Complete answers and sample data are furnished for each experiment. Suggestions are given for evaluating student data and for determining the degree of precision to expect in student analysis of data. Sample graphs are provided for all data that students are required to plot.

The *Laboratory Manual* was written to accompany Merrill *Physics: Principles & Problems.** However, it is well suited for use with any current physics text. The 52 experiments allow for a wide range of choice in selecting those activities best suited to individual class or student needs.

The lab program is interactive with the Lab Partner™ graphing program available for IBM- or Apple II-compatible computers. Data can be easily plotted using the Lab Partner™ Program.

Materials List for Physics *Laboratory Manual*

Quantity needed for 12 lab stations or 24 students

Item	Quantity	Used in Experiment(s)	Item	Quantity	Used in Experiment(s)
acrylic rod	12	20.1	beaker, 100 mL	12	1.1, 2.2, 25.2
alpha source	1	31.1	beaker, 150 mL	12	1.1
aluminum sheet, 5 cm × 5 cm	10	31.1	beaker, 250 mL	24	2.2, 12.1
ammeter, 0–1.0 mA DC	12	21.1	beaker, 500 mL	12	13.1
ammeter, 0–50 mA or 0–100 mA	12	22.1, 23.1, 23.2, 27.1, 29.1	beta source	1	30.1, 31.1
			bicycle air pump	1	19.2
			board, cork	12	17.1
ammeter, 0–5 A	24	22.2, 24.2, 24.3, 26.1	board, flat	12	5.2, 7.1, 11.1
			breadboard	12	29.2
ammeter (microammeter), 0–100 µA	12	27.2	capacitor, 1000 µF	12	21.1
			carbon discs, recording timer	12	2.3, 3.1, 4.1, 4.2, 5.1
apparatus for a collision in 2 dimensions	12	9.1	carbonated water, 100 mL	12	1.1
			cardboard, 8½ in × 11 in	12	24.2
balance	1	5.1, 12.1, 22.2, 24.3	cardboard sheet, 5 cm × 5 cm	10	31.1
battery, 1.5 V, C size	24	27.1, 29.1	cart, laboratory	12	4.1, 5.1
battery, 9 V	12	29.2	clamp, C	24	2.3, 3.1, 4.1, 4.2, 5.1, 9.1
battery clip, 9 V	12	29.2			
battery holder, C size	24	27.1, 29.1	clamp, meter stick	36	10.2

Physics: Principles & Problems, Zitzewitz and Keff. Glencoe Division of Macmillian/McGraw Hill Publishing Company.

Item	Quantity	Used in Experiment(s)
clamp, ringstand	24	7.2, 24.2, 25.2
clock	1	1.1, 19.2
compass, small magnetic	12	24.1, 24.2
computer, Apple II or IBM	1	4.2
constant-velocity vehicle	12	3.1
correction fluid, white, bottle	1	15.1
cross support, with rings or hooks	12	6.1
cup, paper	12	7.2
cup, polystyrene	12	12.1, 13.1, 22.2
current balance	12	24.3
diffraction grating	12	16.1
diode, 1N4004	12	29.1
dish, semi-circular plastic	1	16.1
dowel rod, 30 cm long × 2 cm diam	12	14.1
dowel rods, various diameters	36	26.1
electric model race car set	1	6.2
electronic timer with photogates	12	6.2, 7.2
electroscope, vane or leaf	12	20.1
eye dropper	12	14.1
fiber optic rod or sculpture	1	16.1
film, double slit	12	16.1, 19.1
film, single slit	12	16.1
filter material, red, orange, green, blue, yellow, violet	12	16.1, 19.1, 27.2
flashlight	1	16.1
force table	12	6.1
galvanometer, with centered zero	12	25.1, 25.2
gamma source	1	30.1, 31.1
Geiger counter or scaler	1	30.1, 31.1
glass plate, flat	12	14.1, 16.2, 17.1, 17.2
glass rod	12	20.1
gloves, heat	12	2.2
goggles, safety	24	2.2, 12.1
graduated cylinder, 10 mL	24	2.2
graph paper	48	3.1, 4.1, 4.2
graph paper, polar	24	8.1
gyroscopic bicycle wheel	12	9.2
helping hand project holder	1	19.2
holders, for light, mirror, screen	12	18.1, 18.2
hologram, reflection	1	16.1
hologram, transmission	1	16.1
holographic film	12	19.2
holographic film developer kit	1	19.2
hot plate, electric	12	2.2, 12.1
Iceland spar crystal	12	16.1, 16.2
index card, 5 in × 7 in	24	19.1, 19.2
inner tube, automobile	1	19.2
integrated circuits (CMOS) 4081, 4071, 4001, 4011	12	29.2
iron filings, bottle	1	24.1, 24.2
iron nail	12	24.1, 24.2
kaleidoscope	1	16.1
knife switch	24	21.1, 22.1, 23.1, 23.2, 24.2, 24.3, 27.1, 29.1
laser, He-Ne	1	16.1, 17.1, 18.2, 19.1, 19.2
lead sheet, 5 cm × 5 cm	10	31.1
lens, concave	12	16.1, 18.2
lens, convex	12	16.1, 18.2
Leydon jar	12	20.1
light bulb, 40 W, clear filament with socket and cord	12	16.1, 16.2, 19.1, 27.2, 28.1
light ray box	4	16.1
light source, for lens/mirrors	12	18.1, 18.2
light source, for ripple tank	12	14.1, 14.2
light-emitting diode (LED)— red, green, yellow	12	27.1, 29.2
liquid crystal display, calculator	1	16.1
lodestone	12	24.1
magnet, bar	24	24.1, 25.1
magnet, disk	12	19.2
magnet, horseshoe	24	25.2
magnifier, with scale	12	19.1
mass, 100 g, hooked	12	13.1
mass, 500 g, hooked	12	4.1, 6.1, 10.2, 13.1, 16.1
mass, 1 kg	12	4.2, 5.1
mass, 3 kg	24	9.2
mass of electron apparatus	12	26.1
mass set, hooked	12	10.1
mass set, small masses	12	5.1
metal strip (parabola)	12	14.1
meter stick	24	2.1, 4.2, 5.1, 7.2, 9.1, 10.1, 10.2, 14.1, 14.2, 15.2, 18.1, 18.2, 19.1, 24.2, 30.1
meter stick support	24	18.1, 18.2
metric ruler, grooved	24	1.1, 3.1, 6.1, 7.1, 8.1, 11.1, 14.2, 16.2, 17.1, 17.2, 18.1, 18.2, 19.1
mirror, concave	12	8.1, 19.2
mirror, convex	12	18.1
mirror, plane surface (flat and thick)	12	16.2
mirror, plane surface (flat and thin)	12	16.1, 16.2, 17.1, 17.2
Newton's color disc	1	16.1
Newton's rings apparatus	1	16.1
open pipe tube, adjustable	12	15.2
optic mirage apparatus	1	16.1
oscilloscope	1	29.1
paint brush	1	16.1
paints, red, blue, green, yellow	1	16.1
paper, black	12	19.2
paper, carbon	48	7.1, 9.1
paper, colored (various)	5	16.1
paper, lined	12	7.1
paper, plain white	48	6.1, 14.1, 14.2, 16.1, 17.1, 17.2, 24.1, 24.2
paper, tracing	48	9.1
paper clips, steel, box	1	24.2
paper towel	12	13.1

Item	Quantity	Used in Experiment(s)	Item	Quantity	Used in Experiment(s)
PASCO free fall adapter	1	4.2	spectrum-tube power supply	1	28.1
PASCO game port interface	1	4.2	spoon, plastic	12	1.1
PASCO precision timer software	1	4.2	spotlight	1	16.1
photoelectric effect module, with amplifier	12	27.2	spring scale, 5-N capacity or greater	36	5.2, 6.1, 10.1, 10.2, 11.1, 13.1
pins, straight	24	17.1	stand, for Geiger-Mueller tube	1	31.1
pith ball	12	20.1			
plastic (clear) box or sculpture	12	16.1, 16.2	steel ball	24	7.1, 7.2, 9.1
plastic tray, 4 in × 4 in	3	19.2	steel plate, 12 in × 12 in	1	19.2
polarizing filter	24	16.1, 16.2	stool, rotating	12	9.2
potentiometer, 1000 Ω	12	27.1, 29.1	stopwatch	12	2.2, 2.3, 7.2, 14.2, 19.2, 21.1, 22.2, 30.1, 31.1
power supply, 0–15 VDC	12	14.1, 14.2, 21.1, 22.1, 22.2, 23.1, 23.2, 24.3, 29.1			
			string, various lengths	12	4.1, 5.1, 5.2, 6.1, 7.2, 9.1, 10.1, 11.1, 12.1, 24.3
power supply, 0–5 A	24	24.2, 24.3, 26.1			
power supply, 90–250 VDC	12	26.1	strobe light	1	2.3, 16.1
power supply, 6 VAC	12	29.1	stroboscope, hand	12	14.2
projector, slide	4	16.1	tape, masking	12	3.1, 4.1, 4.2, 5.1, 5.2, 7.1, 7.2, 9.1, 10.2, 14.2, 15.1 18.1, 19.1, 24.2, 25.2, 30.1
protractor	12	5.2, 6.1, 9.1, 14.1, 16.2, 17.1, 17.2			
pulley, double mounted	24	10.1			
pulley, single mounted	24	4.1, 5.1, 10.1			
pulley support	12	10.1			
radio, portable, with earphones	12	15.1	thermal mitt	1	28.1
			thermometer, −10–110°C	48	2.2, 12.1, 15.2, 22.2
raisins	48	1.1			
recording timer	12	2.3, 3.1, 4.1, 4.2, 5.1	thumbtacks	48	17.1
			timer tape, roll	12	2.3, 3.1, 4.1, 4.2, 5.1
reflector, bicycle or light	1	16.1			
resistor, 10 Ω	12	29.1	tongs, beaker	12	2.2
resistor, 22 Ω	12	27.1	tongs, plastic	1	19.2
resistor, 1000 Ω	12	29.1	tube, cardboard	12	25.2
resistor, 10 kΩ	12	21.1	tuning fork hammer	12	15.2
resistor, 27 kΩ	12	21.1	tuning forks, various frequencies	24	15.2
resistors, 100 Ω, 150 Ω, 220 Ω, 0.5-W rating	12	22.1			
resistors, 68 Ω, 82 Ω, 100 Ω, 0.5-W rating	12	23.1	tweezers	12	30.1, 31.1
			U channel, 50 cm or longer	24	7.2
resistors, 180 Ω, 220 Ω, 330 Ω, 0.5-W rating	12	23.2, 29.2	voltmeter, 0–5 VDC or 0–15 VDC	12	21.1, 22.1, 22.2, 23.1, 23.2, 27.1, 27.2, 29.1
rheostat	12	22.2			
ringstand	24	4.2, 6.1, 7.2, 24.2, 25.2			
			voltmeter, 0–250 VDC	12	26.1
ripple tank	12	14.1, 14.2	washer	96	7.2, 9.1, 14.1
rubber bands, assorted sizes	48	16.1, 17.1, 19.1	wave generator, 2-point source	12	14.1, 14.2
rubber gloves, pair	1	19.2			
rubber rod	12	20.1	wire, coil-1-, 25-, 100-turn	12	25.1
safe light, green	1	19.2	wire, connecting, 8 pieces	12	21.1, 22.1, 22.2, 23.1, 23.2, 24.3, 25.1, 25.2, 26.1, 27.1, 29.1, 29.2
sandpaper, fine 2 cm × 2 cm	12	24.3, 25.2			
screen, paper or cardboard	12	16.1, 18.1, 18.2			
silicon spray, can	1	11.1			
silk pad	12	20.1			
solenoid, air core	12	24.3, 26.1	wire, #14-18, 1.5 m	12	24.2
sound level meter	1	15.1	wire, #22-28 magnet, 60 m	12	25.2
specific heat set	12	12.1	wire, with alligator clips	12	20.1
spectroscope	12	16.1, 28.1	wood block	12	2.1, 7.1, 17.1
spectrum tubes—argon, bromine, chlorine, hydrogen, helium, krypton, mercury vapor, neon, nitrogen, xenon, oxygen, carbon dioxide	1	28.1	wood block, with hook at one end	12	11.1
			wood (or paraffin) block	36	14.1
			wool pad	12	20.1

1.1 Bubble Up

Process Skills

observing, interpreting data, predicting, hypothesizing, controlling variables, designing experiments, measuring, communicating, questioning

Teaching Suggestions

1. Soak the raisins overnight, or about 12–15 hours, so that their density is nearly that of water.
2. Have students work in teams of two. Although this activity involves simple procedures, you want to encourage cooperation, collaboration, and communication.
3. Students could test popular brands of carbonated water or soft drinks to see how raisin motion compares in different liquids.
4. Do not provide students with an explanation for why the raisins move up and down. Leave the explanation open ended. As with many scientific phenomena, a complete explanation may not be known. Instead, lead a discussion on which hypothesis seems most correct and why.
5. This is an excellent and simple activity that you can encourage students to do at home to involve their parents.

Observations and Data

Table 1 (Sample data are given.)

Material	Observations
Carbonated water	Clear or colorless; bubbles rising; bubbles coming out of solution; bubbles on bottom of beaker
Soaked raisin	Brown; plumped up; still has wrinkles; mushy; 14 mm–18 mm range in length; 9 mm–12 mm in diameter
Dry raisin	Slightly smaller, more wrinkled and oblong shaped, and not mushy compared to soaked raisins; 12–14 mm in length; 8–12 mm in width.

Table 2 (Sample data are given.)

Observations of Soaked Raisin in Carbonated Water:

Student answers will vary. Small bubbles will accumulate on the surface of the soaked raisin. Some of the bubbles gradually grow in size. The raisins roll around on the bottom of the beaker. After a short time, the raisins rise to the surface. Bubbles are released from the raisin where it surfaces, and the raisin then sinks. The raisin continues to sink and surface every 15–25 seconds, depending on the amount of carbonation in the water.

Analysis

1. those relating to the raisin's appearance
2. those of bubbles attaching to and coming off the raisin and of the rate of sinking and rising
3. Students may have a variety of hypotheses, some of which may not relate to their data. One example of a hypothesis might be the following: the bubbles (carbon dioxide) come from solution and accumulate on the raisin until the density of the raisin has been reduced enough to cause it to float. The raisin then rises to the surface of the liquid.
4. Student hypotheses and experiments will vary. You may wish to let students try a number of approaches, even if they are totally unrelated (e.g., vary the intensity of light used to make observations). Two conditions are necessary to cause the motion of the raisin: soaking and carbonation. To prove this, students will have to manipulate one condition (variable) at a time. You may prefer to guide students in this direction for their investigation of the cause.

Students should develop an experiment to determine if it is the carbonated water that causes the raisin to rise and sink. The tap water can be used as a variable in this investigation. Students should also consider the soaking of the raisin and its effect. This variable can be checked by using a dry raisin, which in carbonated water will sink to the bottom and stay there. Students should manipulate only one variable at a time in their experiments. For example, the effect of tap water, carbonated water, or a mixture of the two should be varied while using only soaked raisins. Next, students can manipulate the type of raisin while keeping the type of liquid constant.

One possible explanation for the observation that soaked raisins float in carbonated water, but not in tap water, could be offered. The density of the soaked raisin is very nearly that of water. It is slightly denser than water until carbon dioxide bubbles accumulate on its surface. The bubbles cause the soaked raisin to become less dense, and it rises.

5. Student answers will vary. Some students will find that their results did not support their original hypothesis. You might encourage them to state a new hypothesis based on their observations. This is a good time to emphasize the importance of developing good investigative skills. The ability to ask the right questions, organize thoughts, make careful and multiple observations, relate data to the problem, and apply the new knowledge is essential, not only to those in scientific fields, but also to everyone in all walks of life. Discrepancies between a hypothesis and experimental outcomes can inspire improvements in technique or alterations in thought.

Application

The overall density of most people is slightly less than that of water, so they float. When people exhale, they become, in effect, more dense. Since they now displace less water, they sink. Each person has a unique body structure and composition, with varying amounts of bone mass, fat, and muscle. This individuality accounts for differences in body density and in the ability to stay above water. Those who are just barely able to float will readily sink after they exhale.

TEACHER NOTES

2.1 Measuring Length

Process Skills

observing, measuring, communicating, inferring, defining operationally

Alternative Materials

A large object such as a table or even the dimensions of the classroom can be substituted for either the wood block or the laboratory manual.

Teaching Suggestions

1. Select several "identical" objects, such as chalk-board erasers, textbooks, and pieces of chalk, and give them to different laboratory groups to measure. Compare each group's results to help stimulate a discussion on precision and accuracy. The point you want to emphasize is that researchers must develop a certain level of confidence in the data derived from experimentation. Careful measuring techniques help in attaining accuracy.

2. Caution students about significant digits. Help them understand that when they perform any mathematical operation with measurements, the end product cannot be more precise (or have more significant digits) than the initial measurements. Students often claim accuracy to more places than they should, simply as a result of the multiplication or division processes.

Observations and Data

Table 1 (Sample data are given.)

	Length (cm)	Width (cm)	Height (cm)	Volume (cm³)
Wood block	11.04	3.00	3.74	124
Laboratory manual				

Table 2 (Sample data are given.)

Number of pages	Total thickness (mm)	Average thickness of a single page (mm)
1	0.1	—
50	4.5	0.09
75	7.0	0.093
100	9.0	0.09

Analysis

1. The ends may be worn or damaged, so that increments are missing.

2. the estimate of one page; The uncertainty is large when measuring the thickness of a single piece of paper.

3. The most accurate value will be the one derived from the measurement of 100 pages. Since the uncertainty in measuring is the same for all of the measurements, any measurement errors are divided by 100 for this 100-page thickness.

Application

In order for a picture frame to look good and function properly, the corners must be square. If the measuring instrument does not produce precise angles, then the frame pieces will not align properly, even if they are cut and assembled by a skillful craftsperson.

TEACHER NOTES 2.2 : Measuring Temperature

Process Skills

observing, classifying, communicating, interpreting data, measuring, hypothesizing, questioning, controlling variables, designing experiments

Alternative Materials

If necessary, small flasks or beakers can be substituted for the graduated cylinders.

Teaching Suggestions

1. The purpose of this experiment is to demonstrate how the acts of observation and measurement may affect results. These effects can be minimized by preparation, comprehension, and skill. Remind students that *before an experiment is conducted* they should read the entire lab, ask questions if there is any confusion or misunderstanding, assemble all materials *before* they begin the procedure, follow directions exactly, and record observations immediately.
2. This experiment is a good way to introduce the topic of accuracy and sources of error in laboratory experiments. Typically, in any experiment, there are a variety of reasons for error. Individually, they may not have a great impact, but collectively they have a significant effect on results. In this experiment, those reasons might include the loss of heat during pouring, the shape of the glass container that regulates the surface area of water exposed to glassware, differences in the temperature of glassware articles, contaminants in the glassware, and inconsistent techniques.

3. Students who have studied chemistry may recall that their experiments often had a small amount of error. Their physics experimental results may have 20 or 30 (or more) percent error. Introduce precision within this discussion of error.

Observations and Data

Table 1 (Sample data are given.)

Time (minutes)	Temperature (°C)		
	80-mL Sample	5-mL Sample	1-mL Sample
0.5	54	44	42
1.0	54	44	41
1.5	53	42.5	40
2.0	53	42	39
2.5	53	41.5	38
3.0	52	41	37

The temperature readings will rise during the first 10–20 seconds and then stabilize (for a short while) before beginning to drop.

Analysis

1. The final temperatures of the two small samples were cooler than that of the large one.
2. Student answers will vary. Some students may reason that the small samples of water have less total heat; therefore, the temperature in these samples falls rapidly within the time period because this small amount of heat is readily transferred to the apparatus.
3. Assume that the constants are the time intervals and the temperature of the air and glassware (room temperature) and that of the hot water (65°C). The experimental variables are the amounts of hot water and the sizes of the water containers.
4. Use three graduated cylinders of the same size instead of two graduated cylinders and one beaker.
5. Heat energy is transferred to or from a thermometer when it measures the temperature of the medium that surrounds its bulb. In the process of measuring the temperature of the water, heat was transferred from the water to the bulb, and the temperature of each sample fell. The smaller the quantity of water, the more the water temperature was lowered by the thermometer.

6. All systems are disturbed when they are observed and measured. The goal is to design and conduct an experiment such that the act of observing has a minimal effect on results.

Application

The moving vehicle is so massive and large in comparison to the radar waves that any disturbance to the vehicle's speed is negligible.

Extension

Student designs will vary, but should provide a statement that clearly expresses their expectations of the results and includes necessary controls to isolate the causative agent(s) of change and appropriate safeguards against accident and injury. One such design could be the following: Fill a 1-L reservoir beaker with warm tap water. Measure the temperature of this water and record it. Pour water from the reservoir into five separate beakers, varying in size from 50 mL to 250 mL, in 50-mL size increments. Measure the temperature of the water in all beakers for two minutes and compare the final temperatures of each beaker to that of the 250 mL of water remaining in the reservoir. If the temperature of a sample matches that of the reservoir, then that sample size is the minimum amount of water needed for the thermometer to produce accurate results. Students may want to try hotter or colder water to test the results from the experiment with warm tap water in a room temperature environment.

TEACHER NOTES

2.3 Measuring Time

Process Skills

observing, using numbers, communicating, interpreting data, measuring, controlling variables

Troubleshooting

Carbon discs often do not make marks when the timer is operating. Causes include a worn patch on the carbon disc where the striker hits, carbon discs installed upside down, improper adjustment of the vibrating arm, and failure to remove the protective tissue facing the carbon side of the disc.

Teaching Suggestions

1. Science Kit offers an economical timer that operates from the standard 120 V, 60 Hertz AC. It always vibrates at the line frequency of 60 Hertz so that the period of the timer is known to be 1/60 of a second. A more expensive spark timer that has switchable 60 Hertz and 10 Hertz spark rates is available from several other suppliers. The spark produces consistent, excellent results, but requires more expensive electrostatic recording paper. However, these types of timers eliminate the need for dry cells or power supplies.

2. If you are using a recording timer that requires a dry cell or power supply, the frequency will vary if the voltage varies. Different power sources may cause student results to be somewhat inconsistent. Divergent results could stimulate a discussion about the reliability of each power source and could introduce the necessity of constant voltage for sensitive machinery. Students may already know that some computers can be disabled or damaged by fluctuations in voltage.

3. An extension of this experiment is to determine the frequency of a timer operated with a dry cell or power source at different voltages. Connect a voltmeter in parallel with the recording timer, turn on the power source, and shine a strobe light on the vibrating arm. Adjust the flash rate to match that of the timer arm. The value of the strobe light flash rate is the same as the frequency of the recording timer. Record the voltage and the frequency for this trial. Try several different voltages. Find the frequency for each voltage, and construct a graph of frequency (y-axis) versus voltage (x-axis). If the voltage is known, the frequency of the recording timer can be found on the line that connects the experimental points on the graph.

4. Give students time to practice using the recording timer. There are several sources of mechanical error: the tape often sticks in the timer and the carbon paper or the vibrating arm may need adjusting to work properly.

Observations and Data

Table 1 (Sample data are given.)

	Data			Calculations	
Trial	Time (s)	Number of dots	Voltage	Frequency (vibrations/s)	Period (s)
1	3.10	190		61.3	0.0163
2	2.94	181		61.6	0.0162
3	3.21	201		62.6	0.0159
4					

Average frequency ___61.8 vibrations/s___

Average period ___0.0162 s___

Flash rate of strobe or known
vibration rate of timer ___60.0 vibrations/s___

Analysis

1. Yes. When the measured times and number of dots are greater, the effect of errors is diminished. The largest source of error is in starting and stopping the timer and stopwatch. Increasing the length of time between starting and stopping will reduce the significance of error.
2. Student answers will vary. Explanations should recognize the sources of error.
3. Relative error

$$= \frac{\text{experimental result} - \text{accepted value}}{\text{accepted value}} \times 100\%$$

$$= \frac{61.8 - 60.0}{60.0} \times 100\%$$

$$= 3\%$$

Student values should be within 15% of the accepted value.

Application

The National Bureau of Standards needs an accurate reference source to define measurements. Scientists attempting to reproduce experimental results where time is used as a reference need standardized units of measurement. A sensitive measuring device that can measure the distance light travels in a fraction of a second provides one such accurate reference source.

Process Skills

observing, measuring, using numbers, communicating, interpreting data, questioning, defining operationally, controlling variables

Alternative Materials

The recording timer can be replaced by an instant-developing camera, using ASA 3000 film, triggered by a shutter release cable. Install an electronic blinky (a flashing light set to flash at regular intervals) on the constant velocity vehicle. An air track car may be substituted for the constant velocity vehicle. Place a photographic meter stick behind the vehicle. Put the camera on a tripod and, in a darkened room, open the shutter with the cable. Turn on the blinky and the vehicle and allow the vehicle to move across the field of view. Turn on the room lights for about five seconds to expose the meter stick, and then close the camera lens by releasing the shutter cable. Develop the photograph. A series of bright dots (the blinky) should appear across the photograph. The moving vehicle will not be visible. Measurements can be taken of the dots using the photographic meter stick.

Teaching Suggestions

1. Be sure students understand that one interval of time is counted as five smaller spaces on the tape. The larger interval is used because the vehicle usually travels at a slow speed, resulting in dots that are close together.
2. Draw a diagram of a typical tape on the chalkboard. Show that five spaces on the tape represent an interval of time and also the distance traveled by the vehicle during this interval of time. This distance divided by one interval of time is the velocity of the vehicle in cm/interval. Dividing by one changes nothing; therefore, the distance traveled through five spaces on the tape is numerically the same as the average velocity through the five spaces.
3. The period of changing velocity is quite small compared to an interval of time on the tape.

Therefore, student tapes may not show a distance value that is lower than those representing the uniform velocity. Explain that this does not mean that there was instantaneous velocity at $t = 0$; rather, that the instruments or the techniques were not sensitive enough to be able to record an intermediate value for the period of changing velocity.

Observations and Data
Table 1 (Sample data are given.)

Time (interval)	Displacement (cm)	Average velocity (cm/interval)	Total displacement (cm)
1	2.70	2.70	2.70
2	3.90	3.90	6.60
3	4.05	4.05	10.65
4	4.10	4.10	14.75
5	3.85	3.85	18.60
6	4.00	4.00	22.60
7	4.00	4.00	26.60
8	3.95	3.95	30.55
9	3.95	3.95	34.50
10	3.85	3.85	38.35

Analysis
1. Sample graph: student answers will vary.

Velocity vs Time

2. Two areas are represented on the graph. In the first area of the graph, the velocity is rapidly increasing, as indicated by the upward sloping line. In the second area, the graph flattens out or becomes horizontal, indicating that the vehicle is traveling at a constant or uniform velocity. Student answers for the vehicle's average velocity for the entire trip will vary. Since the period of changing velocity was so brief, the average velocity will likely be close to the value of the uniform velocity.
3. Sample graph: student answers will vary.

Total Displacement vs Time

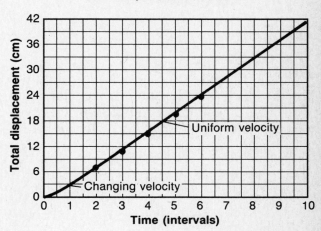

4. Student answers will vary depending on how quickly the vehicle reaches its uniform velocity. The curve at the beginning of the line indicates increasing slope during the period when velocity is increasing. The line then becomes fairly straight when the vehicle moves with constant velocity.
5. The curved portions at the beginning of each graph indicate increasing velocity, while the straight portions of each line indicate constant velocity.
6. The independent variable was time and the dependent variable was displacement.

Extension
1. Student answers will vary. With the sample data given, the average velocity is 0.32 cm/s.
2. a. total displacement
   b. The area under the curve should be within 10% of the total displacement during the interval of time that was measured.
   c. change in velocity

4.1 Accelerated Motion

Process Skills

observing, using numbers, communicating, interpreting data, measuring, questioning, defining operationally

Troubleshooting

The recording timer must make accurate marks. If distinguishable marks do not show up, try replacing the carbon disc. Refer to Teacher Notes 2.3 for other remedies.

Alternative Materials

In place of the recording timer, an electronic blinky can be attached to the cart, and the moving cart can be photographed by using an instant developing camera. The dots can be measured on the developed film. This procedure is discussed in detail in Teacher Notes 3.1.

Teaching Suggestions

1. Prior to the experiment, review with students the three basic graphs of motion (displacement vs. time, velocity vs. time, acceleration vs. time).
2. Students should have completed Experiment 2.3 or 3.1 before performing this experiment.
3. This experiment is easily accomplished because the period of the recording timer is not required. If the period is known, the actual times may be substituted for each interval.
4. The sequence of dots (left to right or right to left) varies with the set-up. Students should make sure they count and mark the intervals in the direction of the movement.

Observations and Data

Table 1 (Sample data are given.)

Time (interval)	Displacement (cm)	Total displacement (cm)
1	1.80	1.80
2	3.50	5.30
3	5.55	10.85
4	6.90	17.75
5	8.95	26.70
6	10.55	37.25
7	12.30	49.55
8		
9		
10		
11		
12		

Table 2 (Sample data are given.)

Time (interval)	Average velocity (cm/interval)	Acceleration ($\Delta v/\Delta t$)
1	1.80	1.80
2	3.50	1.75
3	5.55	1.85
4	6.90	1.73
5	8.95	1.79
6	10.55	1.76
7	12.30	1.76
8		
9		
10		
11		
12		

Analysis

1.

Total Displacement vs Time

2.

Average Velocity vs Time

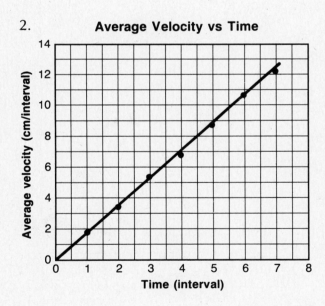

3. The slope of the curve is a parabola. The constantly increasing slope indicates that the cart was traveling greater distances during successive intervals of time.
4. The graph is a straight line passing through the origin. It indicates that the velocity of the cart is increasing at a constant rate.
5. Student answers will vary. The unit for the slope should be cm/interval^2.

6. The graph is a straight line parallel to the *x*-axis. Acceleration is uniform.

Acceleration vs Time

Application

Passengers would experience the same acceleration that exists on Earth. A greater rate of acceleration might cause physical discomfort. If the spacecraft were able to accelerate at that rate for a year, it would be traveling at close to the velocity of light, 3×10^8 m/s.

Extension

1. Student answers will vary. The slopes should be close to the values for average velocity.
2. Student answers will vary. The acceleration of the cart will be less than the acceleration due to gravity since the falling mass is accelerating itself and the cart.

TEACHER NOTES

4.2 Acceleration Due to Gravity

Process Skills

observing, measuring, communicating, using numbers, interpreting data, questioning, controlling variables

Alternative Materials

For Part B, a less expensive and simpler method is to use a PASCO Digital Free Fall apparatus, #ME-9202B, instead of the Apple or IBM computer, game port interface, computer software, and Free Fall Adapter. It is a simple electronic timing device that accurately measures the time required for a steel ball to fall.

Teaching Suggestions

Part A

1. It is important that the mass be stationary before it is dropped to ensure that the initial velocity of the falling mass is zero.
2. Students must not exert any force on the mass by tossing or throwing it to the floor; it must simply be dropped.
3. If student results in Part A have a large relative error, explain that, since the mass falls 1 m or less and the velocity is computed in m/s, even a small error in measurement or technique can have a significant effect.

Observations and Data

Table 1 (Sample data are given.)
Period of recording timer _____0.0167_____ s

Interval	Time (s)	Displacement (m)	Total displacement (m)	Average velocity (m/s)
1	0.017	0.0030	0.0030	0.18
2	0.033	0.0065	0.0095	0.39
3	0.050	0.0090	0.0185	0.54
4	0.067	0.0120	0.0305	0.72
5	0.083	0.0145	0.0450	0.87
6	0.100	0.0170	0.0620	1.02
7	0.117	0.0195	0.0815	1.17
8	0.133	0.0220	0.1035	1.32
9	0.150	0.0250	0.1285	1.50
10	0.167	0.0280	0.1565	1.68
11	0.183	0.0300	0.1865	1.80
12	0.200	0.0330	0.2195	1.98
13	0.217	0.0360	0.2555	2.16
14	0.233	0.0380	0.2935	2.28
15	0.250	0.0410	0.3345	2.46
16	0.267	0.0435	0.3780	2.61
17	0.283	0.0460	0.4240	2.76
18	0.300	0.0490	0.4730	2.94
19	0.317	0.0510	0.5240	3.06
20	0.333	0.0540	0.5780	3.24

Table 2 (Sample data are given.)
Free fall distance _____0.905_____ m

Trial	Time (s)
1	0.4285
2	0.4290
3	0.4288
4	0.4282
5	0.4291
Average	0.4287

g = _9.849_ m/s^2

Table 3 (Sample data are given.)
Free fall distance _____1.900_____ m

Trial	Time (s)
1	0.6226
2	0.6227
3	0.6231
4	0.6222
5	0.6230
Average	0.6227

g = _9.799_ m/s^2

Analysis

Part A

1.

Displacement vs Time

2.

Velocity vs Time

3. The shape of the curve is parabolic. The constantly increasing slope indicates that the mass was traveling greater distances during each successive time interval.
4. The graph is a straight line passing through the origin. It indicates that the velocity of a falling mass increases at a constant rate.
5.

$$\text{slope} = \frac{3.24 \text{ m/s} - 0}{0.333 \text{ s} - 0} = 9.82 \text{ m/s}^2$$

$$\begin{matrix} \text{relative} \\ \text{error} \end{matrix} = \frac{9.82 \text{ m/s}^2 - 9.80 \text{ m/s}^2}{9.80 \text{ m/s}^2} \times 100$$

$$= 0.2\%$$

Part B

1. a.
$$\begin{matrix} \text{relative} \\ \text{error} \end{matrix} = \frac{9.849 \text{ m/s}^2 - 9.80 \text{ m/s}^2}{9.80 \text{ m/s}^2} \times 100\%$$

$$= 0.5\%$$

b.
$$\begin{matrix} \text{relative} \\ \text{error} \end{matrix} = \frac{9.80 \text{ m/s}^2 - 9.799 \text{ m/s}^2}{9.80 \text{ m/s}^2} \times 100\%$$

$$= 0.01\%$$

Student results should have an error of less than 5% for the measurement of g.
2. The uncertainty in measuring the free fall distance, is a smaller percent of the larger distance, so the results for 2 m may be slightly better.
3. Free fall distance was constant. Time was responding.

Application

At higher elevations, the acceleration due to gravity is usually somewhat diminished. A smaller acceleration due to gravity would permit an object, such as the hammer or javelin in the track and field events, to remain in the air slightly longer, yielding a better distance.

TEACHER NOTES

5.1 Newton's Second Law

Process Skills

observing, using numbers, measuring, communicating, interpreting data, questioning, controlling variables

Teaching Suggestions

1. A large-capacity electronic balance (4 kg) will speed the process of determining the mass of the carts and attached tape and string.
2. Be sure that students begin measuring the zero dot as close as possible to the beginning cluster of dots so that the initial velocity is zero.

Observations and Data

Table 1 (Sample data are given.)

	Value
Period of timer (s)	1/60
Mass of laboratory cart (kg)	1.292
Mass needed to equalize friction of cart (kg)	0.015

Table 2 (Sample data are given.)

Trial	Accelerating force (N)	Distance (m)	Number of dots	Time (s)
1	9.80	0.610	33	0.55
2	9.80	0.493	30	0.50
3	9.80	0.550	30	0.50

Table 3 (Sample data are given.)

Trial	Acceleration (m/s²)	Total mass (kg)	$(m)(a)$ (N)
1	4.03	2.308	9.30
2	3.94	2.308	9.09
3	4.40	2.308	10.2

Analysis

1. See Table 2.
2. Trial 1: $a = 2(0.610 \text{ m})/(0.55 \text{ s})^2 = 4.03 \text{ m/s}^2$
   Trial 2: $a = 2(0.493 \text{ m})/(0.50 \text{ s})^2 = 3.94 \text{ m/s}^2$
   Trial 3: $a = 2(0.55 \text{ m})/(0.50 \text{ s})^2 = 4.40 \text{ m/s}^2$
3. less than. The falling mass must move itself plus the cart. Therefore, the force of the falling mass is diminished by that amount of force required to move the cart's mass.
4. total mass = 1.293 kg (cart + string + tape) + 1.000 kg (falling mass) + 0.015 kg (small masses) = 2.308 kg
5. Trial 1: $(2.308 \text{ kg})(4.03 \text{ m/s}^2) = 9.30 \text{ N}$
   Trial 2: $(2.308 \text{ kg})(3.94 \text{ m/s}^2) = 9.09 \text{ N}$
   Trial 3: $(2.308 \text{ kg})(4.40 \text{ m/s}^2) = 10.2 \text{ N}$
6. Error should be less than 20% and, with careful technique, it can be less than 10%. Using the sample data from the three trials, the values for relative error were 5%, 7%, and 4%.
7. $F = mg = (0.015 \text{ kg})(9.8 \text{ m/s}^2) = 0.15 \text{ N}$
8. Frictional forces oppose the force (weight) of the falling mass; the net force is thus reduced by this friction.

Application

The frictional forces acting on an automobile include sliding friction between tires and the road and air resistance to automobile movement. When the frictional forces are equal to the force produced by the engine, the net force is zero. Therefore, there will be no acceleration, and the automobile will travel at a constant velocity.

TEACHER NOTES

5.2 Friction

Process Skills

observing, measuring, using numbers, communicating, interpreting data, predicting, questioning, controlling variables

Teaching Suggestions

1. The large wood blocks used for storage of mass sets are the correct size and weight to use for objects. Chalkboard erasers work well for objects of small mass.

2. Demonstrate another method for determining the coefficient of static friction without using a protractor. The tangent of θ is the ratio of the height of the plane above the horizontal (at which sliding begins) to the length of the plane. Thus

$$\frac{h}{l} = \tan \theta = \mu.$$

Observations and Data

Table 1 (Sample data are given.)

	Description
Object	chalkboard eraser
Surface	cardboard

Table 2 (Sample data are given.)

Weight of object (N)				1.86
	1	2	3	Average
Force of sliding friction (N)				0.39

Table 3 (Sample data are given.)

Motion	Angle (degrees)	$\mu = \tan \theta$
Static	20	0.36
Sliding	13	0.23

Analysis

1. $\mu_{static} = \tan 20° = 0.36$
   $\mu_{sliding} = \tan 13° = 0.23$
2. The coefficient of static friction should be greater. The force needed to overcome the frictional force of an object at rest (static frictional force) is greater than the force needed to keep an object in motion (kinetic frictional force).
3. $\mu = F_{\parallel}/F_{\perp} = 0.39/1.86 = 0.21$
4. They should be the same (or nearly identical). Student explanations for differences will vary.
5. The angles at which the brick begins sliding should be the same regardless of the area of the surfaces in contact. The weight of the brick, $F_{\perp}$, perpendicular to the surface influences the force of friction; the coefficient of static friction is independent of the area of contact.
6. An unwrapped brick begins to slide at an angle greater than that required by a waxed paper-wrapped brick. The waxed paper changes the nature of the surfaces in contact,

essentially acting as a lubricant to reduce the coefficient of static friction, and, thus, the force of friction.

7. The type of surface and the force normal to the surface (perpendicular component of weight) influence the force of friction.

Application

Brand *Y* will give better service since it will have greater traction in wet weather than brand *X*. Both tires have nearly the same coefficient of friction on a dry pavement and, thus, the same amount of traction in dry weather.

Extension

The predicted angle should be very close to the angle at which sliding begins (at a constant speed).

TEACHER NOTES

6.1 Addition of Force Vectors

Process Skills

observing, using numbers, formulating models, classifying, communicating, interpreting data, measuring, predicting, questioning, defining operationally

Troubleshooting

Make sure students check that the scales register zero at no load. Explain how to make zero corrections if the scales are off.

Teaching Suggestions

1. The activity and data collection are easily and quickly performed. Even with a limited number of equipment set-ups, all students should be able to obtain data in a class period if they have previously read and prepared for the experiment.

2. Remind students that the lengths of the vectors are proportional to the forces, not to the lengths of the strings or the spring scales.

Observations and Data

Student drawings will vary, but should be similar to what is shown in Figure 2.

Analysis

1. Student answers will vary.

2. Student answers will vary. Students should have good results, but they will not be perfect. The resultant of $A + B$ should be nearly equal to and opposite C. Relative error should be less than 15%.

3. Student diagrams will vary.

4. The sum of $A + B + C$ is a closed triangle indicating equilibrium. (No net force is exerted on point **P**.)

5. If B is added to C, the resultant should be the negative of the value of A.

6. If C is added to A, the resultant should be the negative of the value of B.

7. The addition of $C + B + A$ should give the same result as the addition of $B + C + A$. The resultant is zero. It might be helpful at this time to remind students that, in vector addition, the order of addition does not affect the final result (commutative law). Also, in the case of two or more vectors, the grouping of vectors as they are added does not affect the final result (associative law).

Application

When a body falls through a fluid such as air, a frictional or drag force acts on it, slowing its downward velocity. As it first begins to fall through the air, its velocity increases, but so does the frictional force acting on it. When the upward frictional force equals the downward force due to gravity, the net force acting on the body becomes zero. At this point, equilibrium is reached, and the body falls at its constant terminal velocity. The frictional force of the air that acts on the skydiver's body, or the body and the parachute, depends on the configuration of the body. When the total surface area of the falling body exposed to the frictional force is increased, the terminal velocity is decreased.

Extension

The results should be the same as those obtained earlier. The sum of $A + B + C$ is zero.

Physics 500

Process Skills

observing, communicating, formulating models, interpreting data, inferring, questioning, controlling variables

Alternative Materials

Speed bumps are available with some race set-ups. Construct substitute speed bumps by attaching small amounts of modeling clay to the track.

Teaching Suggestions

1. Model race car sets are available from a variety of stores, including Radio Shack, hobby stores, and department or discount stores. Most stores will accept a school purchase order if the manager is contacted in advance. Garage sales and students are also excellent sources for used materials.

2. Many of the sets available are compatible with one another. Banked turns, loops, curves from different sources, lane-changing sections, and speed bumps can gradually be added to your collection. Students can make inferences for some of the steps of the procedure even if your layout does not contain all of the race-track features described. For example, if you do not have lane changers, students can make inferences based on their observations of sharp, high-speed turns.

3. In one or two days, the tracks will experience a great deal of wear, and the resulting oxidation. Scrub the tracks each day with a clean pencil eraser to remove this oxidation.

4. If you have an electronic timer with photogates, students' lap times can be measured and recorded. Give award certificates to students with the best times for the inside and outside lanes. When you assemble your track, try to make one of your lanes 500 cm long; thus, this experiment is called the Physics 500.

5. Students may ask numerous questions about the banked turns, curves, and loops and may wonder how forces act on vehicles traveling through them. Their questions can form the base for an introductory discussion of centripetal and centrifugal forces, which are included in the next chapter.

Observations and Data

Outward-banked curve
(a)

Inward-banked curve
(b)

Analysis

1. If the car's brakes are not used, the force of friction, F_f, between the road and the car's tires is the only force that maintains a car's circular motion on a flat curve. Because the car is on a flat surface, $F_W = F_\perp$, and there is no force, $F_\parallel$, from the parallel component of the

vehicle's weight to influence the motion of the car. On an inward-banked curve, the perpendicular force is tilted toward the center of the curvature of the road. The resultant force, $F_{\parallel}$, points radially inward, and the car can travel faster and more easily through the banked curve than it could through a flat curve. If the curve is banked outward, the perpendicular force is tilted away from the center of curvature of the road. $F_{\parallel}$, points radially outward and, if it is greater than F_f, the car may slide off the road, even at a slow rate of speed.

2. The faster the car moves, the harder it is to control the motion of the car.
3. If the car travels too slowly, it will fall out of the loop. Inertia, friction, and the car's weight keep it on the loop.
4. The back end of the car often slides from one side to the other; it is very difficult to control the motion of the car during quick lane changes.
5. At a constant velocity, it is easier to travel through an inward-banked curve than an outward-banked or flat curve. The purpose of an inward-banked curve is to augment the sideways frictional force with a portion of the car's weight, pulling the car toward the center of the curve and making it easier to maintain control of the car as it travels through the curve.

Application

After a cyclist reaches the critical rotational speed, there is no acceleration in the vertical direction. Rather, acceleration is toward the wall of the cylinder or sphere, and the motorcycle does not fall when it is upside down.

Extension

When the car reaches the damp or slippery track, it will skid out of control. The coefficient of friction has been reduced to the point where the car is unable to make the turn. You might point out to students that, since the coefficient of friction is proportional to the square of the velocity, slowing down a little makes a big difference in the ability to maintain control of a vehicle on icy or wet roads.

Projectile Motion

Process Skills

using numbers, observing, formulating models, communicating, interpreting data, measuring, questioning

Alternative Materials

If carbon paper is not available, the steel ball can be coated with tempera paint. Use a cafeteria tray for the incline. When rolled down the incline and across the paper, the steel ball will leave a wide trail, and the tray edge will usually stop the ball.

Teaching Suggestions

1. If students use narrow-ruled notebook paper, they should count every two or three lines as one interval of time. This will give students sufficient space in the table provided to record data from the entire width of the lined paper.
2. Help students understand that the horizontal component of the ball's velocity is constant as it rolls across the inclined board. Since this is true, the lined spaces each represent equal time intervals. While the time in seconds could be determined for each interval, it is not necessary.

Observations and Data

Table 1 (Sample data are given.)

Time interval number	Total vertical distance (m)	Average vertical velocity (cm/interval)
0	0	0
1	0.35	0.35
2	0.80	0.45
3	1.25	0.55
4	1.80	0.55
5	2.35	0.55
6	3.00	0.65
7	3.70	0.70
8	4.45	0.75
9	5.25	0.80

Time interval number	Total vertical distance (m)	Average vertical velocity (cm/interval)
10	6.00	0.75
11	6.80	0.80
12	7.65	0.85
13	8.55	0.90
14	9.50	0.95
15	10.60	1.10
16	11.50	0.90
17	12.60	1.10
18	13.80	1.20
19	14.90	1.10
20	16.20	1.30

4.

Vertical Velocity versus Time Interval

Analysis

1.

Vertical Distance versus Time Interval

2. Since the graph is a parabola, it indicates that the vertical distance traveled by an accelerating object is proportional to the square of the time. The equation,

$$y = v_y t + \tfrac{1}{2}gt^2,$$

in which v_y and g are constants, is the equation of a parabola.
3. The path of the steel ball on the lined paper inscribed half of an arch. In math, this curved line is called a parabola.

5. A change in velocity over a period of time, $\Delta v/\Delta t$, is the definition of acceleration. If this change is uniform or constant, a straight-line graph results. Thus, as a projectile falls to Earth, it is subjected to the uniform acceleration due to gravity, g.
6. Since a projectile is subjected to the uniform acceleration due to gravity, the magnitude of its vertical velocity should increase with time. The data from this experiment show that vertical velocity was increasing as time elapsed.

Application

The bullet will strike the tin can only if it falls off the shelf at the moment the bullet leaves the gun muzzle. If there were no acceleration, or zero gravity, the target would not fall, and the bullet would move along a straight line and strike the can. If the can falls off the shelf, both it and the bullet are accelerated downward by gravity at the same rate. The can will have fallen a vertical distance equal to $\tfrac{1}{2}gt^2$ from the shelf, and the bullet will have fallen the same vertical distance from its starting point when it reaches the line of fall of the target. When the bullet reaches the line of fall, it will be the same distance below the tin can's initial position on the shelf as the tin can, thus it will strike the can. The greater the initial velocity of the bullet, the higher above ground it will hit the tin can. If the tin can does not fall off the shelf, it will not be hit by the bullet.

7.2 Range of a Projectile

Process Skills

observing, measuring, predicting, interpreting data, communicating, questioning, defining operationally

Alternative Materials

Shelving brackets, grooved rulers, or curtain rods can be substituted for the U-channel.

Teaching Suggestions

1. If your laboratory tables are not level, students should use a level to adjust the horizontal sections of track. The leveling assures that there is no initial vertical component of motion.
2. If the steel ball just misses the cup, have students recheck all their measurements and calculations. If the cups are too tall, the ball may hit the edge of the cup. Predictions by students should be within 5% to 10% of the actual distances.

Observations and Data

Table 1 (Sample data are given.)

Trial	Distance (m)	Time (s)
1	0.20	0.153
2	0.20	0.153
3	0.20	0.153
Average	0.20	0.153

Vertical distance, y, = 0.96 m

Analysis

1. $v_x = \Delta d / \Delta t = 0.20$ m/0.153 s = 1.3 m/s
2. $t = [(2)(0.96 \text{ m})/(9.80 \text{ m/s}^2)]^{1/2} = 0.44$ s
3. $x = v_x t = (1.3 \text{ m/s})(0.44 \text{ s}) = 0.57$ m
4. The ball lands in the cup.
5. Yes. The equations used to calculate the horizontal and vertical positions of the ball were based on the premise that the components of motion are independent of each other.
6. The results would probably be different. The displacement of the sponge ball or ping-pong ball will be affected by the significantly large frictional resistance of the air.

Application

$t_{air} = [(2)(6 \text{ m})/(9.80 \text{ m/s}^2)]^{1/2} = 1.1$ s

$x = v_x t = (3.75 \text{ m/s})(1.1 \text{ s}) = 4.1$ m

The diver will land in the water at a point 4.1 m from the edge of the platform.

Extension

1. If $\theta_i = 45°$, $2\theta_i = 90°$ and $\sin 90° = 1$. For all other values of θ_i, $\sin 2\theta_i$ will be less than 1. Student examples will vary. Some possible answers: If $\theta_i = 60°$, $\sin 2\theta_i = 0.8660$; if $\theta_i = 53°$, $\sin 2\theta_i = .9612$; if $\theta_i = 75°$, $\sin 2\theta_i = 0.4999$; and if $\theta_i = 32°$, $\sin 2\theta_i = 0.8829$.

2. $v_i = \dfrac{160\ 000 \text{ m/h}}{3600 \text{ s/h}} = 44.4$ m/s

   $x = \dfrac{(44.4 \text{ m/s})^2}{9.8 \text{ m/s}^2} \times 2(0.8910 \times 0.4540)$

   $x = 162.7$ m

8.1 Kepler's Laws

Process Skills

formulating models, interpreting data, inferring, communicating, questioning, defining operationally

Teaching Suggestions

1. Students should plot data precisely. When plotting radius vectors, they should strive for an error of no more than the width of a sharpened pencil lead. The better the plot, the easier it will be to interpret the result.
2. The eccentricity of an orbit is a measure of the roundness of an orbit. The closer the eccentricity is to zero, the more circular the orbit becomes. The closer the eccentricity is to one, the more oval the ellipse becomes as it approaches a straight line. The eccentricity of an orbit is computed with the following:

$$e = \frac{(\text{longest radius} - \text{shortest radius})}{\text{length of the major axis}}$$

The eccentricity of Mercury's orbit is 0.206 and of Earth's orbit is 0.0167.

Observations and Data

Table 1 is found in the student edition.

Analysis

1. Yes. Mercury's orbit is an ellipse, with the center of the sun at one focus.

The orbit of Mercury.

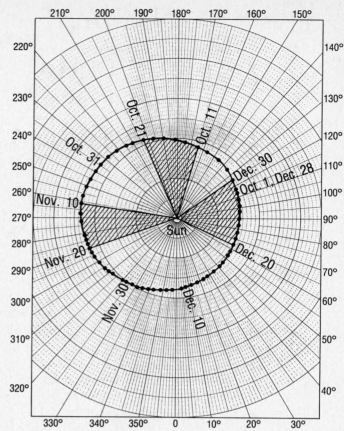

Three areas of the orbit of Mercury.

2. The area for the section of Mercury's orbit between December 20 and December 30 is found with

$$\text{area} = (61°/360°)(\pi)(0.318 \text{ AU})^2$$
$$= 0.054 \text{ AU}^2/10 \text{ days.}$$

3. Student choices for areas may vary. Two choices are the following:
   Oct. 11–21,
$$\text{area} = (38°/360°)(\pi)(0.396 \text{ AU})^2$$
$$= 0.052 \text{ AU}^2/10 \text{ days}$$
   Nov. 10–20,
$$\text{area} = (29°/360°)(\pi)(0.457 \text{ AU})^2$$
$$= 0.053 \text{ AU}^2/10 \text{ days}$$

4. The average area should be about 0.053 AU²/10 days. Students should have errors of less than 5% if their graphs are carefully plotted. Yes, the orbit supports Kepler's law of areas.

5. Average radius = (0.307 AU + 0.467 AU)/ 2
$$= 0.387 \text{ AU}$$

$$\frac{T_M^2}{T_E^2} = \frac{r_M^3}{r_E^3},$$

$$T_M^2 = \frac{(0.387 \text{ AU})^3(365.25 \text{ days})^2}{(1.0 \text{ AU})^3}$$

$$T_M = 88 \text{ days}$$

6. From the graph, the period = 30 days + 30 days + 28 days = 88 days. The values from Questions 5 and 6 for the period of Mercury are the same (88 days). Thus, the results from the graph are consistent with Kepler's law of periods.

Application

$$T_x^2 = \frac{(1.0 \text{ AU})^3(1.0 \text{ yr})^2}{(1.0 \text{ AU})^3} = (1.0 \text{ yr})^2$$

$$T_x = 1.0 \text{ yr}$$

Extension

Figure 3 TE shows the orbit of Mars. Figure 4 TE shows three different areas of the orbit of Mars. The area per day = 0.01 AU²/day. The orbit is an ellipse. Yes, Kepler's law of areas applies.

The orbit of Mars.

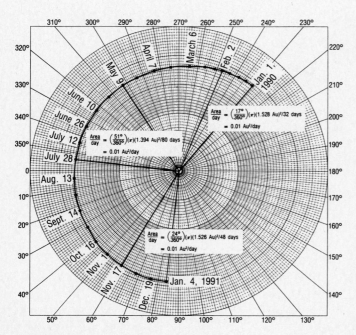

Three areas of the orbit of Mars.

Process Skills

observing, formulating models, interpreting, defining operationally, using numbers, questioning, communicating, measuring

Troubleshooting

If students have trouble making the steel balls land on their paper sheets, lower the starting position of the ball on the incline so that it has a smaller initial velocity.

Teaching Suggestions

1. Use this laboratory investigation only after students are comfortable with the concept of conservation of momentum for a collision in one direction.
2. Remind students that their results may not be perfect, as evidenced by a clustering of the points where the steel balls land. Students will have and should expect some discrepancy between the magnitude and direction of the momentum vector after the collision and those of the momentum vector before the collision.

Observations and Data

Table 1 (Sample data are given.)

Magnitude of Vectors		
$p_{initial}$ (cm)	p_{target} (cm)	$p_{incident}$ (cm)
29.4	23.1	13.4

Analysis

1. $p_{target} + p_{incident}$ = 23.1 cm + 13.4 cm. The sum, 36.5 cm, does not equal $p_{initial}$. These are vector quantities; their sum is the resultant, not the numerical sum of their magnitudes.
2. p_{final} is represented by 27.7 cm.
3. The magnitude of the initial momentum is represented by 29.4 cm while that of the final momentum is represented by 27.7 cm. These values are close. Students should have values that are within 20% of each other.

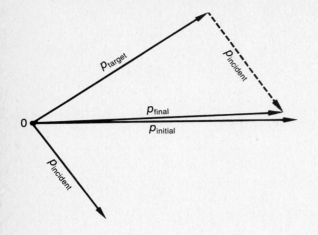

4. The directions of the initial and final momentum vectors are nearly the same. Ideally, the resultant should be equal in magnitude and identical in direction to the initial momentum vector of the incident ball before the collision. Students should realize that their experimental results may not be perfect.

Application

Assuming that the ball is thrown with the same velocity each time, the momentum will be the same. If you let your hands move backwards as you catch the ball, the transfer of momentum will occur over a longer period of time. This extension will relieve the sting your hands feel.

Extension

1. The final momentum of the incident ball and the two target balls will be equal to the initial momentum of the incident ball. The total momentum of a closed, isolated system always remains constant no matter how many objects there are in the system. This relationship is shown by the following:

$$p_a = p'_a + p_b + p_c.$$

2. Mass can be canceled out, and the equation can be recognized as a form of the Pythagorean theorem, $v_a{}^2 = v'_a{}^2 + v_b{}^2$, for a right triangle. Therefore, if this equality holds, the angle between the velocity vectors after the collision must be a right angle.

9.2 Angular Momentum

Process Skills

observing, interpreting data, classifying, communicating, questioning, defining operationally

Alternative Materials

A gyroscope can be substituted for the spinning wheel. However, the results will not be as dramatic for students as when they attempt to cause changes in the angular momentum of the rotating bicycle wheel.

Teaching Suggestions

1. This laboratory activity reinforces the supplemental lesson on rotary motion and angular momentum found in the TRP.
2. If you do not use the TRP lessons on rotational inertia and angular momentum, this experiment can be an enrichment activity after students complete the lessons on conservation of momentum for translational motion.

Observations and Data

1. Observations of student holding masses on spinning stool or platform:

   When the student pulls in his or her arms, the rate of rotation increases. When the arms are extended again, the rate of rotation decreases.
2. Observations of effects of tilting the shaft of a stationary wheel upward:

   Other than being somewhat heavy, the wheel is easily tilted upward.
3. Observations of effects of tilting the shaft of a rotating wheel upward:

   The rotating wheel resists efforts to tilt it upward. When students attempt to tilt it upward quickly, the wheel suddenly swerves to the right.
4. Observations of effects of rotating the spinning wheel:

   When the wheel is rotated to the right, the stool rotates to the left.

Analysis

1. Since the angular momentum must be conserved, the product of $I\omega$ must be constant. When the student's arms are pulled inward, the rotational inertia is reduced. If I has a smaller value, ω must increase to conserve the angular momentum of the system: $I_1\omega_1 = I_2\omega_2$.

2. Student answers may vary. One such condition could be an external torque applied to the system. For example, another student might give the stool an extra spin, thus increasing the rate of rotation and the angular momentum of the student-stool-masses system.

3. When the shaft is tilted, its angular momentum is changed in time by a small amount, ΔL. In order to cause a small change in L during an interval of time, $\Delta L / \Delta t$, a torque must be applied. If the torque is not applied in the same direction as ΔL, the wheel will swerve off to one side or another (depending on the direction of rotation).

4. For angular momentum to be conserved, the stool must rotate to the left when the wheel is rotated to the right. (Students may report the opposite results if their wheels were spinning in the opposite direction.)

Application

Many students will say that the two objects should reach the bottom of the incline at the same time. However, the solid cylinder will reach the bottom first. The thin rim wheel has greater rotational inertia than does the cylinder, and it will roll down the incline at a slower rate.

Extension

1. The moment the diver leaves the springboard, he is a closed, isolated system with a given angular momentum that cannot change while he is in the air. When he goes into the tuck position, his rate of rotation increases and his rotational inertia decreases. When he goes into the layout position prior to hitting the water, he increases his rotational inertia and decreases his rate of rotation. Angular momentum has been conserved throughout the dive.

2. Acceleration due to gravity exerts an external torque on the child-swing system. Without this torque, swinging would be impossible.

TEACHER NOTES

10.1 Pulleys

Process Skills

observing, using numbers, communicating, interpreting data, measuring, inferring, questioning, defining operationally, designing experiments

Teaching Suggestions

1. Grade the results reasonably. Although this investigation should work out well, there are several sources of error in doing the laboratory activity, mostly in getting accurate spring scale readings. Consequently, results usually do not show very close agreement. Demonstrate the proper use of the spring scale in each arrangement. Emphasize the necessity for using the least pull required to keep the mass moving upward at a slow and steady rate. Tell students to consider other potential sources of error and to take precautions that will minimize their effect on results.

2. Demonstrate the measurement of W, h, F, and d. Students often have difficulty measuring d, the distance the force moves.

3. If time and equipment permit, you may want to let students experiment with the pulley systems they have designed in response to the Application suggestion.

Observations and Data

Table 1 (Sample data are given.)

Pulley arrangement	Mass raised (kg)	Weight (W) of mass (N)	Height (h) mass is raised (m)	Force (F) of spring scale (N)	Distance (d) through which force acts (m)
(a)	0.50	4.9	0.25	5.0	0.27
(b)	0.50	4.9	0.25	2.8	0.50
(c)	1.0	9.8	0.25	5.0	0.53
(d)	1.0	9.8	0.25	2.7	1.02

Table 2 (Sample data are given.)

Pulley arrangement	Work output (Wh) (J)	Work input (Fd) (J)	IMA (d_e/d_e)	MA Number of lifting strands	Efficiency %
(a)	1.2	1.4	1	1	86
(b)	1.2	1.4	2	2	86
(c)	2.5	2.7	2	2	93
(d)	2.5	2.8	4	4	89

Analysis

1. Inaccuracies in reading the spring scale, accuracy of the spring scale, and friction are the largest causes of error.
2. The force gets smaller as the mechanical advantage gets larger.
3. The *IMA* and the efficiency should be the same.
4. As the number of pulleys increases, the *IMA* increases. The efficiency may or may not decrease.
5. The values for *IMA* and *MA* should be the same.
6. The amount of work is not reduced, but the force that must be applied is reduced. Considering the losses of energy due to friction, more, not less, work usually must be done.

Application

To boat

10.2 : Torques

Process Skills

observing, using numbers, communicating, interpreting data, predicting, measuring, questioning

Alternative Materials

String or masking tape may be used in place of the meter-stick clamps. However, in doing so, be careful that the spring scales are still able to move freely so that students will be able to obtain fairly accurate readings.

Teaching Suggestion

Explain that since torque is a vector quantity, by definition it includes direction in its specification. Mathematical convention places a negative value on torques in a clockwise direction and a positive value on torques in a counter-clockwise direction. If you prefer, you could use positive values for all torques. Thus, in a condition of equilibrium, the sum of all clockwise torques about an axis would equal the sum of all counterclockwise torques about the same axis.

Observations and Data

Table 1 (Sample data are given.)

	Balance a			Balance c		
Trial	Original reading (N)	Final reading (N)	Real reading (N)	Original reading (N)	Final reading (N)	Real reading (N)
1	0.85	3.15	2.30	0.75	3.10	2.35
2	1.00	3.95	2.95	0.60	2.55	1.95
3	1.30	4.90	3.60	0.35	1.55	1.20

Table 2 (Sample data are given.)

Trial	Distance AB (m)	Distance BC (m)	Clockwise torque (N · m)	Counter-clockwise torque (N · m)
1	0.45	0.45	−1.04	1.06
2	0.30	0.45	−0.89	0.88
3	0.15	0.45	−0.54	0.54

Analysis

1. Since the system in each trial was not rotating about the axis, the sum of the clockwise torques and the sum of the counterclockwise torques had to equal zero.
2. As the length of the lever arm increased, the force exerted decreased.
3. Trial 1: 2% difference; Trial 2: 1% difference; Trial 3: 0% difference
4. The counterclockwise torque should have a value equal to and opposite that of the clockwise torque.
5. When the systems were in equilibrium, there was no rotational movement; the sum of all torques was, therefore, zero. Since $W = \tau\Delta\theta$, if $\Sigma\tau = 0$, then $W = 0$. No work was done.

Application

The total weight supported by the piers of the bridge will be the weight of the bridge plus the weight of the person, or 980 N + 540 N = 1520 N. Since the bridge is not rotating, it is in rotational equilibrium. Therefore, the sum of the clockwise torques equals the sum of the counterclockwise torques. If the force F_1 at one end is the pivot point for possible rotation,

$F_1d = F_{bridge}d + F_{person}d$, where d is the distance from the pivot point. Solve for F_1.

$(F_1)(5.0 \text{ m}) = (980 \text{ N})(2.5 \text{ m}) + (540 \text{ N})(2 \text{ m})$

$F_1 = (2450 \text{ N} \cdot \text{m} + 1080 \text{ N} \cdot \text{m})/5 \text{ m}$

Thus, $F_1 = 710$ N at the end farther from the person, and $F_2 = 1520$ N $- 710$ N $= 810$ N at the end closer to the person.

TEACHER NOTES

11.1 Conservation of Energy

Process Skills

observing, measuring, using numbers, communicating, interpreting data, questioning, defining operationally

Alternative Materials

A non-stick cooking spray can be substituted for the silicone spray.

Teaching Suggestions

1. Emphasize the importance of moving the block up and down the incline at constant speed. If the block is accelerated, the scale reading will be wrong.
2. The quantity $F_{\parallel}d$ is the work done going up the frictionless inclined plane. $F_{up}d$ represents the work input including the work done against friction.

Observations and Data

Weight of the block = 6.0 N

Table 1 (Sample data are given.)

Trial	Length, d (m)	Height, h (m)	F_{up} (N)	F_{down} (N)
1	0.96	0.46	5.0	1.0
2	0.73	0.46	5.5	2.0
3				

Table 2 (Sample data are given.)

Trial	$F_{\parallel}$ (N)	Work done without friction, $F_{\parallel}d$ (J)	Potential energy mgh (J)	Work input $F_{up}d$ (J)
1	3.0	2.9	2.8	4.8
2	3.8	2.8	2.8	4.0
3				

Analysis

1.
$$F_{up} = F_{\parallel} + F_f$$
$$F_{down} = F_{\parallel} - F_f$$
$$\overline{F_{up} + F_{down} = 2F_{\parallel}}$$
$$F_{\parallel} = (F_{up} + F_{down})/2$$

2. Trial 1: $F_{\parallel} = (5.0 \text{ N} + 1.0 \text{ N})/2 = 3.0$ N
Trial 2: $F_{\parallel} = (5.5 \text{ N} + 2.0 \text{ N})/2 = 3.8$ N
3. Trial 1: $W = (3.0 \text{ N})(0.96 \text{ m}) = 2.9$ J
Trial 2: $W = (3.8 \text{ N})(0.73 \text{ m}) = 2.8$ J
4. $PE = (6.0 \text{ N})(0.46 \text{ m}) = 2.8$ J
5. In the absence of friction, the energy within the system is conserved. Students should have nearly the same values for work and potential energy.

Application

Since the hill is frictionless, the gravitational force converts the stored potential energy of the skier at the top of the hill to kinetic energy.

$$mgh = \tfrac{1}{2}mv^2$$
$$(60.0 \text{ kg})(9.80 \text{ m/s}^2)(10.0 \text{ m}) = \tfrac{1}{2}(60.0 \text{ kg})v^2$$
$$v^2 = 196 \text{ m}^2$$
$$v = 14 \text{ m/s}$$

Extension

Trial 1: $F_\parallel = W \sin \theta = (6 \text{ N})(0.46/0.96) = 2.9$ N
Trial 2: $F_\parallel = W \sin \theta = (6 \text{ N})(0.46/0.73) = 3.7$ N
Student answers for differences will vary, but most students will suggest that they may have pulled too hard, causing some acceleration of the block, or they pulled at an angle to the direction parallel to the plane, thus increasing the force reading.

TEACHER NOTES

12.1 Specific Heat

Process Skills

observing, communicating, interpreting data, measuring, using numbers, questioning

Teaching Suggestions

1. Mercury thermometers are dangerous and should be removed from school laboratory supply stock. Use only alcohol thermometers to avoid the risk of a mercury spill.
2. The old-style calorimetry cups (typically aluminum) can be used. However, if this type is used, then the heat lost by the hot metal equals the heat gained by the water, plus the heat gained by the calorimeter.
3. If lead is used, the mass must be large enough (300–400 g) to cause a measurable temperature change.
4. Review with students the values for specific heat of common substances found in Appendix C. They may note that the value for water is very high. Explain that this property of water makes it a particularly good coolant for car engines.

Observations and Data

Table 1 (Sample data are given.)

	Trial 1	Trial 2
Type of metal	brass	aluminum
Mass of calorimeter cup (kg)	0.0016	0.0016
Mass of calorimeter cup and water (kg)	0.1203	0.1251
Mass of metal (kg)	0.2741	0.0905
Initial temperature of room temperature water (°C)	22	23
Temperature of hot metal (°C)	100	100
Final temperature of metal and water (°C)	35	33.5

Table 2 (Sample data are given.)

	Trial 1	Trial 2
Mass of room temperature water (kg)	0.1187	0.1235
ΔT metal (°C)	65	66.5
ΔT room temperature water (°C)	13	10.5

Analysis

1. See Table 2.
2. Trial 1
   $Q_{\text{gained by water}}$
   $= (0.1187 \text{ kg})(13\,°C)(4180 \text{ J/kg} \cdot °C)$
   $= 6450$ J
   Trial 2
   $Q_{\text{gained by water}}$
   $= (0.1235 \text{ kg})(10.5\,°C)(4180 \text{ J/kg} \cdot °C)$
   $= 5420$ J
3. Trial 1
   $C_{\text{brass}} = 6450 \text{ J}/(0.2741 \text{ kg})(65\,°C)$
   $= 362 \text{ J/kg} \cdot °C = 362 \text{ J/kg} \cdot K$
   Trial 2
   $C_{\text{aluminum}} = 5420 \text{ J}/(0.0905 \text{ kg})(66.5\,°C)$
   $= 901 \text{ J/kg} \cdot °C = 901 \text{ J/kg} \cdot K$
4. Trial 1
   relative error $= [(376 - 362) \times 100\%]/\,376$
   $= 4\%$
   Trial 2
   relative error $= [(903 - 901) \times 100\%]/\,903$
   $= 0.2\%$

Student errors should be less than 15%. If samples are of lead or of very small mass, errors will be larger because the temperature changes in these situations will not be great enough to measure.

5. The thermometer may not be reading accurately (however, the difference in temperature should be accurate). Heat may have been lost to the environment from radiation out of the top of the cup. Some hot water from the sample may have dripped into the calorimeter.

Application

$$C_{substance} = \frac{(m_{water})(\Delta T_{water})(4180 \text{ J/kg} \cdot \text{K})}{(m_{substance})(\Delta T_{substance})}$$

$$= 656 \text{ J/kg} \cdot \text{K},$$

From Appendix C, this value for specific heat is closest to that of glass.

Extension

As demonstrated in the application, students should be able to identify the substance by its specific heat. Be sure that the unknown has a large enough mass or the temperature change will be insignificant, and a large error will result.

TEACHER NOTES

13.1 Archimedes' Principle

Process Skills

using numbers, observing, predicting, communicating, interpreting data, measuring, questioning

Teaching Suggestions

1. Be sure that the spring scales are functioning properly. If they stick, a large error is introduced into the results.
2. Each laboratory group could be given different masses, such as 200 g, 400 g, and 1000 g. To prevent damage to the equipment, be sure that the spring scale has the capacity to measure the larger masses.
3. Review with students the equation for buoyant force, $F_b = \rho Vg$. This will help them understand that the buoyant force is related to the weight of the volume of fluid displaced, not the weight of the submerged object.

Observations and Data

Table 1 (Sample data are given.)

Weight of 500-g mass in air	4.9 N
Weight of 500-g mass immersed in water	4.2 N
Volume of water in beaker	300 mL
Volume of water in beaker with 500-g mass immersed	375 mL

Table 2 (Sample data are given.)

Volume of water in beaker	300 mL
Volume of water with 100-g mass immersed	320 mL
Volume of water with 100-g mass in polystyrene cup	400 mL

Analysis

1. $F_{buoyant}$ = 4.9 N − 4.2 N = 0.70 N
2. Volume displaced = 375 mL − 300 mL
   = 75 mL;
   75 mL of water is equivalent to 75 g of water.

   $$F = (0.075 \text{ kg})(9.8 \text{ m/s}^2) = 0.73 \text{ N}.$$

   Student explanations will vary, but may include errors in measuring volume and force. Students might also note the effect of air bubbles that adhere to the surface of the mass.
3. It rose. The 100-g mass in the boat has an average density less than that of water, and the boat (with mass) floats. But the weight of the fluid it displaces is now greater than the weight of the water displaced by the mass alone. Whereas the volume of water displaced by the weight of the mass alone was 20 mL, now the 100-g mass displaces 100 g of water when it is placed in the boat. Since 100 g of water is equivalent to 100 mL of water, this is the difference between the observed volumes.

Application

The water level in the pool drops because Tim and Sally are heavier than the weight of the water they displace while submerged. When they fall into the water, they displace a volume of water that is less than their weight; the volume of water displaced is equal to the buoyant force acting on them. Since they displace less water while submerged than when floating, the pool water level drops when they fall off the raft.

14.1 Ripple Tank Waves

Process Skills

observing, formulating models, communicating, measuring, interpreting data, predicting, questioning, defining operationally

Troubleshooting

If students have difficulty in producing good images, suggest that they either increase or decrease the water depth in the ripple tank.

Alternative Materials

A straight-wave generator can be substituted for the dowel rod, but students often have difficulty adjusting them to work effectively. The dowel rod will usually generate a straight wave.

Teaching Suggestions

1. This is a long experiment and will probably require two laboratory periods.
2. Several point-source generators can be assembled and shared among lab groups.
3. If you use paraffin blocks, separate and store them in a cool place because they will melt in warm weather.

Observations and Data

Reflection

Table 1 (Sample data are given.)

1. Observations of straight pulses striking a straight barrier at 0° and at another angle:
   Pulses strike the barrier and bounce off. If they strike straight on, 0° to the normal, they reflect at an angle of 0°. If they strike the barrier at an angle to the normal, they reflect at an equal angle to the normal.

2. Sketch of incoming pulses and reflected pulses:

3. Statement of the relationship between the angle of incidence and the angle of reflection:
   The angle of incidence equals the angle of reflection.

4. Description of the shape of the reflected pulse from a concave surface:
   Straight waves reflected from a concave surface converge at a common point.

5. Description of the reflection of circular waves originating at the focus:
   The waves originating at the focal point of a concave barrier are reflected as straight waves.

Refraction

Table 2 (Sample data are given.)

Observations of refraction of straight waves:

(a)   (b)

Diffraction

Table 3 (Sample data are given.)

1. Observations of diffraction:
   a. large opening

   b. small opening

2. Observations of decreased wavelength:

Blocks

Interference

Table 4 (Sample data are given.)

1. Interference Pattern:

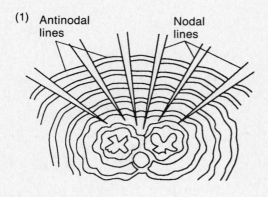

(1) Antinodal lines   Nodal lines

2. Interference Pattern (higher frequency than Item 1):

(2)

Analysis

1. The angle of incidence equals the angle of reflection.
2. As a water wave passes from deep to shallow water, its velocity decreases, wavelength decreases, and frequency remains the same.
3. Diffraction becomes more noticeable when the slit opening is smaller than the wavelength.

4. As the wavelength decreases, the angle of spread of the diffracted waves becomes smaller.
5. As the wavelength increases, the emerging interference pattern and nodal lines radiate outward at a greater angle. The smaller the wavelength, the greater the number of nodal (and antinodal) lines.
6. The diffracted waves will have an interference pattern similar to that produced by a two-point source.
7. Light is diffracted through the opening and creates an interference pattern with nodal and antinodal lines.

Applications

1. The ocean waves bend and slow down as they pass over a submerged reef or sandbar.
2. If you understand that the angle of reflection equals the angle of incidence, you are better able to position yourself to hit the returning ball (platform tennis or racquet ball) or to line up your next shot (pool).

Extension

The waves spread out, forming an interference pattern similar to the one produced by the two-point source. This result should match student's predictions from Question 6.

TEACHER NOTES

14.2

Velocity, Frequency, and Wavelength in Ripple Tanks

Process Skills

observing, using numbers, measuring, interpreting data, communicating, hypothesizing, questioning, controlling variables

Alternative Materials

Straight-wave generators may be substituted for the point source. Students may have difficulty using one side of the wave generator; if the plunger is off center or leaning, waves of poor quality are produced.

Teaching Suggestions

1. If students complain, encourage them to be patient. The lab activity will work well if they carefully follow each step.
2. If the images are not clear and sharp, try adding or removing a little water. The wave generator must be able to move up and down without touching the bottom of the ripple tank.
3. If students have never used stroboscopes, devote some time to explaining their use.

Observations and Data

Table 1 (Sample data are given.)

Trial	Width of five wavelengths (m)	Time for ten revolutions (s)	Time for one revolution (s)
1	0.105	4.1	0.41
2	0.116	4.8	0.48
3			

Table 2 (Sample data are given.)

Length of object (cm)	Length of shadow (cm)	Magnification ratio (length of shadow/length of object)
12	24	24/12 = 2

Table 3 (Sample data are given.)

Trial	Observed wavelength (m)	Corrected wavelength (m)
1	0.021	0.011
2	0.023	0.012
3		

Table 4 (Sample data are given.)

Trial	Frequency (Hz)	Wavelength (m)	Velocity (m/s)
1	9.76	0.011	0.107
2	8.33	0.012	0.100
3			

Analysis

1. The frequency of the wave was manipulated, and the wavelength responded to the change in frequency.
2. The velocities should show fairly good agreement. They should vary no more than 10–15%. The velocity should be the same but, with the procedure used, may show some variation.
3. Yes. Since the velocities calculated from $f\lambda$ are nearly equal, velocity of a wave in a given medium is constant.

Applications

1. Frequency is $1/T$, with T being the period of the wave, and the wavelength is the distance between waves, so $v = \lambda/T$, which is equivalent to $v = \Delta d/\Delta t$.
2. a. $f = v/\lambda$
      $= 217$ m/s $/ 3.5$ m $= 62$ Hz
   b. $T = 1/f$
      $= 1/62$ Hz $= 0.016$ s^{-1}

The Sound Level of a Portable Radio or Tape Player

TEACHER NOTES

15.1

Process Skills

using numbers, communicating, interpreting data, measuring, predicting, questioning, defining operationally

Teaching Suggestions

1. To improve results, record a 1000-Hz tone on a cassette tape to serve as the sound source.
2. Make arrangements with your school nurse to have students' hearing tested. Let students make copies of their hearing records. They should look for changes in hearing sensitivity levels and for trends, such as gradual hearing loss in one or both ears.

3. Have students investigate various areas in your school, such as the office, copy center, maintenance area, and cafeteria, recording sound levels and types of equipment producing the sounds. Compare the measured levels with the time exposure permitted at these levels.

Observations and Data

Table 3 (Sample data are given.)

Setting	Sound Level (dB)		
	Trial 1	Trial 2	Trial 3
0	—	—	
1	60	67	
2	60	79	
3	66	90	
4	70	96	
5	74	101	
6	77	106	
7	83	109	
8	86	111	
9	90		
10	94		

Table 4 (Sample data are given.)

Volume setting for listening	8
Estimate of time at preferred volume setting	1 h

Analysis

1. See Figure 1TE. Answers will vary depending on the type of volume control in each radio or tape player. Some will be linear and some will be logarithmic.
2. Student answers will vary. In Trial 1, volume setting 8 corresponds to a sound level of 86 dB.
3. Student answers will vary. At a sound level of 86 dB, the maximum exposure per day should not exceed eight hours.
4. Student answers will vary depending on the sound level that each portable radio or tape player produces. Both tape players represented in the sample data are potentially dangerous, since they can produce sound levels in excess of 90 dB.

This graph of sound level versus volume setting was produced using the Lab Partner™ graphing program.

Applications

1. Jack needed a sound level 5 dB greater than normal, which is three times as intense. Sam needed a sound level 25 dB greater than normal to detect sound, which is approximately 300 times as intense.
2. $(10 \text{ dB}) \log \dfrac{I_2}{I_1} = \beta_2 - \beta_1, \dfrac{I_2}{I_1} = 100\,000$

   The rock group makes 100 000 times as much noise as does normal conversation at 1 m.

Extension

1. In an enclosed room, sound is reflected from the ceiling, walls, floor, and furniture. It doesn't weaken as quickly and may be focused or amplified.
2. a. $I = \dfrac{100 \text{ W}}{4\pi \,(2.5 \text{ m})^2} = \dfrac{100 \text{ W}}{78.5 \text{ m}^2} = 1.27 \text{ W/m}^2$

   b. $\beta = (10 \text{ dB}) \log \dfrac{1.27 \text{ W/m}^2}{10^{-12} \text{ W/m}^2}$

   $= 1 \text{ dB} + 120 \text{ dB} = 121 \text{ dB}$

   The sound level that can be generated by a 150-W amplifier is just above the threshold of pain and could cause severe hearing damage. This hazard is compounded because the system will be installed in his small room where sounds are reflected off walls, ceiling, etc., rather than dissipated in open space. To save his hearing, the student should not buy this powerful amplifier.
3. While the student has doubled the intensity of the sound, the increase in the sound level is 3 dB. The new sound level is 103 dB.

15.2 Resonance in an Open Tube

Process Skills

observing, using numbers, measuring, communicating, interpreting data, predicting, questioning, hypothesizing, designing experiments

Alternative Materials

Small cardboard tubes, such as those found in rolls of toilet paper, paper towels, or gift wrap, work well. A selection of different tubes should provide several sets that slide into each other and can be fashioned into tubes of adjustable lengths.

Teaching Suggestions

1. The resonance in an open tube will not be as loud as resonance in a closed tube. However, it is still easy to adjust the tube length to produce the maximum sound. Cardboard tubes do not produce sounds as loud as those generated in a smooth tube, such as those made of glass that were used to produce resonance in a closed tube.
2. Using the information from Figure 1, you can prepare in advance a variety of tubes that are close to the length needed to produce resonance. For example, a tube adjustable from 25–45 cm can be used with tuning forks of frequencies between 512 and 384 Hz.

Observations and Data

Table 1 (Sample data are given.)

Trial	Frequency (Hz)	Pipe diameter (m)	Measured length of pipe (m)
1	256	0.0480	0.630
2	384	0.0480	0.415

Table 2 (Sample data are given.)

Trial	Corrected length (L) of air column (m)	Wavelength $\lambda = 2L$ (m)
1	0.668	1.34
2	0.453	0.906

Table 3 (Sample data are given.)

Trial	Air temperature (°C)	Velocity correction for temperature (m/s)	Accepted velocity of sound (m/s)
1	21	12.4	344
2	21	12.4	344

Analysis

1. $v_1 = f\lambda = (256 \text{ Hz})(1.34 \text{ m}) = 343 \text{ m/s}$
   $v_2 = f\lambda = (384 \text{ Hz})(0.906 \text{ m}) = 348 \text{ m/s}$
2. $\text{Error}_1 = (344 - 343)(100\%)/344 = 0.3\%$
   $\text{Error}_2 = (348 - 344)(100\%)/344 = 1.2\%$
   Students should have relative errors of less than 10%.
3. Students should answer that the steam will cause the velocity of sound to change due to the greater temperature and density of steam compared with those of air. They should reason that the velocity will increase. The velocity of sound is actually about 25% faster in steam than in air.
4. Resonance should recur when the wavelength of the tone is approximately four times the length of the open tube. Students should find a tube of approximately twice the length that produced resonance for a given tuning fork and repeat the procedure. Students should be able to detect the second harmonic, but it is not as loud as the fundamental resonant sound.

Application

The frequency of the note produced is 55 Hz.
$v = 331.5 \text{ m/s} + (0.59 \text{ m/s/}°\text{C})(20°\text{C})$
  $= 343.3 \text{ m/s}$
$\lambda = 2(L + 0.8d) = 2[3.0 \text{ m} + (0.8)(0.15\text{m})]$
  $= 6.24 \text{ m}$
Thus, $f = v/\lambda = (343.3 \text{ m/s})/(6.24 \text{ m}) = 55 \text{ Hz}$

16.1 Light Days

Process Skills

observing, interpreting data, communicating, classifying, hypothesizing, questioning

Alternative Materials

If specific lab station activities are not appropriate for your needs or for the equipment available, then substitute other activities.

Teaching Suggestions

1. Review laser light safety with the class before beginning this activity.
2. This activity is designed to be motivating and exploratory and serves very well as an introduction to light. Allow students ample time to complete all activities, which may take a minimum of two laboratory periods. Do not expect students to have all the correct answers, but do emphasize and insist on good, comprehensive observations.
3. Some lab station activities, such as viewing holograms or working with colored shadows, are best done in small groups so that students can spend as much time as they need to make their observations. Time spent in these introductory activities should facilitate later class discussions.
4. Maintaining a darkened room is important for observation of many of the light phenomena.
5. This activity is fun and exciting, and it can be used to attract the attention of prospective students of physics. A little music, a light chaser, a mirror ball with a spotlight, and some signs on your door will contribute to the overall effect.

Observations and Data

1. A single slit and double slit will produce alternating vertical dark and light lines. The spacing will vary, depending on the slit width. Rainbows will be observed with the diffraction grating. The red filter will produce alternating vertical black and red bands.
2. The converging lens will magnify the writing or object, while the diverging lens will make it appear smaller. Students may also note that the object is clearest at a certain distance, but appears fuzzy, or out of focus, at other distances.
3. Students will observe concentric circles, which may be colored if enough white light is available. This is an example of thin film interference. Students should suggest that this looks similar to soap bubbles or oil on the surface of water (or on the street).

4. The disc contains all color pigments. As it is spun in daylight, the colors combine, and the disc appears to be white.
5. Filter color   Shadow colors
   a. Red filter   red, blue-green (cyan)
   b. Yellow filter   yellow, bluish
   c. Green filter   green, pinkish (magenta)
   d. Blue filter   blue, yellow
6. Each filter covering the light absorbs all other colors and transmits its own color. A red filter transmits only red light.
7. Light is reflected inside the fiber optic rod. Total internal reflection occurs, keeping the light within the fiber optic medium.
8. The strobe light shows a few lines in the blue region of the spectrum.
9. The object of the hologram appears three dimensional, and different sides of the image can be viewed from different angles. Ordinary photographs are two dimensional and look the same from all viewing angles. The three-dimensional image is created by interference of light, not by reflection only as in photographs.
10. The observed pattern of light follows the law of reflection, where the angle of incidence equals the angle of reflection.
11. The laser beam has a small divergence; the flashlight beam spreads out very quickly.
12. The beam bends as it passes through water. It is bent toward the normal as it passes into the denser medium (air to water).
13. An incandescent bulb shows a continuous spectrum from violet through red. The fluorescent light also shows a continuous spectrum, but has several bright lines in the red, yellow, and green regions. The bright lines comprise the pattern unique to mercury, which is found in a fluorescent tube.
14. When one filter is rotated, the field becomes black. When the filter is rotated another 90°, the field clears. The plastic box appears very colorful. The polarized light is bent as it passes through the different areas of the plastic. This bent light interferes with similar adjacent rays as it passes through the second polarizing filter. The result is the colorful pattern observed.
15. Some possible combinations include red + blue = purple, red + yellow = orange, red + green = brown, blue + green = bluish-green, yellow + blue = green, and yellow + green = yellow-green.

16. The object appears to be projected into the air, but cannot be projected onto a screen. The parabolic mirrors reflect light from each other, creating an image the same size as the object.
17. The surface of a reflector has 3- or 6-sided facets that reflect light striking them back toward the light source.
18. This hologram is not as strikingly three dimensional as the transmission hologram. When seen in white light, the image appears colorful.
19. Student observations may vary, depending on the quality of the filters used and the amount of white light present in the room.

Table 1

Color of paper in white light	Color of paper when incident light is				
	red	orange	yellow	green	blue
red	red	red	orangish	brown	dark purple
orange	red-orange	orange	orange	brown	brown
yellow	orange	orange	yellow	greenish	bluish
green	brownish	brownish	green	green	dark green
blue	brown	brownish	greenish	bluish	blue

20. Students should draw geometric patterns, which will vary with the type of kaleidoscope. Mirrors reflect the particles inside, creating multiple images that combine and look like a geometric pattern.
21. The liquid crystal display numbers are produced by polarized light. Rotating a polarizing filter over the display blocks out the light, and no numbers are observed.
22. Students should see a double image. The separate images are polarized and out of phase by 90°. This phase difference is revealed by rotating a polarizing filter over the crystal. First one image is visible, and then the other.
23. The drawing should show a parabolic mirror with the filament located near the focus. When the filament is located at the focal point, the reflected rays of light leave the parabolic mirror in a parallel beam.
24. The concave lens spreads the light rays apart (they diverge), while the convex lens causes the light rays to converge to a point.

25.

Table 2

Mixture of lights	Observed color of mixture
red + blue	violet (magenta)
red + green	yellow
red + yellow	white
green + yellow	greenish
green + blue	aqua (cyan)
blue + green + yellow	white
red + blue + green	white
red + blue + yellow	white

a. Any combination containing red, blue, and green (yellow is made of red + green) produces white light.
b. The three primary colors of light that together produce white light are:
1. red 2. blue 3. green
c. The complementary color for primary color 1 is cyan (blue-green).
The complementary color for primary color 2 is yellow.
The complementary color for primary color 3 is magenta (red-violet).
(Note: Student answers for 25 c will vary depending on the order of their answers for 25 b.)

Suggest a method for detecting the complement of any color. If students stare at a certain color for 20 seconds, then transfer their gaze to a sheet of white paper, they will see the complementary color. Explain that retinal fatigue causes this effect.

Applications

1. Yellow light is produced by the combination of red and green light. The intensity and tint controls must be adjusted simultaneously to affect the yellow.
2. A certain level of illumination is required for the human eye to perceive color.
3. Store lighting is often tinted, or not white light. Clothing seen in the store's lighting may reflect a different color outside the store.

16.2 Polarized Light

Process Skills

observing, classifying, communicating, interpreting data, measuring, inferring, questioning

Alternative Materials

Special elastic-stress, optical plastic can be purchased from science supply houses. It can be used in place of the plastic object for Step 8.

Teaching Suggestions

1. Small plastic boxes or protractors, which have been stamped with holes or notches, are excellent materials for observation of stress.
2. The laboratory extension can correlate with polarization or be delayed until refraction is more fully explained in the next chapter.

Observations and Data
Table 1

Observations of light source with 1 polarizing filter:
The light intensity does not change.

Observations of light source with 2 polarizing filters, rotating the filter closer to the light:
During one rotation, the intensity changes twice, from minimum to maximum intensity.

Observations of light source with 2 polarizing filters, rotating the filter closer to your eye:
The same variation as above was observed.

Table 2

Drawing of a word viewed through Iceland spar:

The word appears twice, and the images are side by side and slightly off center. If the crystal is rotated, one of the words moves around the other as a radius transcribing a circle around the stationary word.

Observations of a word viewed through Iceland spar, with one rotating polarizing filter:

As the filter is rotated, one image disappears, and then reappears as the other image fades away.

Table 3

Observations of light reflected from plane mirror:
The light intensity does not change.

Observations of light reflected from glass plate:
The light intensity changes.

Observations of light reflected from shiny table top:
The light intensity changes.

Table 4

Observations of plastic:

A pattern of color is observed in the plastic. The colors change quickly and move together as stress is applied to the plastic. Where the strain is greatest, the colors are closest.

Analysis

1. Light from a light bulb is not polarized since the intensity does not change as the filter is rotated.
2. The intensity changes twice from minimum to maximum brightness as one of the filters is rotated through 360°. It makes no difference which of the filters is rotated. The maximum brightness change occurs when one filter is rotated 90°.
3. The light images were polarized, and one image was shifted away from the other. The light rays of the images travel at different speeds, so they are bent (refracted) at different angles. Materials like Iceland spar are called double refracting, because they have two indices of refraction.
4. Light reflected from a plane mirror is not polarized. Its intensity does not change when observed through one rotating polarizing filter. If students are using a thick glass mirror, they may observe some polarization, but generally, polarization will not be seen.
5. Light reflected from a glass plate or a shiny surface is polarized because the light changes intensity when viewed through one rotating polarizing filter.
6. Color bands, some wide and some narrow and closely spaced, were seen. The bands moved together as the material was squeezed.

Applications

1. A piece of polarizing material oriented in one plane, say vertically, could be placed over the high-beam lights, while polarizing material oriented in the opposite direction, horizontally, could be placed on the windshield. Glare from headlights could thus be reduced. However, the drawback to this scheme is the need to outfit all cars with these materials in these orientations. Also, the filter material does block some light, not always a desirable result at night when visibility is already reduced.
2. Engineers could build a transparent plastic model of the product and subject it to various stresses and strains. When viewed through polarized light, the model would show the locations of greatest stress. Thus, the engineers would know where reinforcements are needed or whether a new design is required.

Extension

Students should measure angles of about 55°–60° for plate glass. This corresponds to an index of refraction of about 1.5. The index of refraction of water is 1.33.

TEACHER NOTES

17.1 Reflection of Light

Process Skills

observing, measuring, using numbers, interpreting data, inferring, predicting, hypothesizing, defining operationally

Teaching Suggestions

1. If students have difficulty constructing their triangles in Part B, tell them to repeat the procedure, but emphasize that they must sight very carefully along the lines to the image of the pin in the mirror.
2. One set-up for Part C can be used for all students. As they work on Parts A and B, each lab group can take a turn with the laser. In this way, the laser remains in a separate, protected area of the room.

Observations and Data

Table 1 (Sample data are given.)

Object distance	4.1 cm
Image distance	3.8 cm
Angle of incidence, i_1, **PXN**	13°
Angle of reflection, r_1, **AXN**	13.5°
Angle of incidence, i_2, **PYN'**	24°
Angle of reflection, r_2, **BYN'**	25°

Table 2 (Sample data are given.)

Points	Distance to mirror line (cm)
A	1.7
B	5.4
C	1.8
A'	1.8
B'	5.2
C'	1.9

Table 3

Drawing of reflected laser light from a thin plane mirror: A single large spot should appear.

Drawing of reflected laser light from a thick plane mirror:

Figure 1 TE. The second spot is brightest; this is the reflection from the mirrored surface.

Observation of reflected laser beams:
Students should note a series of reflected beams, becoming progressively narrower as they are more distant from the incident beam.

Analysis

1. They are equal (or should be nearly so).
2. The image is the same distance behind the mirror as the object is in front of the mirror.
3. The image should be the same size as the object. Students may have some small errors due to sighting inaccuracies.
4. Images formed by plane mirrors are as far behind the mirror as the object is in front of the mirror. The image is reversed right to left and is the same size as the object.
5. The image appears where the light rays apparently cross, not where they actually cross. This image does not exist behind the mirror, where it appears to be.

6. The second spot is brightest, because this beam is the reflection from the mirrored surface. The first spot is the reflection from the glass.

7. The thin mirror reflects light from the glass and mirrored surface, but the reflected spots are nearly in the same location. The thick mirror has multiple reflections, spaced farther apart, from the glass at the top and the silver at the bottom of the mirror, as shown in Figure 2 TE.

Figure 2 TE. Partial reflection occurs at the mirror-air interface.

Application

Students should state that some of the light is transmitted while most light is reflected. One-way mirrors generally reflect a large portion of the incident light, such as 50%–60%, while allowing a smaller portion, such as 5%–15%, to pass through. Since a smaller portion of the light is transmitted, the viewing area is usually darker than the observed area.

Extension

The distances should be equal.

TEACHER NOTES

17.2 Snell's Law

Process Skills

observing, using numbers, measuring, inferring, interpreting data, questioning, communicating

Teaching Suggestions

1. This activity should be easy to understand and complete, even for students who have not studied trigonometry. However, review the relationships of triangles prior to the lab and introduce Snell's law as a relationship between the opposite side and the hypotenuse of a triangle. The results should be apparent, even if the math is not.

2. A dish of water or oil could be substituted for the glass plate to provide a different index of refraction. The activity is conducted in the same manner. However, the oil is messy if it is spilled.

Observations and Data

Table 1 (Sample data are given.)

θ_i	θ_r	$\sin \theta_i$	$\sin \theta_r$	$\theta_{r'}$	Index of refraction, n
30°	19°	0.5	0.326	30°	1.53
45°					

Analysis

1. They should be equal or nearly equal. Students might have as much as 10% error if they are not careful while sighting along their rulers.

2. As the light rays pass at an angle from a less dense to a more dense medium, they bend toward the normal.

3. As the light rays pass at an angle from a more dense to a less dense medium, they bend away from the normal.

4. The two angles are equal. According to Snell's law, as the light ray passes back to the optically less dense medium, it should resume its original speed and bend away from the normal.

5. $v_s = c/n_s = (3.00 \times 10^8 \text{ m/s})/1.53$
   $= 1.96 \times 10^8$ m/s
   Light travels 3.00×10^8 m/s $- 1.96 \times 10^8$ m/s $= 1.04 \times 10^8$ m/s faster in a vacuum.
   % increase $= 1.04 \times 10^8/1.96 \times 10^8 = 53\%$ faster in a vacuum.

Application

Light will bend more traveling from air into water than from water into glass. Using the general form of Snell's law, $n_i \sin \theta_i = n_r \sin \theta_r$, light traveling from air into water yields an effective $n = 1.34$, while light traveling from water into glass yields an effective $n = 1.14$, determined from $(1.34)(\sin \theta_i) = (1.53)(\sin \theta_r)$. The greater the index of refraction, the greater the amount of refraction.

Extension

The sample materials should be easy to identify. The samples will take on a ghostlike appearance and be just barely visible in the liquid with nearly the same index of refraction. Glass normally has an index of refraction of about 1.5. You probably will not have any glass with $n = 1.7$.

18.1 Concave and Convex Mirrors

Process Skills

observing, measuring, interpreting data, communicating, questioning, designing experiments

Troubleshooting

If students have difficulty locating sharp images, check the mirror. The mirror must be clean and of good quality to produce clear, sharp images. To check the quality of the mirrors, take clean mirrors and focus sunlight onto a screen. Those mirrors that are of good quality will produce a small image of the sun while those of poorer quality will not focus the sunlight.

Alternative Materials

1. Object markers may be used with the light sources. However, students usually have no trouble identifying the orientations of the images. Light bulbs generally have flat bases or glowing filaments, which indicate upright or inverted positions.
2. Candles can be substituted for light sources. If candles are used, caution should be observed around the flames.

Teaching Suggestions

1. Allow ample time to complete this investigation. A prelab discussion of the types of images formed by mirrors and a demonstration of how to find focal lengths may be helpful.

2. Use a concave mirror to project an outdoor scene from outside a window onto a screen. This demonstration will familiarize students with mirrors and real images. They should also be fascinated by the color image.

Observations and Data

Table 1 (Sample data are given.)

Focal length of mirror, f	33 cm
Center of curvature of mirror, **C**	66 cm
Height of light source, h_o	1 cm

Table 2 (Sample data are given.)

Position of object	Beyond C		At C	Between C and F	At F	Between F and A
d_o	1.0 m	66 cm		48 cm	33 cm	16 cm
d_i	49 cm	66 cm		98 cm	—	—
h_i	0.8 cm		1.0 cm	6 cm	—	larger than object
Type of image: real, none, or virtual	real		real	real	none	virtual
Direction of image: inverted or erect	inverted		inverted	inverted	no image	erect

Table 3 (Sample data are given.)

Trial	Position of object	Position of image	Type of image: real or virtual	Image size compared to object size	Direction of image: inverted or erect
1	for all positions	behind mirror	virtual	smaller	erect
2					
3					

Analysis

1. a. The image is between **C** and **F**, inverted, real, and smaller than the object.
   b. The image is at **C**, real, inverted, and the same size as the object.
   c. The image is beyond **C**, inverted, real, and larger than the object.
   d. No image is formed.
   e. The image is behind the mirror, erect, and larger than the object.

2. The images are virtual, smaller and erect, and located behind the mirror.
3. For beyond **C**, $f = 33$ cm; at **C**, $f = 33$ cm; between **C** and **F**, $f = 32$ cm. Student values should be in good agreement.
4. The average is 33 cm, relative error = 0%. Students should have an error of no more than 10%–15% if they have made careful observations and have reasonably good mirrors.

Application

The top edge of the box should be along the principal axis, while the light bulb socket should be located at **C** to produce an image equal in size to the object and inverted.

18.2 Convex and Concave Lenses

Process Skills

observing, measuring, interpreting data, communicating, questioning, predicting, designing experiments

Troubleshooting

When using sunlight to determine the focal length of the concave lens, the contrast between the circle of light projected on the screen and the ambient light can be increased by placing a piece of paper around the lens so that sunlight is blocked from falling directly on the screen.

Teaching Suggestion

To find the focal length of the convex lens, arrange your lens, meter stick, and screen, as shown in Figure 3. When sunlight is used, the focal length can be determined by projecting a focused image of the sun onto a screen and measuring the distance from the lens to the focused spot on the screen. Measure the dis-

tance quickly, since a focused spot can become hot and cause the screen to burn. Supervise students and be sure to caution them to avoid looking directly at the sun.

Observations and Data

Table 1 (Sample data are given.)

Focal length	18	cm
$2F$	36	cm
Height of light source, h_o	1.2 cm	

Table 2 (Sample data are given.)

Position of object	Beyond $2F$ (cm)	At $2F$ (cm)	Between $2F$ and F (cm)	At F (cm)	Between F and lens (cm)
d_o	50	37	25	17.5	10
d_i	29.2	37.2	66.5	—	—
h_i	1.0	1.2	1.8	—	appears larger as viewed through lens
Type of image: real, none, or virtual	real	real	real	none	none
Direction of image: inverted or erect	inverted	inverted	inverted	—	erect

Table 3

Distance from lens (m)	Diameter of screen image (cm)
0.0	0.15
0.5	0.5
1.0	0.75
1.5	1.1
2.0	1.4
2.5	1.8
3.0	2.0

Analysis

1. a. The image is between F and $2F$, real, about the same size, and inverted.
   b. The image is at $2F$, the same size as the object, real, and inverted.
   c. The image is beyond $2F$, larger, real, and inverted.

d. No image was readily apparent.

e. The image is virtual, larger, erect, and on the same side of the lens as the object.

2. a. f = 18.4 cm; b. f = 18.5 cm; c. f = 18.2 cm There should be good agreement for all measurements.

3. Average f = 18.4 cm; relative error = (18.4 − 18)(100%)/18 = 2%. Students should have a relative error of less than 10%.

4. The intersection provides a focal length of −0.25 m. The accepted value is −0.20 m, therefore the relative error = (0.25 − 0.20)(100%)/0.20 = 25%. Student error may vary greatly, since the observed diameters are usually not clearly defined at the edges.

Image Size vs Distance

This graph of image size versus distance from the lens was produced using the Lab Partner™ graphing program. The x-intercept is −0.26 m.

Application

If the direction of the reflected laser pattern is opposite to that of the observer's head, then this person is nearsighted. If the direction of the reflected laser pattern is the same as that of the observer's head, then this person is farsighted. If the observer does not perceive any relative motion, then his or her eyesight is normal. To simulate near- or farsightedness, students could hold various lenses in front of their eyes and observe the laser light spot.

Extension

The object appears about normal when viewed through a convex or a concave air lens in air. However, the object appears smaller when viewed through the convex air lens immersed in water and larger when viewed through the concave air lens immersed in water. Note the reversal of the usual effects of glass lenses on these shapes. In water, light rays are traveling from the object through a more dense medium (water) to a less dense medium (air in the lenses). This reversal of media accounts for the opposite effects of the lenses.

TEACHER NOTES
19.1 Double-Slit Interfer-ence

Process Skills

observing, communicating, interpreting data, measuring, predicting, questioning

Troubleshooting

If students have difficulty measuring x for the violet filter, suggest that they move farther away (increase L). This color is the most difficult to observe and measure, especially if the room lights are on.

Alternative Materials

Double slits can be purchased or constructed. If you wish to have students construct their own double slits, tape a pair of razor blades together and lightly pull the unit across a microscope slide covered with dried graphite emulsion. An alternative to graphite emulsion is aluminum foil, placed over a microscope slide and cut with the razor-blades unit.

Teaching Suggestions

1. Suggest that students use the red filter material first, since it provides the best observations of diffraction and interference.

2. If students have difficulty when the filter material is placed on the light bulbs, they can try holding the filter material in front of their slits.

3. If a variety of color filter material is available, give each lab partnership a red piece and two other colors, so that the variety of other colors is different for different lab partners. This individualizes the lab, and partners are less inclined to copy data.

Observations and Data

Table 1 (Sample data are given.)

Observations of Light	
Close	The bright bands of red are close together.
Far away	The bright bands of red move farther apart and are easier to see.

Table 2 (Sample data are given.)

Color	d (mm)	x (m)	L (m)
Red	0.15	0.017	4.0
Yellow	0.15	0.015	4.0
Violet	0.15	0.012	4.0

Analysis

1. The pattern spreads out, so the first-order, second-order, etc., lines are farther apart.
2. $\lambda_{red} = xd/L$
   $= (0.017\ m)(0.15 \times 10^{-3}\ m)/4.0\ m$
   $= 640\ nm$
   $\lambda_{yellow} = xd/L$
   $= (0.015\ m)(0.15 \times 10^{-3}\ m)/4.0\ m$
   $= 560\ nm$
   $\lambda_{violet} = xd/L$
   $= (0.012\ m)(0.15 \times 10^{-3}\ m)/4.0\ m$
   $= 450\ nm$
   Student answers will vary and will be dependent on how carefully they measure x. Answers should be within the visible spectrum (in the range of 400–700 nm).
3. Red light is diffracted most. Using the same values for L and d, the angle will be larger, since x is greater for the larger wavelength, $x = \lambda L/d$.
4. Student answers will vary. However, the distance should be greater than the measured distance of x for the red light. The infrared light will be diffracted more than visible red light, since it has a larger wavelength.
5. Student answers will vary. However, the distance should be less than the measured distance for x for the violet light. The ultraviolet light will be diffracted less than visible violet light, since it has a smaller wavelength.

Applications

1. Since $\tan \theta = x/L$ and $\theta = 0.8°$, $\lambda = xd/L = d(\tan \theta) = (0.05 \times 10^{-3}\ m)(\tan 0.8) = 700\ nm$, which is the wavelength of red light.

2. $L = xd/\lambda$
   $= \dfrac{(14.7 \times 10^{-3}\ m)(1.50 \times 10^{-5}\ m)}{5.00 \times 10^{-7}\ m}$
   $= 0.441\ m$
3. $x = L\lambda/d$
   $= \dfrac{(4.41 \times 10^{-1}\ m)(5.89 \times 10^{-7}\ m)}{1.5 \times 10^{-5}}$
   $= 0.0173\ mm$

Extension

The solutions will vary, depending on the values for L and x. However, when students substitute their values into $d = \lambda L/x$, the resulting value for d should be very close to the actual value.

Process Skills

observing, communicating, questioning, interpreting data

Alternative Materials

1. Small, plastic microwave trays can be substituted for the glass or plastic trays. Keep the trays as close to the size of the film as possible to minimize waste of chemicals.
2. A massive object, such as an oscilloscope placed on its side, can be substituted for the steel plate.
3. A small steel plate can be taped on any large non-steel object and used as the base plate for the experiment. The magnets stick easily to this surface.

Teaching Suggestions

1. Provide one classroom setup of the laser and photographic platform. Each lab group can, in turn, arrange its materials and make its hologram. A small night-light with a green Christmas light bulb works well as a safelight.

2. For purposes of supervising chemical use, it is recommended that the teacher develop the holograms at a central location. The teacher should wear the protective apron, goggles, and rubber gloves. Follow the manufacturer's included directions for mixing and using the photographic chemicals. Lab partners can arrange their own materials and take their picture, and then bring the hologram to the teacher for developing. After it is developed, the hologram can be returned to the students for viewing. The plastic tongs are used to transfer the plate from the developer to the bleach and to the water rinse.
3. A diverging lens used as a beam expander can be substituted for the small concave lens. In this case, alter the procedure by placing the glass plate vertically, rather than horizontally. Place the object to be photographed behind the glass plate.
4. You may need exposure times as long as 30 seconds to provide a good image; however, if your laser is close and more powerful than 1.5 mW, shorter exposure times will work.

Observations and Data
Table 1

Observations of Hologram
Looking through hologram:
The plate is transparent and greenish. No image is visible.
Looking at reflection:
The image of the photographed objects appears in great detail. The objects have three dimensions, and the sides of the objects can be viewed as the hologram is tilted back and forth.

Analysis

1. The hologram appeared only in the reflected light and was not visible in the transmitted light. The reflected light recreated the interference pattern that produced the original hologram, thus making the image visible only in reflected light.
2. Students will say that the hologram is three dimensional and has depth; it is not two dimensional, as is a picture or photograph. They should also comment that the hologram does not appear as sharp or as clear as the photograph.
3. The color comes from the interference pattern resulting from the white light, not from anything on the film.

Application

Holograms can be utilized to reduce or prevent counterfeiting of money and credit cards. Holograms of rare coins produce a three-dimensional record of the coin collection and can be used for positive identification.

Extension

The transmission hologram will be of much better quality and will appear sharper than the white light reflection hologram. However, it must be viewed in the laser light.

TEACHER NOTES

20.1 Investigating Static Electricity

Process Skills

observing, classifying, communicating, interpreting data, inferring, hypothesizing, questioning

Troubleshooting

On a humid day, it may not be possible to produce a positive charge with the glass rods. In these weather conditions, you will find that many of the lucite or acrylic materials produce adequate positive charges. The strength of the positive charge produced by these materials can be verified by comparison with the negative charge produced by a hard rubber rod.

Alternative Materials

Nylon or cotton scraps can also be used for rubbing pads.

Teaching Suggestions

1. Encourage students to make detailed observations. Often students rush through this experiment and are unsure of what they saw.
2. On a dry day, the vane type of electroscope should perform well. This type requires more charge to cause a deflection than does the leaf electroscope. On more humid days, it is better to use a leaf electroscope; it responds better with a smaller charge.

Observations and Data

Table 1
A. Negatively Charging a Pith Ball

Observations of pith ball with nearby charged rod:
The pith ball is attracted toward the charged rod.

Observations of pith ball after it has been touched with a charged rod:
The pith ball is attracted toward the rod but, after it has been touched, it is repelled.

Table 2
B. Positively Charging a Pith Ball

Observations of pith ball with nearby charged rod:
The pith ball is attracted toward the charged rod.

Observations of pith ball after it has been touched with a charged rod:
The pith ball is attracted toward the rod but, after it has been touched, it is repelled.

Table 3
C. Charging an Electroscope by Conduction

Observations of uncharged electroscope when negatively-charged rod touches it:
The vane deflects (or the leaves separate).

Observations of negatively-charged electroscope when negatively-charged rod is brought near:
The electroscope vane is (or leaves are) further deflected while the rod is nearby; the original charged position is assumed when the rod is removed.

Observations of negatively-charged electroscope when a positively-charged rod is brought near:
The vane moves back toward zero (or the leaves collapse). When the rod is removed, the electroscope again indicates the presence of charge.

Observations of deflection of leaves or vane when plastic material charges the electroscope and a negatively-charged rod is brought near:
The rubber rod causes the electroscope to move back toward zero, indicating that it has a charge opposite that of the rod. The electroscope is positively charged.

Table 4
D. Charging an Electroscope by Induction

Observations of electroscope when charged rod is brought near:
The electroscope vane or leaves move, indicating the presence of charge, but when the rod is removed, the vane returns to zero or the leaves fall.

Observations of electroscope after touching with finger:
The electroscope indicates the presence of charge when the charged rod is brought near, but drops to zero when it is touched by a finger. After the finger and then the charged rod are removed from the electroscope top, the electroscope again indicates the presence of charge.

Observations to determine the type of charge:
The electroscope has a charge opposite that of the charged rod that was originally brought near. The leaves converge or the vane returns to zero, indicating that the original charged rod is attracting the charge of the electroscope.

Table 5
E. Charging a Leyden Jar

Observations of charging a Leyden jar-electroscope combination:
The electroscope charges easily by itself, but does not (apparently) charge when the Leyden jar is attached. The charge travels through the wire to the Leyden jar, which stores charge.

Analysis

1. The ball touches the charged rod, becomes charged, and then is repelled.
2. The ball touches the charged rod, becomes charged, and then is repelled.
3. The process is the same for either type of charge.
4. When the charged rod touches the electroscope ball, the vane deflects (leaves diverge). The vane or leaves return to normal when the electroscope ball is touched by a finger.
5. Electrons were transferred to the electroscope, the vane (leaves) became negatively charged and deflected (repelled each other).
6. The leaves were still negatively charged.
7. The charge was positive. Student results may vary depending on the type of material available. The charge type can be confirmed by testing it with a known negatively-charged rod.
8. The finger provided a path to ground for the charge that was the same type as that of the charged rod brought near the electroscope. The net charge remaining on the electroscope, after the finger and rod were removed from the electroscope top, was opposite that of the charged rod.
9. It was the charge opposite that of the rod.
10. It acted as a ground, removing some of the charges.

11. Conduction produces the same charge; induction produces the opposite charge.
12. The charge was transferred to the Leyden jar (it stores static charges) from the electroscope. The electroscope does not retain the charge, as shown by the action of the leaves (they come together) or the vane (it returns to zero).

Application

When the record is slid out of its plastic cover, static electricity is produced as a result of the rubbing together of these two materials. These static charges can damage the needle if, when it comes down onto the record, a discharge (electrical spark) occurs. Record cleaners serve two purposes — to remove dust and to eliminate static electricity. Dust may accumulate on or be attracted to a record, which is easily charged with static electricity. The fluid or water causes static charge to dissipate quickly.

TEACHER NOTES

21.1 The Capacitor

Process Skills

observing, measuring, communicating, predicting, hypothesizing, questioning, controlling variables

Alternative Materials

Larger capacitors may be substituted for the 1000 μF value; however, if smaller capacitors are used, the time constant, RC, will be small. The capacitor will charge too quickly, making measurements difficult.

Teaching Suggestions

1. Discuss polarity for meters, batteries, and capacitors prior to the experiment. This preparation will minimize the chances that students will wire the circuit incorrectly. Before they close the switch, have students trace the circuit path with a finger while looking at the circuit diagram. Review with students the "Rules for Using Meters" in Appendix D.

2. The initial value of the current will rise very quickly, and then begin dropping off. In analog meters, there will be a slight delay while the meter reaches the initial reading, so students probably will not have an accurate recorded value for time = 0. At time = 0, the capacitor acts like a short, so the actual value of current is $I = V/R$, where V is the potential difference of the power source and R is the value of the circuit resistor. When the graph is plotted, the initial reading will not make a significant difference in the curve.
3. Show students how the unit of RC (seconds) can be traced from the derived SI units of resistance (ohms) and capacitance (farads).

Observations and Data

Table 1 (Sample data are given.)

Battery voltage	15.0 VDC
Capacitance	1000 μF

Table 2 (Sample data are given.)

Time (s)	27 kΩ Current (mA)	10 kΩ Current (mA)
0	1.100	0.510
5	0.900	0.450
10	0.640	0.400
15	0.450	0.340
20	0.320	0.300
25	0.230	0.250
30	0.170	0.210
35	0.130	0.190
40	0.100	0.160
45	0.080	0.140
50	0.060	0.120
55	0.050	0.100
60	0.046	0.095
65	0.039	0.083
70	0.035	0.075
75	0.032	0.064
80	0.030	0.058
85	0.028	0.052
90	0.025	0.048

Analysis

1. With no current on the capacitor plates, the current begins as a maximum. As the capacitor becomes charged, the current flow gradually becomes smaller until it approaches zero as the capacitor becomes fully charged.
2. The resistor controls the amount of current flowing to the capacitor; thus, it regulates the charging rate. The larger the value of resistance, the longer it will take to charge the capacitor.

3.

Charging Capacitor

Trial 1   Time (s)

Charging Capacitor

Trial 2   Time (s)

These graphs of current versus time for a charging capacitor were produced using the Lab Partner™ graphing program.

4. Charge $= Area_{27 k\Omega} = \frac{1}{2}bh$
   $= \frac{1}{2}(35 \text{ s})(1.1 \times 10^{-3} \text{ A})$
   $= 1.9 \times 10^{-2} \text{ C}$

Charge $= Area_{10 k\Omega} = \frac{1}{2}bh$
   $= \frac{1}{2}(90 \text{ s})(0.4 \times 10^{-3} \text{ A})$
   $= 1.8 \times 10^{-2} \text{ C}$

5. Trial 1: $C = q/V = (1.9 \times 10^{-2} \text{ C})/15.0 \text{ V} = 1.3 \times 10^{-3} \text{ F} = 1300 \ \mu F$
   Trial 2: $C = q/V = (1.8 \times 10^{-2} \text{ C})/15.0 \text{ V} = 1.2 \times 10^{-3} \text{ F} = 1200 \ \mu F$

6. Trial 1: relative error $= (1300 - 1000)(100\%)/1000 = 30\%$
   Trial 2: relative error $= (1200 - 1000)(100\%)/1000 = 20\%$

7. Without a resistor, the capacitor would become charged almost instantly; the current would as quickly drop to zero.
8. The capacitor value and the power source voltage remained constant while the resistance was manipulated. The current in the circuit varies inversely with time.

Application

Since a capacitor requires a specific time to charge through a resistor, the *RC* combination can be used for timing applications, such as for a burglar alarm or a timer to turn on or off a light. For a short time of charging or discharging, the *RC* circuit can be used to produce musical notes for an electronic instrument or keyboard.

Extension

Answers will vary depending on the capacitor used. The exponential decay of current shown on the graph will drop more slowly as the capacitance increases.

TEACHER NOTES

22.1 Ohm's Law

Process Skills

observing, measuring, using numbers, interpreting data, communicating, predicting, inferring, questioning, controlling variables, defining operationally

Alternative Materials

An excellent source for an inexpensive, high quality voltmeter is Radio Shack. The versatile multitester unit provides several voltage ranges and current ranges from the same meter. The multitester can measure resistance if it is powered by a battery which, of course, you would not include if students are expected to find the values of unknown resistors.

Teaching Suggestions

1. Variable power supplies work well for this experiment. Remind students not to exceed the values each meter is designed to measure.
2. The recommended resistors are readily available and inexpensive, particularly if they are purchased from an electrical supply house or ordered from Radio Shack. Use of milliammeters and these resistors reduces the circuit currents; however, the resistors can still become warm. Caution students not to touch resistors when current flows in the circuit.
3. Unknown resistors can be made by covering other known resistors with heat-shrink tubing. To prevent current readings from being small and difficult to measure, try not to exceed values of more than about 470 Ω for unknowns. A couple of resistors can be placed in parallel or in series to create various resistance values. When resistors are sealed in heat-shrink tubing, the color bands are not visible. The use of unknowns encourages students to do their own work.
4. Tell students to open the switch immediately if the meter "pegs" or travels all the way to the far side of the meter.

Observations and Data

Table 1 (Sample data are given.)

Resistor	Printed value of resistor (Ω)	Tolerance range (+/− %)	Voltage (V)	Current (mA)	Current (A)	Resistance (Ω)
R_1	100	20	1.5	14	0.014	110
	100	20	5.0	49	0.049	100
R_2	150	20	1.5	10	0.010	150
	150	20	5.0	30	0.030	170
R_3	220	20	1.5	7.0	0.0070	210
	220	20	5.0	24	0.024	210

Analysis

1. See Resistance column of Table 1.
2. R_1 error: $(105 - 100)(100\%)/100 = 5\%$
R_2 error: $(160 - 150)(100\%)/150 = 7\%$
R_3 error: $(220 - 210)(100\%)/220 = 5\%$

These sample values agree fairly well; however, student answers (values) may be more divergent.
3. The resistors may have overheated, causing the values to change. The voltmeter may introduce some error in the circuit, since it requires some current to cause deflection of the needle.
4. The ammeter must be placed in series with the circuit element.
5. The voltmeter must be placed in parallel with the circuit element to be measured.
6. The current in a circuit is equal to the voltage divided by the resistance.

Application

$$R = \frac{V}{I} = \frac{120\ V}{0.5\ A} = 240\ \Omega$$

Extension

Student answers will vary. Graphs of voltage versus current should be linear and should have a positive slope.

TEACHER NOTES

Electrical Equivalent of Heat

22.2

Process Skills

observing, using numbers, measuring, interpreting data, communicating, questioning

Alternative Materials

A rheostat and a constant-voltage power supply may be substituted for the variable power supply.

Teaching Suggestions

1. Be sure to remind students to stir the water gently so that mixing takes place and localized heating is prevented.
2. A large rheostat may be used to control the current flow from a constant-voltage power supply. Most of the new power supplies are variable and have a built-in rheostat.

Observations and Data

Table 1 (Sample data are given.)

Mass of polystyrene cup	1.1 g
Mass of water and cup	189.3 g
Mass of cold water	188.2 g
Initial temperature of water	14.1°C
Room temperature	25.0°C
Final temperature of water	36.2°C
Change in temperature of water	22.1°C
Average current	2.5 A
Average voltage	10.0 V

Table 2 (Sample data are given.)

Time (min)	Current (A)	Voltage (V)
1	2.5	10.0
2	2.5	10.1
3	2.5	10.1
4	2.5	10.0
5	2.5	10.0
6	2.5	10.1
7	2.5	10.0
8	2.6	10.3
9	2.4	9.7
10	2.5	10.0
11	2.5	10.1
12	2.5	10.0
13		
14		
15		

Analysis

1. $E = IVt = (2.5 \text{ A})(10.0 \text{ V})(720 \text{ s}) = 18\ 000 \text{ J}$
2. $Q_W = m_W C_W \Delta T_W =$
   $(188.2 \text{ g})(4.18 \text{ J/g} \cdot \text{C}°)(22.1°C) = 17\ 400 \text{ J}$
3. % difference $= \dfrac{(E - Q_W)(100\%)}{E}$

   $= \dfrac{(18\ 000 - 17\ 400)(100\%)}{18\ 000} = 3.4\%$
4. Not accounted for were the energy used to raise the temperature of the coil and associated metal supports and the energy used to raise the temperature of the thermometer.

5. Yes. Students should realize that the polystyrene cup calorimeter is not an ideal set-up.
6. % conversion = (17 400 J/18 000 J)(100%) = 97%. Student answers will vary, but should be no less than 90%.
7. 100% − 16% = 84% converted to heat, so (0.84)(100 W) = 84 W expended as heat. Since there is 1 J/s per watt, (84 W)(1 J/s/W) = 84 J/s.

Applications

1. $\Delta PE = mgh = (9.8 \text{ m/s}^2)(1 \text{ kg})(50 \text{ m}) = 490 \text{ J}$
   $= \Delta$thermal energy (ΔQ)
   $\Delta T = \Delta Q/mC = 490 \text{ J}/(1000 \text{ g})(4.18 \text{ J/g} \cdot °C)$
   $= 0.12°C$
   This is not sufficient to produce a warm shower.
2. $Q_W = (4.18 \text{ J/g} \cdot \text{C}°)(90 \text{ g})(89°C) = 33\ 482 \text{ J}$
   $t = 33\ 482 \text{ J}/200 \text{ J/s} = 167 \text{ s or 2 min 47 s}$

23.1 Series Resistance

Process Skills

observing, measuring, using numbers, communicating, interpreting data, predicting, questioning

Alternative Materials

Resistors of 5, 10, or 15 Ω can be used, but they are more expensive and difficult to obtain and must have 10-W ratings to prevent overheating in Part A (use of a single resistor). In this case, an ammeter with a range of 0–1 A must be used instead of the smaller milliammeter.

Teaching Suggestions

1. Caution students that, even though the resistors are small, they can still become hot if too large a voltage is applied. Do not exceed the recommended voltage and do not handle the resistors while the current is flowing through the circuit.

2. Remind students to check the polarity of their meters before activating the circuit to prevent damage to the meters.
3. Remind students to convert milliamps to amps before applying Ohm's law.

Observations and Data

Table 1 (Sample data are given.)

	R_1 (Ω)	Ammeter reading (mA)	Voltmeter reading (V)
	100	50	5.0
Tolerance (%)	10		

Table 2 (Sample data are given.)

	R_1 (Ω)	R_2 (Ω)	Ammeter reading (mA)	Voltmeter reading (V)
	100	82	28	5.0
Tolerance (%)	10	10		

Table 3 (Sample data are given.)

	R_1 (Ω)	R_2 (Ω)	R_3 (Ω)	Ammeter reading (mA)	Voltmeter reading (V)			
					$V_{1,2,3}$	V_1	V_2	V_3
	100	82	68	20.0	5.0	2.0	1.6	1.4
Tolerance (%)	10	10	5					

Analysis

1. Measured value of resistance $= \dfrac{V}{I}$

$= \dfrac{(5.0 \text{ V})}{(0.05 \text{ A})} = 100 \ \Omega$. The two values agree.

2. Measured value of the equivalent resistance $= \dfrac{V}{I} = \dfrac{(5.0 \text{ V})}{(0.028 \text{ A})} = 180 \ \Omega$. The equivalent resistance $= 100 \ \Omega + 82 \ \Omega = 182 \ \Omega$. $180 \ \Omega$ is within the 20% tolerance range. Student answers will vary, but should be within the tolerance range.

3. Measured equivalent resistance $= \dfrac{V}{I}$

$= \dfrac{(5.0 \text{ V})}{(0.02 \text{ A})} = 250 \ \Omega$. The calculated equivalent resistance $= R_1 + R_2 + R_3 = 100 + 82 + 68 = 250 \ \Omega$. The two values agree. Student answers should fall within the sum of the tolerances for the resistors.

4. The equivalent resistance is determined by adding the individual resistances together.

5. The sum of the individual voltages $= 2.0 \text{ V} + 1.6 \text{ V} + 1.4 \text{ V} = 5.0 \text{ V}$. The sum of the voltage drops across individual resistances is equal to the total voltage drop around the circuit.

6. The amount of (equivalent) resistance determines the current in the circuit as long as the voltage remains constant.

Application

The equivalent resistance is found by

$$R = \frac{V}{I} = \frac{120 \text{ V}}{1.0 \text{ A}} = 120 \ \Omega.$$

Since there are 50 lights of equal resistance, the resistance of an individual light is $120 \ \Omega/50 = 2.4 \ \Omega$. The voltage drop per light is $V = IR = (1.0 \text{ A})(2.4 \ \Omega) = 2.4 \text{ V}$.

TEACHER NOTES

23.2 Parallel Resistance

Process Skills

observing, predicting, measuring, using numbers, interpreting data, communicating, inferring

Teaching Suggestions

1. Remind students to convert milliamps to amps before applying Ohm's law.
2. Caution students to use care when touching the resistors and to leave switches closed no more than a few seconds at a time.
3. Depending on the internal resistance of the ammeters, student data may not match perfectly. Remind them to take careful measurements.
4. Be sure to allow sufficient time for students to complete this experiment. It takes time to move the meters about and obtain circuit measurements.

Observations and Data

Table 1 (Sample data are given.)

R_1 (Ω)	Ammeter reading (mA)	Voltmeter reading (V)
180	17	3.0
Tolerance (%) 10		

Table 2 (Sample data are given.)

R_1 (Ω)	R_2 (Ω)	Ammeter reading (mA)			Voltmeter reading (V)		
		I	I_1	I_2	V	V_1	V_2
180	220	30	17	14	3	3	3
Tolerance (%) 10	10						

Table 3 (Sample data are given.)

R_1 (Ω)	R_2 (Ω)	R_3 (Ω)	Ammeter reading (mA)				Voltmeter reading (V)			
			I	I_1	I_2	I_3	V	V_1	V_2	V_3
180	220	330	39	17	14	10	3	3	3	3
Tolerance (%) 10	10	10								

Analysis

1. $R_1 = \dfrac{3.0 \text{ V}}{0.017 \text{ A}} = 176 \ \Omega$.

   Student answers will vary; the sample data yield a result within the tolerance range.

2. a. $R = \dfrac{V}{I} = \dfrac{3.0 \text{ V}}{0.03 \text{ A}} = 100 \ \Omega$

   b. $I = 17 \text{ mA} + 14 \text{ mA} = 31 \text{ mA}$

   c. $R_1 = \dfrac{3.0 \text{ V}}{0.017 \text{ A}} = 176 \ \Omega$

   d. $R_2 = \dfrac{3.0 \text{ V}}{0.014 \text{ A}} = 214 \ \Omega$

   e. $R = 99 \ \Omega$

3. Student values may have a greater difference, depending on the quality of the ammeters used.

   a. The measured current should equal the sum of the currents (or very nearly).

   b. Using the sample readings, the calculated equivalent resistance (99 Ω) equals the measured equivalent resistance (97 Ω) within the tolerance of the resistors.

4. a. $R = \dfrac{3.0 \text{ V}}{0.039 \text{ A}} = 77 \ \Omega$

   b. $I = 17 \text{ mA} + 14 \text{ mA} + 10 \text{ mA} = 41 \text{ mA}$

   c. $R_1 = \dfrac{3.0 \text{ V}}{0.017 \text{ A}} = 176 \ \Omega$

   d. $R_2 = \dfrac{3.0 \text{ V}}{0.014 \text{ A}} = 214 \ \Omega$

   e. $R_3 = \dfrac{3.0 \text{ V}}{0.010 \text{ A}} = 300 \ \Omega$

   f. $R = 76 \ \Omega$

5. Student values may have a greater difference, depending on the quality of the ammeters used.

   a. The two currents are very nearly equal (they should be equal).

   b. Using the sample readings, the calculated equivalent resistance (76 Ω) equals the measured equivalent resistance (73 Ω) within the tolerance of the resistors.

6. The sum of the current in the branches of a parallel circuit equals the total current in the circuit.

7. The voltage drop across each branch of a parallel circuit is the same as the voltage drop across the entire circuit.

8. The total current increases.

Application

Since the equivalent resistance is 0.5000 Ω and the meter resistance is 500.0 Ω, the shunt resistance is found from

$$\frac{1}{R} = \frac{1}{R_1} + \frac{1}{R_2}, \text{ or } \frac{1}{0.5000 \ \Omega} = \frac{1}{500.0 \ \Omega} + \frac{1}{R_s}.$$

Solving for $\dfrac{1}{R_s}$,

$$\frac{1}{R_s} = 2.0 \ \Omega - 0.002 \ \Omega = 1.998 \ \Omega.$$

Therefore, $R_s = \dfrac{1}{1.998} = 0.5005 \ \Omega$.

Extension

There are many ways to solve this problem. In one solution, the circuit can be reduced to two parallel sets, each having four 100-Ω resistors in parallel connected in series with a pair of 100-Ω resistors in parallel. This reduces to two 75-Ω resistors in parallel, which is equivalent to one 37.5-Ω resistor in series with the 1.0-V battery.

The current $= I = \dfrac{V}{R} = \dfrac{1.0 \text{ V}}{37.5 \ \Omega} = 27 \text{ mA}$.

24.1 The Nature of Magnetism

Process Skills

observing, communicating, inferring, formulating models

Teaching Suggestions

1. Some magnets may lose their magnetism if they are exposed to heat or dropped. They can be remagnetized in commercially available magnetizers.
2. To prevent iron filings from becoming attached to the magnets, you may want to place the magnets in a plastic sandwich bag.
3. If the lodestones are weak, you may substitute staples for the paper clips.

Observations and Data

B. Magnetic Field Lines
The field lines are continuous from one pole to another.

C. Magnetic Field Lines Between Poles
The like poles repel while the unlike poles attract.

(a)

(b)

D. Direction of the Magnetic Field Lines

E. Lodestone Properties
Observations of lodestone:
The lodestone attracts paper clips and behaves like a magnet. The compass points to different north and south poles on the lodestone.

F. Induced Magnetism
Observations of nail:
The nail by itself does not pick up the paper clips. The nail becomes a magnet when it is attached to the bar magnet and picks up the paper clips. The free end of the nail and the end of the magnet to which it is attached have the same pole type.

Analysis

1. The magnetic field is most concentrated near the poles.
2. The magnetic field lines between two like poles show that like poles repel each other.
3. The magnetic field lines between two unlike poles show that unlike poles attract each other.
4. The magnetic field lines extend from the north pole to the south pole outside a bar magnet. This is the direction in which the north pole of a compass points when it is placed in the magnetic field.
5. Lodestones attract iron (ferrous) materials. They act like small magnets with poles.
6. The free end of the nail has the same polarity as that of the end of the magnet to which it is attached.

Application

Earth's north magnetic pole behaves like the south pole of a magnet. Remind students that Earth's magnetic axis does not coincide with the true or geographic N–S axis. The angle between the two north poles is called the angle of magnetic declination.

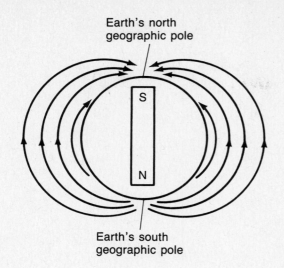

Earth's north
geographic pole

S

N

Earth's south
geographic pole

C. The Field Around a Coil
The compass needle lines up as indicated by the labels in the figure.

D. An Electromagnet
1. Sample electromagnet picks up six clips.
2. Sample electromagnet picks up ten clips; increasing the number of loops increases the magnet's strength.
3. Sample electromagnet picks up 16 clips; increasing the current increases the magnet's strength.

Analysis
1. The direction of the magnetic field follows the direction of the fingers of the right hand when the right thumb points in the direction of the conventional current (from positive to negative).
2. It increases electromagnetic strength.
3.

S   N

+   —

4. The number of turns, the current strength, and the type of core determine the strength of an electromagnet.
5. A bar magnet maintains its magnetism for a long time, while an electromagnet is a temporary magnet, which loses its magnetism as soon as the current flow is stopped.

Application
Continuously applied current: strong electromagnets—such as in junk yards, magnetic-resonance-imaging equipment

Intermittently applied current: telephone ringers, door bells, buzzers, door locks, electric switches (relays)

TEACHER NOTES
24.2 : Principles of Electromagnetism

Process Skills
observing, communicating, formulating models, classifying, interpreting data, predicting, questioning

Teaching Suggestions
1. Review the right-hand rule with students before beginning the lab.
2. Remind students to leave the switches closed only long enough to make observations.

Observations and Data
A. The Field Around a Long, Straight Wire
With current flowing upward, the north pole points counter-clockwise about the wire.

With current flowing downward, the north pole points clockwise about the wire.

B. Strength of the Field
The filings are oriented in circular patterns about the wire. The smaller the current, the less distinct the patterns. With 0.5 A of current, almost no pattern is observed.

24.3

Magnetic Field About a Coil

Process Skills

observing, measuring, interpreting data, communicating, hypothesizing, questioning

Troubleshooting

If the ammeter that is measuring loop current gives erratic readings, have students clean the contacts on the current balance and the supports for it.

Alternative Materials

1. A single large DC power supply, 12 V, 5 A, can be used with two rheostats to provide the necessary current to operate the coil and the loop. Separate power supplies and rheostats can also be used for the coil and loop.

Teaching Suggestions

1. It would be convenient to determine the mass of a long length of the string that you will be using to have a value for the mass/length before students begin the activity.
2. If students will be performing Experiment 26.1, they should record the coil number (number or identify the coils prior to the lab) and use the same coil for that experiment. Numbering the coils also encourages students to do their own work, particularly if they believe that each coil will produce different results.

Observations and Data

Table 1 (Sample data are given.)

Trial	Length of wire, L (m)	Current in wire, I (A)	Current in coil, I_c (A)	Length of string (m)	Force per length of string (N/m)
1	0.03	1.0	4.0	0.15	0.0032
2	0.03	1.0	4.4	0.17	0.0032
3	0.03	1.0	2.3	0.096	0.0032
4	0.03	1.0	1.0	0.040	0.0032
5	0.03	1.0	1.5	0.064	0.0032

Table 2 (Sample data are given.)

Trial	Force (N)	Magnetic induction, B (T, N/A · m)
1	4.80×10^{-4}	0.016
2	5.44×10^{-4}	0.018
3	3.07×10^{-4}	0.010
4	1.28×10^{-4}	0.0043
5	2.05×10^{-4}	0.0068

Analysis

1. See Table 2 for the values of force.
2. See Table 2 for the values of magnetic induction. For example, Trial 1:

$$B = \frac{F}{IL} = \frac{(4.8 \times 10^{-4} \text{ N})}{(1.0 \text{ A})(0.03 \text{ m})} = 0.016 \text{ T}$$

3. This straight-line graph shows that magnetic induction varies directly with the current through the solenoid.

The graph of magnetic induction (magnetic field strength) versus solenoid coil current was produced using the Lab Partner™ graphing program.

Application

$F = mg = (1.0 \text{ kg})(9.8 \text{ m/s}^2) = 9.8 \text{ N}$, and $F = BIL$;

therefore, $L = \dfrac{F}{BI} = \dfrac{(9.8 \text{ N})}{(5.0 \times 10^{-5} \text{ T})(1.0 \text{ A})}$

$= 2.0 \times 10^5 \text{ m}$ (nearly 200 km!).

It is not reasonable to use Earth's magnetic field since it is so weak. The weight of 200 km of wire is much more than 9.8 N.

25.1 Electro-magnetic Induction 1

Process Skills

observing, communicating, interpreting data, measuring, hypothesizing, predicting, questioning

Alternative Materials

Students can wind the coils around cardboard tubes, such as toilet-paper tubes or paper-towel tubes, using 20- or 22-gauge copper wire. A few pieces of masking or electrical tape keep the coils together. Commercially made coils are available or use a galvanoscope block with wound coils.

Teaching Suggestions

1. Help students understand that while the conversion of electrical energy to mechanical energy in a magnetic field is the principle of the electric motor, the conversion of mechanical energy to electrical energy in a magnetic field is the principle of the electric generator. Emphasize that this correspondence of opposites prevails in many areas of science and provides guidance and structure to researchers and students alike.
2. Remind students to keep magnets away from their wrist watches.

Observations and Data

1. The galvanometer just barely moves. Student answers will vary, depending on the strength of the magnet and the sensitivity of the galvanometer.
2. Students should see movement of the galvanometer needle, indicating that a current was produced.
3. Students should find that a much stronger current is produced, compared to that produced by the 25-turn coil.
4. The galvanometer needle deflects in one direction when the magnet is thrust into the coil and in the opposite direction when the magnet is pulled out. The needle deflects in opposite directions when the north or south pole is thrust into the coil, due to the different directions of the magnetic fields.
5. The stronger magnet produces the stronger current. The greater the speed of the magnets' motion, the stronger the current.
6. No current is induced when the magnets are stationary. A current is produced when the coil moves over the magnets.

Analysis

1. The end of the coil into which the north pole of the magnet is thrust becomes a south pole, and then reverses when the magnet is pulled out. An induced current acts in such a direction that its magnetic properties oppose the change by which the current is induced.
2. The EMF, measured in volts, depends on the strength of the magnetic field, the number of loops in the coil, and the speed at which the wire cuts through the magnetic flux. If the moving wire is part of a closed circuit, the induced current is equal to the voltage divided by the resistance of the circuit.
3. From Ohm's law, $V = IR$. If resistance is constant, the voltage (EMF) is proportional to the current. This experiment showed that the strength of the magnetic field, B, affected the magnitude of the current; the number of turns, I, affected the current; and the rate of movement, v, of the wire through the magnetic field affected the current. Therefore $EMF \propto B$, $EMF \propto I$, and $EMF \propto v$, and the equation, $EMF = Blv$, is substantiated.
4. No current flows in the wire. An electric current is produced only when the wire cuts the magnetic field lines.
5. No matter what its source, each field exerts a force, $q'E$, on a test charge, q'.

Application

A changing magnetic field appears in the iron core due to the alternating current in the primary coil. Through the iron core, the field moves over the loops of the secondary coil, causing an induced current, and an induced EMF, to appear in that coil. The transformer does not work with direct current since no changing magnetic field is produced; thus, no current can be induced.

Extension

1. $EMF = Blv \sin \theta$
   $= (0.75 \times 10^{-2} \text{ T})(0.40 \text{ m})(5.0 \text{ m/s})(\sin 45°)$
   $= 1.1 \times 10^{-2} \text{ V}$

2. *EMF* is greatest when $\theta = 90°$ and diminishes to zero as θ approaches $0°$.
3. The output is an alternating current that varies sinusoidally over a period of time; the amplitude of the current changes with the sine of the angle between *v* and *B*. In the U.S., the frequency of the AC is 60 cycles per second; the current changes direction (alternates) 120 times per second.

Electromagnetic Induction 2

25.2

Process Skills

observing, inferring, communicating, interpreting data, questioning

Teaching Suggestions

1. If the horseshoe magnets are weak, try remagnetizing them. To increase the magnetic field strength, two magnets may be placed side by side, with like poles together, and secured with pieces of tape.
2. Different lab groups could wind different sizes (number of turns) of coils to determine which size coil works best.
3. Smaller size wire, such as 26- or 28-gauge wire, makes the best coils because of its lighter weight.
4. It is useful to discuss Lenz's law either prior to or at the beginning of the experiment.

Observations and Data

1. The swinging coil has an induced current that changes direction as the swinging coil changes direction. The coil generates 200–500 μA per swing. The faster the coil swings, the stronger the induced current. The stronger the magnetic field, the stronger the induced current.

2. When one coil starts swinging, the other also begins to swing. The coils swing in opposite directions and gradually come to rest.
3. The unhooked coil swings faster than it does when it is attached to the other coil.
4. The galvanometer shows that current flows from one coil through the galvanometer to the other coil, causing it to move. When the second coil swings back, it generates current in the opposite direction; this current flows back to the first coil. The entire process continues back and forth until friction brings the system to a rest.

Analysis

1. Factors affecting the strength of the induced current include the relative speed of the wire through the magnetic field and the strength of the magnetic field.
2. The current produced when one coil is set in motion flows to the other coil through the connecting wires. This current interacts with the magnetic field surrounding the second coil, causing it to move. When the second coil swings back, it generates current in the opposite direction, which flows back to the first coil. The entire process continues until friction brings the system to rest.
3. The unattached coil swings faster. Lenz's law states that the direction of the induced current is such that the magnetic effects produced by the current oppose the change in flux that caused the current. When the generator coil is attached to the second coil, a load exists on the generator, which creates an opposing force.
4. The first coil set into motion acts like the generator; its induced current causes the second coil, which is the motor, to swing. The process reverses itself as the coils swing in the opposite directions.

Application

When the lights are turned on, a larger current flows from the generator. When the current increases, the opposing force also increases, and it is more difficult to turn the generator. A larger opposing force means that a larger amount of mechanical energy must be supplied to turn the generator.

26.1 Mass of an Electron

Process Skills

observing, inferring, communicating, interpreting data, measuring, questioning, using numbers, designing experiments

Teaching Suggestions

1. The older, 6AF6G-style tuning-eye tube is no longer in production. However, the new, 6E5 version of a mass-of-the-electron apparatus is available from science supply houses.
2. Remind students that they must use the same coil they used in Experiment 24.3 and the graph they made of magnetic induction versus solenoid coil current.

Observations and Data

Table 1 (Sample data are given.)

Trial	Coil current, I (A)	Magnetic induction, B (T, N/A·m)	Potential difference, V (V)	Radius, r (m)
1	1.4	0.006	160	0.0075
2				
3				

Table 2 (Sample data are given.)

Trial	B^2 (N/A·m)^2	r^2 (m^2)	Charge on one electron, q (C)	mass/charge (kg/C)	Mass of electron (kg)
1	3.6×10^{-5}	5.63×10^{-5}	1.6×10^{-19}	6.33×10^{-12}	1.0×10^{-30}
2					
3					

Analysis

1. See Table 2
2. 1.0×10^{-30} kg; student answers will vary.
3. Relative error = $(1.0 \times 10^{-30} - 9.1 \times 10^{-31})$ $(100\%)/(9.1 \times 10^{-31})$ = 10%. Student error will vary depending on the accuracy of their graphs from the previous experiment and the accuracy in approximating the radius. In general, all answers should be within an order of magnitude.

4. Regardless of even a large error, such as 50–100% or more, the mass of an electron has been approximated with relatively simple equipment, and it is very, very small.

Application

The magnetic induction of Earth is about 100 times smaller than the coil. To effect the same displacement, a very large tube would be needed since Earth's magnetic field would cause a very small deflection, which is probably not measurable in one of our laboratory tubes. The students might propose using a larger tube or suggest using a long straight tube and measuring the deflection parallel with the field to compare it to the deflection perpendicular to the field.

27.1 Planck's Constant

Process Skills

observing, measuring, using numbers, communicating, interpreting data, predicting, questioning

Alternative Materials

A variable power supply can be used instead of the battery; however, it should provide well-filtered, clean DC power. Most new variable power supplies meet these criteria. Using a variable power supply permits elimination of the battery and potentiometer.

Teaching Suggestions

1. The packing material of many LEDs displays the wavelength of their emitted radiation. However, if you have some LEDs that are not identified, the following table will help in approximating the wavelengths of light for typical LEDs.

Color	Wavelength (nm)
red	635, 650, 660, 675, 690 (standard red is 650 or 660)
yellow	590, 610
green	550, 563, 570

2. The purpose of the 22-Ω resistor is to limit current to the LED, thus preventing instantaneous destruction of the LED if students accidentally apply too large a voltage. Resistance could be increased to as much as 33 Ω, if desired, or eliminated. If it is eliminated and a potential difference of 3 V is applied to the LED, excessive current will flow through the junction and destroy it.

Observations and Data

Table 1

LED	LED Color	Wavelength (nm)
1	red	650
2	yellow	590
3	green	563

Table 2 (Sample data are given.)

LED 1		LED 2		LED 3	
Voltage (V)	Current (mA)	Voltage (V)	Current (mA)	Voltage (V)	Current (mA)
1.50	0	1.50	0	1.50	0
1.55	0	1.55	0	1.55	0
1.60	0	1.60	0	1.60	0
1.65	1	1.65	0	1.65	0
1.70	2	1.70	0	1.70	0
1.75	3.7	1.75	0	1.75	0
1.80	5.0	1.80	1	1.80	0
1.85	7.5	1.85	1.7	1.85	1
1.90	11.0	1.90	3.1	1.90	1.8
1.95	13.5	1.95	5.5	1.95	3.2
2.00	17.5	2.00	7.0	2.00	5.1
2.05	22.0	2.05	13.5	2.05	9.0
2.10	25.0	2.10	17.0	2.10	13.0
2.15		2.15	21.0	2.15	15.0
2.20		2.20		2.20	18.0
2.25		2.25		2.25	21.0
2.30		2.30		2.30	23.0
2.35		2.35		2.35	

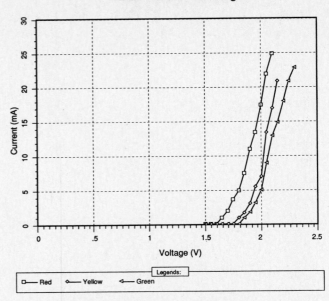

LED Current vs Voltage

Legends: □—— Red   ◇—— Yellow   ◁—— Green

This graph of LED current versus voltage was produced with the Lab Partner™ graphing program.

Analysis

1. a. red voltage: 1.75 V
   b. yellow voltage: 1.95 V
   c. green voltage: 2.05 V
2. red LED, $h = qV\lambda/c = (1.6 \times 10^{-19}\text{ C})$ $(1.75\text{ V})(650\text{ nm})/(3.0 \times 10^8\text{ m/s})$ $= 6.1 \times 10^{-34}\text{ J} \cdot \text{s}$
   yellow LED, $h = qV\lambda/c = (1.6 \times 10^{-19}\text{ C})$ $(1.95\text{ V})(590\text{ nm})/(3.0 \times 10^8\text{ m/s})$ $= 6.14 \times 10^{-34}\text{ J} \cdot \text{s}$
   green LED, $h = qV\lambda/c = (1.6 \times 10^{-19}\text{ C})$ $(2.05\text{ V})(563\text{ nm})/(3.0 \times 10^8\text{ m/s})$ $= 6.2 \times 10^{-34}\text{ J} \cdot \text{s}$
3. red error $= (6.6 \times 10^{-34} - 6.1 \times 10^{-34})$ $(100\%)/6.6 \times 10^{-34} = 8\%$
   yellow error $= 7\%$
   green error $= 6\%$
   Student answers will vary but should be within 10–15% of h.
4. A blue LED should have a voltage greater than that of the green LED, which may be approximately 2.4–2.6 V. The infrared LED will have a voltage less than that of the red LED, or less than 1.6 V, possibly 1.2–1.4 V.

Application

The light-emitting diode is more durable because it has no fragile filament. Light from an incandescent light bulb comprises the entire visible spectrum, while light from the LED has only one wavelength (monochromatic light). The wavelength of an LED is a very narrow band around its computed value, with a band width of about 25–30 nm. When wavelength is closely controlled and the light is produced in a cavity at the junction, a laser diode results.

The Photo-electric Effect

Process Skills

observing, measuring, using numbers, inferring, predicting, interpreting data, communicating, questioning

Alternative Materials

The photoelectric-effect modules with associated amplifiers are available from most science suppliers or from Thornton Associates. Different manufacturers have equipment that is generally compatible only with their own product line.

Teaching Suggestions

1. Since many filters are of the broad-band type that allows a range of frequencies to pass through, selection of a shorter wavelength works best.
2. A sensitive voltmeter, such as a digital voltmeter, may be used to measure more accurately the stopping voltage.

Observations and Data

Table 1 (Sample data are given.)

Filter color	Stopping voltage (V)	Energy (J)
red	0.20	3.2×10^{-20}
blue	0.45	7.2×10^{-20}
green	0.40	6.4×10^{-20}
yellow	0.41	6.6×10^{-20}
ultraviolet	1.45	2.3×10^{-19}

Table 2 (Sample data are given.)

Filter color	Wavelength (m)	Frequency (Hz)
red	6.6×10^{-7}	4.5×10^{14}
blue	4.8×10^{-7}	6.3×10^{14}
green	5.2×10^{-7}	5.8×10^{14}
yellow	5.8×10^{-7}	5.2×10^{14}
ultraviolet	4.2×10^{-7}	7.2×10^{14}

Analysis

1. See Table 2.
2.

This graph of photoelectron kinetic energy versus frequency of incident light was produced using the Lab Partner™ graphing program.

3. The intersection of the x-axis represents the value of the threshold frequency where photoelectrons are just emitted with zero kinetic energy.
4. The slope of the graph should be Planck's constant. With the sample data, the slope equals 6.5×10^{-34} J·s. This is only a 2% difference from the accepted value of Planck's constant.

Application

From the use of $E = hf = hc/\lambda$, you know that red light has a relatively low frequency (high wavelength) compared to other colors of light. Since red photons contain less energy than green or blue photons, they are less likely to further expose the film.

28.1 Spectra

Process Skills

observing, measuring, interpreting data, communicating, questioning

Teaching Suggestions

1. If two spectrum-tube power supplies are available, they can be located in different parts of the room. Students can move from one to the other and collect data. The teacher can change the spectrum tubes, reducing the risk to students of shock or burns.
2. The emission spectra transparency from Chapter 28 (Transparency 41) can be used for a post-lab discussion or for evaluation of laboratory data. Element names can be covered and the transparency can be used as an evaluation instrument if you decide to give students unknowns for analysis and identification.

Observations and Data
Table 1

Analysis

1. The color of the glowing gas tube is different from that of the bright lines visible in the spectroscope. The tube color is produced by a mixture of the individual spectral color lines.
2. The spectral lines for each element vary in intensity. Some are quite bright in comparison to others.
3. The spectrum observed is identical to that of mercury gas. The fluorescent tube is filled with mercury gas.

Applications

1. Emission spectra of gases from the sun and other stars can be analyzed to determine the elements present in these distant objects.
2. Some practical uses might include analysis of unknown substances or determination of components of substances.

29.1 Semi-conductor Properties

Process Skills

observing, measuring, using numbers, communicating, interpreting data, predicting, questioning

Alternative Materials

Any diode or rectifier can be substituted for the 1N4004 series diode as long as the diode working voltage is greater than the voltage you are using.

Teaching Suggestions

1. The 10-Ω resistor serves as a current-limiting device to prevent damage to the ammeter in case students accidently turn the potentiometer control and apply the full battery or power-supply voltage to the meter. If the power-supply voltage is over 3 V, such as 6 V, the resistance can be increased to 33–47 Ω.

2. You can use any of the laboratory power supplies with an AC power output. The small transformer adapters with an AC output can be substituted. Use only a low-voltage AC power supply, not the 120-VAC line current.

Observations and Data

Table 1 (Sample data are given.)

Forward-Biased Diode									
Voltage (V)	0.00	0.10	0.20	0.30	0.40	0.50	0.60	0.70	0.80
Current (mA)	0	0	0	0	0	0	2	17.5	180

Table 2 (Sample data are given.)

Reverse-Biased Diode									
Voltage (V)	0.00	0.10	0.20	0.30	0.40	0.50	0.60	0.70	0.80
Current (mA)	0	0	0	0	0	0	0	0	0

Table 3

Diode with AC Power

AC wave shape

AC wave shape through a diode

Analysis

1.
Current versus Voltage for Forward and Reverse Biasing of a Diode

2. With a resistor in the circuit, a linear relationship between current and voltage exists for both negative and positive values of voltage. With a diode in the circuit, no current flows when it is reverse biased (for negative voltages), but the current increases exponentially when the diode is forward biased and the voltage is increased.

3. The diode conducts current in only one direction.

4. The diode is made of silicon because it begins to conduct current with a forward bias at a voltage of about 0.6 V.

5. An alternating current source has a sinusoidal wave shape. The wave shape of a current across the resistor that passes through the diode is only the positive portion of the alternating current. The negative portion of the alternating current is blocked.

6. The shape is the opposite half (negative portion) of the AC wave shape that was drawn in Table 3 (AC wave shape through a diode).

Application

The figure shows full-wave rectification. Each diode alternately conducts current for one-half of the time.

Extension

The wave shape observed should be the same as the one predicted in the application.

TEACHER NOTES
29.2

Integrated Circuit Logic Devices

Process Skills

observing, using models, classifying, communicating, measuring, predicting, questioning

Troubleshooting

Have students check that their probes are working. Students must apply power to the IC or the circuit will not work and may be destroyed.

Alternative Materials

Batteries, which have low current drain, should be used instead of power supplies, which often create problems with integrated circuits.

Teaching Suggestions

1. To simplify the test-probe arrangement, you can solder the 330-Ω resistor to one lead of the LED. Then attach two long, sturdy wires to the remaining LED lead and the resistor. Electrical tape or heat-shrink tubing can now be placed around the wires and covering the resistor. Label the negative lead. A simple test probe can be constructed by using a 2-lead, bicolor LED. A red light indicates current is flowing in one direction, while a green light indicates current is flowing in the other direction. Regardless of the direction of the leads' placement, the LED will light.
2. Requiring students to demonstrate their circuits before they continue ensures that each group does its own work. Ask different members to demonstrate different combinations.

Analysis

1. The combination produces a logical OR.
2. The NOR function is a negative OR (not OR).
3. The NAND function is a negative AND (not AND).
4. The result is an inverter. A logical 1 input produces a 0 output or a logical 0 input produces a 1 output.
5. The result is an inverter. A logical 1 input produces a 0 output or a logical 0 input produces a 1 output.

Application

$$A = (I \cdot G) \cdot [(L \cdot B_L) + (R \cdot B_R)]$$

Table 5

NAND Gate Combination

Inputs A	B	Output Z
0	0	0
0	1	1
1	0	1
1	1	1

Extension

XOR Truth Table

Inputs A	B	Output Z
0	0	0
0	1	1
1	0	1
1	1	0

Observations and Data

Table 1

AND Gate Truth Table

Inputs A	B	Output Z
0	0	0
0	1	0
1	0	0
1	1	1

Table 2

OR Gate Truth Table

Inputs A	B	Output Z
0	0	0
0	1	1
1	0	1
1	1	1

Table 3

NOR Gate Truth Table

Inputs A	B	Output Z
0	0	1
0	1	0
1	0	0
1	1	0

Table 4

NAND Gate Truth Table

Inputs A	B	Output Z
0	0	1
0	1	1
1	0	1
1	1	0

TEACHER NOTES

30.1 Radiation Properties

Process Skills

observing, using numbers, formulating models, communicating, interpreting data, measuring, questioning

Alternative Materials

An ionization-type smoke detector, which often contains americium, could be used as a radioactive source. Mantles for gasoline camping lanterns may contain radioactive thorium, which also can be used as a radioactive source.

Teaching Suggestions

1. To facilitate measurements, students can take readings for a shorter period of time, such as 15 seconds. The value for that time period can be multiplied appropriately to determine the activity in counts per minute.
2. Remind students that the decay process is spontaneous and probably will vary during the time that readings are taken. A smooth curve that best fits the data will take this into account.

Observations and Data

Background radiation = 36 c/min

Table 1 (Sample data are given.)

Distance (cm)	Measured activity (c/min)	Adjusted activity (c/min)	Distance^2 (cm^2)	1/Distance^2 (cm^{-2})
2	2616	2580	4	0.25
3	1416	1380	9	0.11
4	732	696	16	0.65
5	564	528	25	0.04
6	426	390	36	0.028
7	312	276	49	0.02
8	276	240	64	0.016
9	240	204	81	0.012
10	168	132	100	0.01
11	150	114	121	0.008
12	114	78	144	0.007
13	126	90	169	0.006
14	72	36	196	0.005
15	72	36	225	0.004
16	42	6	256	0.004
17	66	30	289	0.003
18	66	30	324	0.003
19	50	14	361	0.003
20	36	0	400	0.003

Analysis

1. See Table 1.
2.

Activity vs Distance for a Beta Source

These graphs were produced using the Lab Partner™ graphing program.

3. Activity vs 1/Distance Squared for a Beta Source

4. Background radiation originates from cosmic radiation and from naturally decaying materials (from such sources as rocks or the soil).
5. The graphs show that the intensity of radiation varies inversely with the square of the distance from the source. The graph of adjusted activity versus distance decreases exponentially as the distance increases. The graph of adjusted activity versus 1/distance^2 is a straight line, thus confirming the relationship.

6. The curves have the same shape whether or not the background radiation is subtracted. It is important to subtract the background radiation when the source is weak compared to the background level, or the graph of activity versus distance will be asymptotic.

Application

Since the radioactive activity decreases at the rate of the reciprocal of the distance squared, the measured activity should be one-ninth of that measured at 5 cm, or about 1100 c/min.

Extension

The results for gamma radiation are similar to those for the beta radiation.

Background radiation = 26 c/min

Gamma Radiation			
Distance (cm)	Measured activity (c/min)	Distance (cm)	Measured activity (c/min)
2	612	12	42
3	360	13	50
4	228	14	42
5	186	15	42
6	120	16	66
7	114	17	24
8	120	18	
9	72	19	
10	78	20	
11	30		

31.1 Radioactive Shielding

Process Skills

observing, communicating, interpreting data, measuring, predicting, questioning

Teaching Suggestions

1. Before starting, check that the alpha source activity is measurable. If the activity is too weak, have students skip this part.

2. Organize small groups of three or four. Students are then busy manipulating layers of shielding material, timing, resetting the Geiger counter, and recording data and can move quickly through the experiment.

Observations and Data

Background radiation = 7 c/10 s

Table 1 (Sample data are given.)

Number of sheets	Measured Activity (c/10s)							
	Cardboard			Aluminum			Lead	
	alpha	beta	gamma	alpha	beta	gamma	beta	gamma
0	280	670	190	255	484	184	521	173
2	9	656	200	5	409	162	4	147
4		585	173		152	135		114
6		560	154		20	142		120
8		452	162		2	160		96
10		371	169			107		63

Analysis

1. Alpha particles are most easily absorbed; gamma rays are least easily absorbed.
2. Cardboard is not an effective absorber of beta or gamma radiation. Beta radiation is reduced to one-half by approximately three sheets of aluminum. Gamma radiation is reduced to one-half by approximately eight sheets of lead.
3. Alpha particles are effectively blocked by a pair of cardboard or aluminum sheets, while beta and gamma rays pass through the same amount of shielding. A pair of lead sheets blocks beta rays, while gamma rays pass through the same amount of shielding.
4. The gamma radiation is not eliminated, but is reduced as it passes through lead.

Application

The number of lead sheets required varies, depending on the sheet thickness. With the samples used in this experiment, approximately 12 sheets reduced the intensity to one-fourth.

Extension

Since the intensity of a photon beam is reduced exponentially as it penetrates a particular type of absorber, theoretically, an absorber of infinite thickness would be required to reduce the beam intensity to zero.

STUDENT EDITION

Merrill

Physics

*Principles
and Problems*

AUTHOR

Craig Kramer
Physics Teacher
Bexley High School
Bexley, Ohio

GLENCOE
Macmillan/McGraw-Hill

New York, New York   Columbus, Ohio   Mission Hills, California   Peoria, Illinois

A Glencoe/McGraw-Hill Program

Merrill Physics: Principles & Problems

Student Edition
Teacher Wraparound Edition
Problems and Solutions Manual
Teacher Resource Package
Transparency Package
Laboratory Manual:
  Student and Teacher Editions

Study Guide, Student Edition
Lesson Plan Booklet
English/Spanish Glossary
Computer Test Bank

ISBN 0-02-826724-9

Send all inquiries to: **GLENCOE DIVISION, Macmillan/McGraw-Hill**
936 Eastwind Drive
Westerville, Ohio 43081

Printed in the United States of America

3 4 5 6 7 8 9 POH 99 98 97 96 95

Contents

Chapter	Title	Page

Preface

The Laboratory Manual contains 52 experiments for the beginning student of physics. The experiments illustrate the concepts found in this introductory course. Both qualitative and quantitative experiments are included, requiring manipulation of apparatus, observation, and collection of data. The experiments are designed to help you utilize the processes of science to interpret data and draw conclusions.

The laboratory report is an important part of the laboratory experience. It helps you learn to communicate observations and conclusions to others. Special laboratory report pages are included with each experiment to allow the most efficient use of lab-report time. The report sheets are designed as a self-contained lab report or as a guide for a more formal report. Graph paper is necessary for those labs requiring construction of graphs.

While accuracy is always desirable, other goals are of equal importance in laboratory work that accompanies early courses in science. A high priority is given to how well laboratory experiments introduce, develop, or make the physics theories learned in the classroom realistic and understandable and to how well laboratory investigations illustrate the methods used by scientists. The investigations in the *Laboratory Manual* place more emphasis on the implications of laboratory work and its relationship to general physics principles, rather than to how closely results compare with accepted quantitative values.

PROCESSES OF SCIENCE

The scientifically literate person uses the processes of science in making decisions, solving problems, and expanding an understanding of nature. The *Laboratory Manual* utilizes many processes of science in all of the lab activities. Throughout this manual, you are asked to collect and record data, plot graphs, make and identify assumptions, perform experiments, and draw conclusions. In addition, the following processes of science are included in the *Laboratory Manual*.

Observing: Using the senses to obtain information about the physical world.
Classifying: Imposing order on a collection of items or events.
Communicating: Transferring information from one person to another.
Measuring: Using an instrument to find a value, such as length or mass, that quantifies an object or event.
Using Numbers: Using numbers to express ideas, observations, and relationships.
Controlling Variables: Identifying and managing various factors that may influence a situation or event, so that the effect of any given factor may be learned.
Designing Experiments: Performing a series of data-gathering operations that provide a basis for testing an hypothesis or answering a specific question.
Defining Operationally: Producing definitions of an object, concept, or event in terms that give it a physical description.

Formulating Models: Devising a mechanism or structure that describes, acts, or performs as if it were a real object or event.

Inferring: Explaining an observation in terms of previous experience.

Interpreting Data: Finding a pattern or meaning inherent in a collection of data, which leads to a generalization.

Predicting: Making a projection of future observations based on previous information.

Questioning: Expressing uncertainty or doubt that is based on the perception of a discrepancy between what is known and what is observed.

Hypothesizing: Explaining a relatively large number of events by making a tentative generalization, which is subject to testing, either immediately or eventually, with one or more experiments.

THE EXPERIMENT

Experiments are organized into several sections. Each experiment opens with a statement describing the purpose of the activity. The Purpose is followed by a Concept and Skill Check, which reviews or introduces relevant physics concepts and background information. Numerous illustrations are provided to help you assemble the apparatus and understand the principles under investigation.

The Materials section lists the equipment used in the experiment and allows you to assemble the required materials quickly and efficiently. All of the equipment listed is either common to the average high school physics lab or can be readily obtained from local sources or a science supply company. Slight variations of equipment can be made and will not affect the basic integrity of the experiments in the *Laboratory Manual*.

The Procedure section contains step-by-step instructions to perform the experiment. This format helps you take advantage of limited laboratory time. Safety symbols alert you to potential dangers in the laboratory investigation, and caution statements are provided where appropriate.

The Observations and Data section helps organize the lab report. All tables are outlined and properly labeled. In more qualitative experiments, questions are provided to guide your observations.

In the Analysis section, you relate observations and data to the general principles outlined in the purpose of the experiment. Graphs are drawn and interpreted and conclusions concerning data are made. Questions relate laboratory observations and conclusions to basic physics principles studied in the text and in classroom discussions.

The Application section allows you to apply some aspect of the physics concept investigated. Often this section illustrates a current application of the concept.

Many of the experiments include an Extension section. Extensions are supplemental procedures or problems that expand the scope of the experiment. They are designed to further the investigation and to challenge the more interested student.

Introduction

PURPOSE OF LABORATORY EXPERIMENTS

The laboratory work in physics is designed to help you to better understand basic principles of physics. You will, at the same time, gain a familiarity with the scientific methods and techniques employed in the laboratory. In each experiment, you will be seeking a definite goal, investigating a specific principle, or solving a definite problem. To find the answer to the problem, you will make measurements, list your measurements as data, and then interpret the data to find the results of your measurements.

The values you obtain may not always agree with accepted values. Frequently this result is to be expected because your laboratory equipment is usually not sophisticated enough for precision work, and the time allowed for each experiment is not extensive. The relationships between your observations and the broad general laws of physics are of much more importance than strict numerical accuracy.

PREPARATION OF YOUR LAB REPORT

One very important aspect of laboratory work is the communication of your results obtained during the investigation. This laboratory manual is designed so that laboratory report writing is as efficient as possible. In most of the laboratory experiments in this book, you will write your report on the report sheets placed immediately following each experimental procedure. All tables are outlined and properly labeled for ease in recording data and calculations. Adequate space is provided for necessary calculations, discussion of results, conclusions, and interpretations. For instructions on writing a formal laboratory report, see Appendix F.

Using Significant Digits

When making observations and calculations, you should stay within the limitations imposed upon you by your equipment and measurements. Each time you make a measurement, you will read the scale to the smallest calibrated unit and then obtain one smaller unit by estimating. The doubtful or estimated figure is significant because it is better than no estimate at all and should be included in your written values.

It is easy, when making calculations using measured quantities, to indicate a precision greater than your measurements actually allow. To avoid this error, use the following guidelines.

- When adding or subtracting measured quantities, round off all values to the same number of significant decimal places as the quantity having the least number of decimal places.
- When multiplying or dividing measured quantities, retain in the product or quotient the same number of significant digits as in the least precise quantity.

Accuracy and Precision

Whenever you measure a physical quantity, there is some degree of uncertainty in the measurement. Error may come from a number of sources, including the type of measuring device, how the measurement is made, and how the measuring device is read. How close your measurement is to the accepted value refers to the accuracy of a measurement. In several of these laboratory activities, experimental results will be compared to accepted values.

When you make several measurements, the agreement, or closeness, of those measurements refers to the precision of the measurement. The closer the measurements are to each other, the more precise is the measurement. It is possible to have excellent precision, but to have inaccurate results. Likewise, it is possible to have poor precision, but to have accurate results when the average of the data is close to the accepted value. Ideally, the goal is to have good precision and good accuracy.

Relative Error

While absolute error is the absolute value of the difference between your experimental value and the accepted value, relative error is the percentage deviation from an accepted value. The relative error is calculated according to the following relationship:

$$\text{relative error} = \frac{|\text{accepted value} - \text{experimental value}|}{\text{accepted value}} \times 100\%.$$

Graphs

Frequently an experiment involves finding out how one quantity is related to another. The relationship is found by keeping constant all quantities except the two in question. One quantity is then varied, and the corresponding change in the other is measured. The quantity that is deliberately varied is called the independent variable. The quantity that changes due to the variation in the independent variable is called the dependent variable. Both quantities are then listed in a table. It is customary to list the values of the independent variable in the first column of the table and the corresponding values of the dependent variable in the second column.

More often than not, the relationship between the dependent and independent variables cannot be ascertained simply by looking at the written data. But if one quantity is plotted against the other, the resulting graph gives evidence of what sort of relationship, if any, exists between the variables. When plotting a graph, use the following guidelines:

- Plot the independent variable on the horizontal x-axis (abscissa).
- Plot the dependent variable on the vertical y-axis (ordinate).
- Draw the smooth line that best fits the most plotted points.

Chapter 2 of the textbook provides information about linear, parabolic, and inverse relationships between variables.

LAB PARTNER™ GRAPHING TOOLKIT

A menu-driven graphing toolkit is available from the publisher to help plot graphs of experimental data. Graphs can be produced quickly, allowing time previously spent plotting data to be used for interpreting results. Student-collected data are entered, in column format, into a spreadsheet. A graph can be made by plotting any one or more columns of data against another. The axes are self-scaling to produce the best-size graph. With the software, you can either plot individual data points as a scatter graph or connect the points. A statistics treatment procedure in the software can determine the best curve fit for your data, using a linear relationship to a ninth-order equation. The statistics procedure provides the equation for your data, the intercepts, the slope, the data correlation coefficient, and the standard error of the curve fit. Another unique feature of the program allows a data column to be treated by any standard mathematical function, including a derivative and integral to establish a new column.

Data are easily saved to a disk. Samples of the printouts of Lab Partner™ are printed in the Teacher Annotated Edition of the *Laboratory Manual*. The program is set up for Epson®-compatible printers and can be adapted for most other printers. Included is a utility program that allows users to define their own printer code parameters. The Lab Partner™ program is available from the publisher for IBM®-compatible computers with a 1.2-m, 5¼-inch drive, a 3½-inch drive, or a hard drive. A full-page graph is produced on 9 pin, 24 pin, or laser quality printers. A more basic version of the program is available for the Apple II® series computers, which produces a smaller size plot.

Safety in the Laboratory

If you follow instructions exactly and understand the potential hazards of the equipment and the procedure used in an experiment, the physics laboratory is a safe place for learning and applying your knowledge. You must assume responsibility for the safety of yourself, your fellow students, and your teacher. Here are some safety rules to guide you in protecting yourself and others from injury and in maintaining a safe environment for learning.

1. The physics laboratory is to be used for serious work.
2. Never bring food, beverages, or make-up into the laboratory. Never taste anything in the laboratory. Never remove lab glassware from the laboratory, and never use this glassware for eating or drinking.
3. Do not perform experiments that are unauthorized. Always obtain your teacher's permission before beginning an activity.
4. Study your laboratory assignment before you come to the lab. If you are in doubt about any procedure, ask your teacher for help.
5. Keep work areas and the floor around you clean, dry, and free of clutter.
6. Use the safety equipment provided for you. Know the location of the fire extinguisher, safety shower, fire blanket, eyewash station, and first aid kit.
7. Report any accident, injury, or incorrect procedure to your teacher at once.
8. Keep all materials away from open flames. When using any heating element, tie back long hair and loose clothing. If a fire should break out in the lab, or if your clothing should catch fire, smother it with a blanket or coat or use a fire extinguisher. NEVER RUN.
9. Handle toxic, combustible, or radioactive substances only under the direction of your teacher. If you spill acid or another corrosive chemical, wash it off immediately with water.
10. Place broken glass and solid substances in designated containers. Keep insoluble waste material out of the sink.
11. Use electrical equipment only under the supervision of your teacher. Be sure your teacher checks electric circuits before you activate them. Do not handle electric equipment with wet hands or when you are standing in damp areas.
12. When your investigation is completed, be sure to turn off the water and gas and disconnect electrical connections. Clean your work area. Return all materials and apparatus to their proper places. Wash your hands thoroughly after working in the laboratory.

First Aid in the Laboratory

Report all accidents, injuries, and spills to your teacher immediately.

YOU MUST KNOW safe laboratory techniques.

where and how to report an accident, injury, or spill.

the location of first aid equipment, fire alarm, telephone, and school nurse's office.

SITUATION	SAFE RESPONSE
Burns	Flush with cold water.
Cuts and bruises	Treat as directed by instructions included in your first aid kit.
Electric shock	Provide person with fresh air, have person recline in a position such that the head is lower than the body; if necessary, provide artificial respiration.
Fainting or collapse	See electric shock.
Fire	Turn off all flames and gas jets; wrap person in fire blanket; use fire extinguisher to put out fire. DO NOT use water to extinguish fire, as water may react with the burning substance and intensify the fire.
Foreign matter in eyes	Flush with plenty of water; use eye bath.
Poisoning	Note the suspected poisoning agent, contact your teacher for antidote; if necessary, call poison control center.
Severe bleeding	Apply pressure or a compress directly to the wound and get medical attention immediately.
Spills, general acid burns	Wash area with plenty of water; use safety shower; use sodium hydrogen carbonate, $NaHCO_3$ (baking soda).
Base burns	Use boric acid, H_3BO_3.

Safety Symbols

In this *Laboratory Manual* you will find several safety symbols that alert you to possible hazards and dangers in a laboratory activity. Be sure that you understand the meaning of each symbol before you begin an experiment. Take necessary precautions to avoid injury to yourself and others and to prevent damage to school property.

	DISPOSAL ALERT This symbol appears when care must be taken to dispose of materials properly.		**LASER SAFETY** This symbol appears when care must be taken to avoid staring directly into the laser beam or at bright reflections.
	BIOLOGICAL HAZARD This symbol appears when there is danger involving bacteria, fungi, or protists.		**RADIOACTIVE SAFETY** This symbol appears when radioactive materials are used.
	OPEN FLAME ALERT This symbol appears when use of an open flame could cause a fire or an explosion.		**CLOTHING PROTECTION SAFETY** This symbol appears when substances used could stain or burn clothing.
	THERMAL SAFETY This symbol appears as a reminder to use caution when handling hot objects.		**FIRE SAFETY** This symbol appears when care should be taken around open flames.
	SHARP OBJECT SAFETY This symbol appears when a danger of cuts or punctures caused by the use of sharp objects exists.		**EXPLOSION SAFETY** This symbol appears when the misuse of chemicals could cause an explosion.
	FUME SAFETY This symbol appears when chemicals or chemical reactions could cause dangerous fumes.		**EYE SAFETY** This symbol appears when a danger to the eyes exists. Safety goggles should be worn when this symbol appears
	ELECTRICAL SAFETY This symbol appears when care should be taken when using electrical equipment		**POISON SAFETY** This symbol appears when poisonous substances are used.
	PLANT SAFETY This symbol appears when poisonous plants or plants with thorns are handled.		**CHEMICAL SAFETY** This symbol appears when chemicals used can cause burns or are poisonous if absorbed through the skin.

EXPERIMENT
1.1
Bubble Up

Purpose

Develop your ability to use observations to form hypotheses.

Concept and Skill Check

When you perform the laboratory activities in this manual, you will acquire data by making observations. The observations will be either qualitative, such as color or shape, or quantitative, such as a measurement of length, mass, or rate of activity. The quality of your observations and how you organize and communicate data can affect your ability to draw inferences, form hypotheses, or predict outcomes.

Materials

100-mL beaker	4 raisins	plastic spoon
150-mL beaker	clock	metric ruler
100 mL carbonated water	100 mL tap water	

Procedure

1. Soak two raisins overnight in a 100-mL beaker filled with tap water. CAUTION: *Remember that eating and drinking in the school science laboratory is never safe. Do not eat the raisins or drink the liquids used in this experiment.*
2. Pour about 100 mL of carbonated water into a 150-mL beaker and observe the water closely for one minute. Record your observations in Table 1.
3. Using a spoon, remove one raisin from the tap water. In Table 1, describe how this raisin appears. Compare the appearance of the soaked raisin to that of a dry, normal raisin. Use a metric ruler to measure each type of raisin. Record your observations in Table 1.
4. Place the soaked raisin in the carbonated water. Watch closely for the next five minutes and record your observations of the soaked raisin in Table 2 .

Observations and Data
Table 1

Material	Observations
Carbonated water	
Soaked raisin	
Dry raisin	

1.1 Bubble Up

Table 2

Observations of Soaked Raisin in Carbonated Water:

Analysis

1. Which of your observations do you think are not related to the motion of the raisin?

2. Which of your observations do you think are related to the motion of the raisin?

3. Form a hypothesis, or generalization, to explain the observed motion of the raisin.

4. Using the materials listed for this lab, design an experiment to test your hypothesis. Write down your procedure. Identify which variables will remain constant and which will be manipulated. Predict how the motion of the raisin could be stopped.

5. Describe your experiment to your teacher. With the teacher's permission, perform your experiment. Was your prediction correct? Did the outcome support or refute your hypothesis? Explain.

Application

Why do you exhale before you do a surface dive in a lake or a swimming pool? Why do some people float better than others?

EXPERIMENT
2.1 Measuring Length

Purpose

Measure the dimensions of several objects, learn the metric system of measurement, and observe the use of significant digits to express measured values and results of calculations.

Concept and Skill Check

Proper measurement is critical in all laboratory experiments. Measurements can be made using a variety of different measuring instruments, such as an electrical meter, a thermometer, or a meter stick. Any physical measurement is uncertain. The degree of uncertainty depends upon the measuring instrument and the skill of the individual using it. Before continuing with this lab, review the introductory material on uncertainty in the front of this manual.

Examine a meter stick. Notice that it is divided into one hundred equal, numbered parts called centimeters (cm). Each centimeter is further divided into ten equal, nonnumbered parts called millimeters (mm). How accurately can you measure with a meter stick? Suppose that there are no subdivisions on the meter stick. Measure the height of your desk to the nearest meter. The desk should be one meter high. Actually it is less than one meter. You may have estimated that it is about 0.7 m high. If the meter stick is marked only in one-meter intervals, you will have a great deal of uncertainty about the desk's true height. A meter stick with centimeter subdivisions has greater precision than a meter stick with no subdivisions. Likewise, a meter stick with millimeter subdivisions has greater precision than does one with only centimeter subdivisions.

Place the meter stick with its marked edge along the top of the wood block. Read the measurements from directly in front of the meter stick and at eye level. Doing this will improve the accuracy of the readings. For a more accurate reading, use a mark farther along the meter stick, rather than at the beginning. The desired reading is obtained by subtracting the initial reading from the final reading, as shown in Figure 1.

Materials

meter stick
wood block
laboratory manual

7.35 cm − 5.00 cm = 2.35 cm

Figure 1. Subtract the first reading from the second to obtain an accurate length measurement.

Procedure

1. Measure and record in Table 1 the length, width, and height in centimeters of a block of wood. While making your measurements, read the meter stick to the nearest millimeter, and then estimate to a tenth of a millimeter. The final estimated reading and all figures to the left of it are significant digits.

2. Measure the length, width, and height in centimeters of your laboratory manual. Record the measurements in Table 1.

3. Calculate the volume of the block in cubic centimeters. Include only as many significant digits as you have in the value for one dimension of the block. Record the volume in Table 1.

2.1 Measuring Length

NAME ————————————————————————

4. Calculate the volume of the laboratory manual in cubic centimeters. In your volume calculation, include only as many significant digits as you have in the value for one dimension of the laboratory manual. Record the volume in Table 1.
5. Place the meter stick next to the edge of one page of your laboratory manual. Estimate the thickness of one page in millimeters. Record your estimate in Table 2.
6. Measure the thickness of 50, 75, and 100 pages of your laboratory manual in millimeters. Record your results in Table 2. For each quantity of pages, determine the average thickness of a single page. Record your calculations in the table.

Observations and Data
Table 1

	Length (cm)	Width (cm)	Height (cm)	Volume (cm³)
Wood block				
Laboratory manual				

Table 2

Number of pages	Total thickness (mm)	Average thickness of a single page (mm)
1		—
50		
75		
100		

Analysis

1. Why is it less accurate to use either end of the meter stick for measuring length?

2. Of all the measurements you made, which one do you feel is least precise? Explain.

3. If the values in Table 2 for the average thickness of a single page are different, which value is probably the most accurate? Explain.

Application

How important are measuring instruments with a high degree of precision to a craftsperson manufacturing picture frames?

EXPERIMENT 2.2

Measuring Temperature

Purpose

Measure the temperature of water while investigating the effects that observations have on an experimental system.

Concept and Skill Check

As you perform the experiments in this laboratory manual, you will make many observations and measurements of physical phenomena. Some measurements will be done with timers, some with heat sensors such as thermometers, and some with electrical meters such as ammeters and voltmeters. To ensure accuracy and precision, you must be familiar with laboratory techniques and apparatus. In this experiment, you will measure the temperature of three samples of hot water at constant intervals of time. You will record these measurements in tables, taking careful note of changes in each sample and of differences between the samples. Before starting the procedure, review with your lab partner how to read the scale on a thermometer.

Materials

2 250-mL beakers	4 thermometers,	electric hot plate (or Bun-
100-mL beaker	−10°C to 110°C range	sen burner with ringstand
2 10-mL graduated cylinders	safety goggles	and wire gauze)
tap water	gloves or tongs	stopwatch

Procedure

CAUTION: *Wear safety goggles while performing this experiment. Use gloves or tongs while handling containers of hot water.*

1. Place three of the thermometers in a 250-mL beaker containing cold tap water until they register the same temperature reading.

80 mL   5 mL   1 mL

Measuring Temperature

2. Heat 150 mL of water in the second 250-mL beaker until the remaining thermometer placed in it reads 65°C. Turn off the heat source.
3. Pour 80 mL of hot water into the 100-mL beaker, 5 mL of hot water into one 10-mL graduated cylinder, and 1 mL of hot water into the other 10-mL graduated cylinder.
4. Immediately place one of the three thermometers in each sample of water, as shown in Figure 1. Begin timing. Support the thermometers or hold them so their weight does not cause the small graduated cylinders to fall over.
5. Record in Table 1 the temperature of each sample every 30 seconds for three minutes. This will allow time for the thermometer readings to stabilize.

Observations and Data
Table 1

Time (minutes)	Temperature (°C)		
	80-mL Sample	5-mL Sample	1-mL Sample
0.5			
1.0			
1.5			
2.0			
2.5			
3.0			

Analysis

1. Compare the temperatures of the samples at the end of the timed period. Were the final temperatures of all samples the same?

2. How do you account for temperature differences, if any, among the samples of water?

Measuring Temperature

3. For this experimental system, list the factors that were the same (constant) and those that were different (variable).

4. How could this experiment be revised to yield more precise results?

5. Form a hypothesis about the final temperatures of the samples.

6. Explain the following statement: The act of observing a system affects the system.

Application

Radar guns transmit radio waves, which spread outward from the radar gun. The waves strike a moving vehicle and are partially reflected back to a receiver in the gun. Electronic circuitry in the radar gun then converts the received signal to the vehicle's corresponding speed. Why does the radar wave not cause a change in the speed of the moving vehicle?

Measuring
Temperature

Extension

Design an experiment to investigate the minimum quantity of water needed for the thermometers to produce accurate results. Ice water can also be investigated and the results compared to those from the hot water experiment. In the space below, write all the details of your experiment. Then show the procedure and safety precautions to your teacher and obtain permission before proceeding.

In your design, include a data table with appropriate labels and column heads that will help you record data for later analysis. Give careful consideration to the data you will need to support your hypothesis. A well-designed table allows you to collect and record all important measurements in an orderly fashion. Remember to record your measurements immediately; do not trust your memory of multiple readings taken over a period of time. Describe your results.

EXPERIMENT 2.3 : Measuring Time

Purpose

Determine the period of a recording timer.

Concept and Skill Check

The recording timer is a device that helps you study motion. It consists of a simple electric vibrator through which paper tape can be drawn. A carbon paper disc placed between the vibrating arm and the paper tape leaves a mark on the tape each time the arm goes up and down. When the recording timer is connected to a power source with constant voltage, its arm will vibrate regularly. The period of the timer is the time it takes for the arm to complete one vibration all the way up and all the way down. The frequency (f) of the timer is the number of times it vibrates per second. The period (T) of the timer is the reciprocal of the frequency ($T = 1/f$), or the time for one vibration. If the arm vibrates 60 times per second (frequency), its period is 1/60 second.

Materials

recording timer with necessary power supply
C-clamp

timer tape
carbon paper discs
stopwatch

strobe light
voltmeter (optional)

Procedure

1. Assemble the apparatus as shown in Figure 1. If your timer operates from a dry cell or an electrical power supply, attach a voltmeter to the circuit according to your teacher's instructions. Record the operating voltage for each trial of the timer.

2. Place a short strip of timer tape in the recording timer under the carbon paper. Make sure that the paper tape moves freely through the timer. Turn on your recording timer and pull the tape through. If no dots appear on the tape, check to see that the timer tape was placed under the carbon paper and that the inked side of the carbon disc was facing the timer tape. If the timer still makes no dots on the tape, ask your teacher for assistance. The distance between dots varies and is the distance the

tape moved during one complete vibration of the recording timer. The number of dots on the tape is the number of times the arm vibrated while you pulled the tape through the timer.

3. Place the end of a 3-m strip of tape into the timer. Pull the tape through the timer with a gentle, constant motion. As you pull the tape through the timer, your partner will operate the timer and stopwatch. After you have begun to pull the tape through the timer, ask your partner to start the timer and to begin timing for three seconds. At the end of three seconds, turn off the timer.

EXPERIMENT 2.3 Measuring Time

4. Count the number of dots on the tape and calculate the frequency and the period of the recording timer. Record your data in Table 1.
5. Repeat Steps 3 and 4 several times, switching places with your partner. Record all your trial data in Table 1. Compute the frequency and period of the recording timer for each trial and record these calculations in the table. Calculate the timer's average frequency and average period and write these values on the lines provided.
6. Shine a strobe light on your vibrating recording timer. Adjust the rate of flash until the vibrating arm appears to have stopped. Record the value of the strobe light flash rate (frequency) on the line provided. If your recording timer is designed to vibrate at a constant frequency and your teacher has provided that information, record that value instead of the strobe light rate.

Observations and Data
Table 1

Trial	Time (s)	Number of dots	Voltage	Frequency (vibrations/s)	Period (s)
1					
2					
3					
4					

Average frequency ————————————

Average period ————————————

Flash rate of strobe or known vibration rate of timer ————————————

Analysis

1. Would your value of the period for the timer be more accurate if you had drawn each tape through the timer for five seconds rather than for three seconds? Explain.

2. Compare your calculated average period to the strobe flash rate or known period. Calculate the relative error.

Application

Discuss the importance of a device that measures time very accurately. Hint: Time is used to define the length of a meter.

EXPERIMENT
3.1 : Uniform Motion

Purpose

Use graphical methods to analyze the motion of a vehicle.

Concept and Skill Check

You were introduced to the operation of the recording timer in Experiment 2.3. Please review the timer procedures you practiced before continuing with this experiment. In the previous laboratory activity, you were concerned with measurement of time, and you calculated the average period of the timer from your experimental results. In this investigation, the actual time in seconds that it takes for the arm to go up and down and make a dot on the tape is not important. However, it is important to understand that the time interval represented by each successive dot on the timer tape is constant.

In this laboratory activity, a strip of timer tape will be attached to a constant-velocity vehicle as shown in Figure 1. The movement of the attached tape through the timer equals the distance the vehicle travels. Therefore, the distance between two successive dots on the tape is the same as the displacement of the moving body during the time required for the timer arm to go up and down once. If the distance between dots is large, the tape was moving rapidly; if the distance between the dots is small, the tape was moving slowly.

Because the time intervals represented by successive dots are the same throughout the tape, it is possible to use this time period as a standard unit of time. For the purposes of this experiment, you will use the time represented by six successive dots on the timer tape (five full vibrations of the timer arm, or five spaces) as one time interval, Figure 2.

The distance represented by five spaces between dots on the tape is equivalent to the actual displacement of the moving vehicle during that time interval. This distance divided by one interval of time is the average velocity ($\bar{v}$) of the moving tape, which is equivalent to the average velocity of the moving vehicle during that time interval (t).

Constant-velocity vehicle

Masking tape

Paper tape

Timer

Figure 1.

$$\bar{v} = \Delta d / \Delta t$$

If the distance is measured in centimeters, the velocity of the vehicle is expressed in centimeters per time interval. If the actual time per interval is known, the velocity of the vehicle is expressed in centimeters per second or, more properly, in meters per second.

Uniform Motion

First distinguishable dot

Start 0   1   2   3   4

Time interval 1 distance

Time interval 2 distance

Figure 2. Measure the distance from the first distinguishable dot to the dot at the end of the first interval. Measure the distances for all other intervals.

Materials

recording timer with
  necessary power supply
C-clamp

timer tape
carbon paper discs
metric ruler

masking tape
constant-velocity vehicle
graph paper

Procedure

1. With your lab partner, set up the recording timer as shown in Figure 1. Insert about 1.5 m of timer tape into the timer. Make sure the tape moves freely through the timer. Using a piece of masking tape, attach the timer tape to the constant-velocity vehicle.

2. Start the timer. Then start the vehicle and allow it to pull the timer tape through the recording timer. Stop the vehicle and the timer after all the tape has been pulled through the timer. Insert another piece of recording tape into the timer and repeat the procedure so that each lab partner has a tape to analyze.

3. Write "start" at the end of the tape that was attached to the vehicle, as shown in Figure 2. Examine the dots at the "start" end of the tape. Notice that several dots are crowded close together. Find the first easily distinguishable dot and mark this dot "0." Count off five dots (spaces) from the 0 dot. Mark this dot "1." Count off five more dots from the dot marking interval 1 and label this dot "2." Continue counting five dots and marking intervals 3, 4, 5, etc. These numbers represent the intervals of time that elapsed as the vehicle traveled the distance between dot 0 and each fifth numbered dot.

4. Beginning at the "0" dot, measure in centimeters the distance on the recording tape of the first interval (between dot 0 and dot 1). Record this distance in Table 1 as the displacement during interval 1. Continue measuring the displacement of the vehicle for each successive interval and recording each value in Table 1.

5. The average velocity during a given interval is the displacement divided by one interval of time. Since the time for each measurement is one interval ($t = 1$ interval), the velocity will be numerically equal to the displacement during the interval. For example, a vehicle that traveled 3.5 cm during the first interval will have an average velocity of 3.5 cm/interval since 3.5 cm/ 1 interval = 3.5 cm/interval. Record each average velocity next to the corresponding time interval.

6. The total displacement of the vehicle at the end of any given interval is the sum of the displacements during each preceding interval plus the current measurement. The total displacement at the end of interval 1 is the displacement during interval 1. The total displacement at the end of interval 2 is the sum of the displacement during interval 1 plus the displacement during interval 2. The total displacement for each remaining interval is found in the same manner. Calculate the total displacement of the vehicle for each interval and record the values in Table 1.

3.1 Uniform Motion

NAME _____

Observations and Data
Table 1

Time (interval)	Displacement (cm)	Average velocity (cm/interval)	Total displacement (cm)
1			
2			
3			
4			
5			
6			
7			
8			
9			
10			

Analysis

1. On a sheet of graph paper, plot the velocities (vertical axis) versus the corresponding time intervads (horizontal axis). Be sure that each graph you plot in this experiment has a title and that all axes are properly labeled.
2. Write an explanation for what the graph shows. Point out any location on the graph that shows constant velocity or changing velocity. Calculate the vehicle's average velocity for the entire trip. How does it compare to the velocities during each interval? Using a colored pencil or a pen, draw a line on your graph indicating this average velocity.

3. On another sheet of graph paper, plot the total displacement (vertical axis) versus the time intervals (horizontal). Use the same size scale on the x-axis for time intervals as you did for your preceding graph.

4. Write an explanation for what the graph shows. Point out any changes in the slope of the line and describe what the slope represents.

5. Look at both graphs. Explain how the shape of the second graph correlates with the shape of the first graph.

6. In your experiment, which was the independent variable and which was the dependent variable?

Extension

1. Using the actual period for your recording timer, convert each interval to actual time in seconds. Each interval consists of five spaces (dots) from the initial dot, so the actual time for the interval will be five times the period of your recording timer. Calculate the average velocity in cm/s for each interval.

2. Using your velocity-time graph, answer the following.
   a. What does the area under the line on the graph represent?

   b. Make an estimate of the area under the curve. How does the area compare to the total displacement for the same number of intervals?

   c. What does the slope of the line represent?

EXPERIMENT
4.1 : Accelerated Motion

Purpose

Observe and analyze the motion of a uniformly accelerated body moving in a straight line.

Concept and Skill Check

The recording timer can be used to record the movement of a small cart as it is pulled across a table top by a falling mass. The resulting timer tape measures displacement of the moving cart per interval of time. From Experiment 3.1, you know that average velocity is equivalent to displacement for a given interval of time. The ratio of a change in velocity to a change in time yields acceleration $[a = (v_2 - v_1)/(t_2 - t_1)]$; this is the equation for the slope of a velocity versus time graph. With the data from this experiment, you will construct three graphs to analyze the motion of the cart: displacement versus time, velocity versus time, and acceleration versus time.

Materials

laboratory cart	timer tape	pulley
recording timer with	500-g mass	2 C-clamps
necessary power supply	masking tape	graph paper
carbon discs	heavy string (1 m)	

Procedure

1. Set up the apparatus as shown in Figure 1, placing the recording timer about 1 m from the edge of the table. Attach a 1-m length of timer tape to one end of the cart with a piece of masking tape. Tie a 1-m length of string to the opposite end of the cart and thread the string through the pulley. Do not attach the 500-g mass to the string at this time.

Figure 1

2. While one student holds the cart still, another student will attach the 500-g mass to the loose end of the string that is hanging over the table.
3. While still preventing the cart from moving, turn on the recording timer. Now release the cart, allowing the 500-g mass to pull the cart across the table.

4.1 Accelerated Motion

4. Catch the cart at the edge of the table to prevent it from knocking the pulley loose or plunging to the floor.
5. Turn off the recording timer and inspect the timer tape. A dark dot should be visible at the beginning of the tape followed by a series of recognizable and distinct dots along the length of the tape.
6. Repeat Steps 1 through 5 so that each lab team member has a tape with recognizable dots to analyze.
7. Label the first distinguishable dot "0." Count off five dots (spaces) from 0 and mark this dot "1." Continue counting off five dots from each previous numbered one and marking them "2," "3," "4," etc., as shown in Figure 2. Each set of five spaces represents one time interval.

First distinguishable dot

Figure 2. Begin counting each set of five dots from the first distinguishable dot.

8. Carefully measure the distance the cart traveled during each interval of time. Record that displacement in Table 1. Calculate the total displacement of the cart at each interval by summing the current displacement plus the displacements during the preceding intervals. Record the total displacement values in Table 1.
9. The average velocity of the laboratory cart during one interval of time has the same value as the displacement for that interval. Record the values for average velocity per interval in Table 2.

Observations and Data
Table 1

Time (interval)	Displacement (cm)	Total displacement (cm)
1		
2		
3		
4		
5		

Table 2

Time (interval)	Average velocity (cm/interval)	Acceleration $(\Delta v/\Delta t)$
1		
2		
3		
4		
5		

4.1 Accelerated Motion

Table 1 (continued)

Time (interval)	Displacement (cm)	Total displacement (cm)
6		
7		
8		
9		
10		
11		
12		

Table 2 (continued)

Time (interval)	Average velocity (cm/interval)	Acceleration ($\Delta v/\Delta t$)
6		
7		
8		
9		
10		
11		
12		

Analysis

1. On graph paper, plot the total displacement of the cart versus the time interval. Use the values from Table 1.
2. On graph paper, plot the average velocity versus the time interval. Use the values from Table 2.
3. Describe the graph of displacement versus time. What is the meaning of the graph?

4. Describe the velocity versus time graph. What is the meaning of the graph?

Accelerated Motion

5. Calculate the slope of the velocity versus time graph for each time interval. Write the results of your calculations in Table 2. What is the unit for the slope?

6. On graph paper, plot acceleration versus time. Describe this graph. What does your graph show about the acceleration of the cart?

Application

What would be the advantage of building an interplanetary spacecraft that could accelerate at 1 g (9.8 m/s^2) for a year?

Extension

1. At several different points along the total displacement versus time graph, draw a tangent to the curve and find the slope at each of the points. Compare the slopes to the average speeds for the various time intervals.

2. Using the actual period of your timer, convert the time unit (interval) to seconds. Compute your acceleration in m/s^2. How does your cart's acceleration compare to acceleration due to gravity?

EXPERIMENT 4.2 : Acceleration Due to Gravity

Purpose

Observe a falling object and determine the acceleration due to gravity.

Concept and Skill Check

The recording timer can be used to record the displacement of a falling mass. The resulting tape is used to analyze the accelerated motion of the mass. In this experiment, you must know the period of the timer. If the period is unknown, use the procedure described in Experiment 2.3 to determine this value.

The average velocity during an interval of time is found by the equation

$$v = \frac{\Delta d}{\Delta t},$$

where Δd is the distance traveled during an interval of time, Δt. A uniformly accelerated object will produce a straight (but not horizontal) line on a graph that plots velocity versus time. The slope of the velocity versus time graph is the acceleration. The slope is found from the ratio

$$\text{slope} = \frac{\text{rise}}{\text{run}} = \frac{(v_f - v_i)}{(t_f - t_i)}.$$

An object dropped from rest will travel a distance given by the following equation

$$d = \frac{1}{2} gt^2.$$

Therefore, since d and t have been measured, g may be calculated from

$$g = \frac{2d}{t^2}.$$

The Free Fall Adapter apparatus uses the computer to measure accurately the time required for a steel marble to fall from the top of the free fall apparatus to a sensor pad. The computer software averages the times for the trials and, after the free fall distance is entered, calculates the acceleration due to gravity.

Materials

Part A

recording timer with necessary power supply
timer tape

carbon discs
C-clamp
masking tape

1-kg mass
meter stick
graph paper

Part B

Apple II+, IIe, or IIGS computer or IBM computer
PASCO game port interface, #AI-6575 (Apple) or #CI-6588 (IBM) and IBM interface card #SE-6590

PASCO Free Fall Adapter, #ME-9207A (Apple) or #ME-9207 (IBM)
PASCO Precision Timer III software, #SV-7401 (Apple) or #SV-7413 (IBM)

meter stick
ringstand

EXPERIMENT 4.2 Acceleration Due to Gravity

Procedure

Part A

1. Record the period of your recording timer on the line provided above Table 1.
2. Set up the apparatus as shown in Figure 1. Insert a 1.5-m strip of timer tape into the recording timer. Use the masking tape to attach the timer tape to the 1-kg mass.
3. Start the recording timer and drop the mass. Stop the recording timer when the mass hits the floor.
4. Remove the timer tape from the mass and write a zero below the first distinguishable dot. Number every subsequent dot consecutively 1, 2, 3, 4, 5, and so on. The elapsed time for the intervals can be determined by finding the product of the interval number and the period of the timer. Calculate the time for each interval and record these values in Table 1.
5. Carefully measure in meters the distance traveled during each interval of time (the space between dots). Record the displacement during each interval in Table 1.
6. The total displacement from zero to any numbered point along the timer tape is the sum of the measured distances between consecutive numbers on your tape. Record in Table 1 the total displacement of the mass during the corresponding intervals.
7. Calculate the average velocity during each interval and record these values in Table 1.

Figure 1.

Part B

1. Set up the apparatus according to the instructions for the Free Fall Adapter and as shown in Figure 2. Allow a distance of 1 m between the sensor pad and the release mechanism.
2. Insert the ball into the Free Fall Adapter mechanism. Carefully measure in meters the distance from the bottom of the ball to the sensor pad (the distance the ball will fall). Record this distance in Table 2.
3. Release the ball. The elapsed time is automatically recorded into the computer data table. Record this time in Table 2.

Figure 2.

4. Replace the ball in the Free Fall Adapter and drop it again. Repeat this step at least five times. Record the elapsed time for each trial in Table 2.
5. Select the Analysis section of the program. The software automatically calculates and displays on the screen the average time and standard deviation of the times. Record the average time in Table 2. Enter the free fall distance into the computer when prompted to do so. The computer calculates the value for the acceleration due to gravity. Record this value in Table 2.
6. Increase the free fall distance to about 2 m. Repeat Steps 2 through 5. Record your data in Table 3.

EXPERIMENT 4.2 Acceleration Due to Gravity

Observations and Data

Table 1

Period of recording timer _____ s

Interval	Time (s)	Displacement (m)	Total displacement (m)	Average velocity (m/s)
1				
2				
3				
4				
5				
6				
7				
8				
9				
10				
11				
12				
13				
14				
15				

4.2 Acceleration Due to Gravity

NAME _____

Table 1 (continued)

Period of recording timer _____ s

Interval	Time (s)	Displacement (m)	Total displacement (m)	Average velocity (m/s)
16				
17				
18				
19				
20				

Table 2

Free fall distance _____ m

Trial	Time (s)
1	
2	
3	
4	
5	
Average	

$g =$ _____ m/s^2

Table 3

Free fall distance _____ m

Trial	Time (s)
1	
2	
3	
4	
5	
Average	

$g =$ _____ m/s^2

EXPERIMENT
4.2 Acceleration Due to Gravity

Analysis

Part A

1. On graph paper, plot the total displacement of the mass versus time. Use the values in Table 1.
2. On graph paper, plot the average velocity versus time. Use the values in Table 1.
3. Write a brief explanation describing what the graph of total displacement versus time indicates about the motion of the falling mass.

4. Study the graph of velocity versus time. Write a brief explanation of what the graph indicates about the motion of a falling mass.

5. Calculate the slope of the velocity versus time graph. Compare your results for acceleration due to gravity to the reference value, 9.80 m/s^2, by finding the relative error.

$$\text{relative error} = \frac{(\text{experimental result} - \text{reference value})}{\text{reference value}} \times 100\%$$

Part B

1. Calculate the relative error by comparing your results for each free fall distance to 9.80 m/s^2.
   a.

   b.

Acceleration
Due to Gravity

2. If the free fall distance is increased to about 2 m, what effect does it have on the results? Explain.

3. Which variable remained constant in each set of trials? Which variable responded in this experiment?

Application

Would there be any potential benefit to athletes when the Olympic games are held in a country having a relatively high elevation?

EXPERIMENT
5.1 Newton's Second Law

Purpose

Investigate Newton's second law of motion.

Concept and Skill Check

Newton's second law of motion states that the acceleration of a body is directly proportional to the net force on it and inversely proportional to its mass. In mathematical form, this law is expressed as $a = F/m$. An object will accelerate if it has a net force acting on it, and the acceleration will be in the direction of the force. In this experiment, a laboratory cart will be accelerated by a known force, and its acceleration will be measured using a recording timer. The product of the total mass accelerated and its acceleration equals the force causing the acceleration.

In order to calculate the net force acting on the laboratory cart, frictional forces that oppose the motion must be offset. If the cart moves at a constant velocity, then the net force acting on the cart is zero because the acceleration is zero. The frictional force can be neutralized by providing enough small masses at the end of the string to make the cart move forward at a constant velocity.

If you assume that the laboratory cart experiences a uniform acceleration due to the falling mass, then the relationship

$$d = v_i t + \frac{1}{2}at^2$$

applies. If the cart has an initial velocity of zero, the equation becomes

$$d = \frac{1}{2}at^2.$$

If the displacement in a given time is known, you can solve for acceleration with

$$a = 2\frac{d}{t^2}.$$

Materials

recording timer with necessary power supply	1000-g mass	heavy string (1.5 m)
timer tape	set of small masses	masking tape
carbon-paper discs	pulley	balance
laboratory cart	2 C-clamps	meter stick

Procedure

1. Record the period of the timer in Table 1. If you do not know the period, use the procedure described in Experiment 2.3 to determine the period.
2. Determine the combined mass of your laboratory cart and attached timer tape and string. Record the mass in Table 1. Record the weight, $F = mg$, of the 1000-g mass in Table 2 as the accelerating force.
3. Assemble the cart, pulley, recording timer, string, and timer tape as shown in Figure 1 on the next page. Tie a small loop in the end of the string hanging from the pulley.
4. Give the cart a small push. It should roll to a stop in a few centimeters. Attach a 10-g mass with a piece of masking tape to the end of the string that is hanging from the pulley. Give the cart a

Figure 1.

small push toward the pulley and observe its motion. If the cart moves at a constant velocity, then the weight of the 10-g mass is equal to the force of friction in the cart's wheels and from the timer tape sliding through the recording timer. If the cart rolled to a stop, then the total mass on the string must be increased. If the cart's velocity increased after it was released, then the total mass on the string must be decreased. Adjust the total mass until the cart moves at a constant velocity after you have given it a small push. Record in Table 1 the mass needed to equalize the friction of the cart. Leave the small masses attached to the string.

5. Move the cart next to the recording timer. Attach the timer tape to the cart. Insert the timer tape into the recording timer. Carefully hang the 1000-g mass from the loop in the string. Adjust the string length so that the mass is hanging just under the pulley. Hold the cart to prevent it from moving. Turn on the recording timer. Release the cart, allowing it to accelerate across the table top. Catch the cart before it collides with the pulley or plunges to the floor. Turn off the recording timer. Remove the timer tape and inspect it. A dark area should occur at the beginning of the tape where the timer made numerous dots close together before the cart was released. Note a series of dots, each an increasing distance from the previous one, as shown in Figure 2. It is in this interval on the tape that the cart was accelerating. Write a zero by the first distinguishable dot. Continue counting and marking dots 1, 2, 3, 4, 5, and so on. After the mass hits the floor, the dots will clump together, indicating the end of the acceleration phase. Stop counting at a dot located about 10 cm before the clump of dots.

Figure 2.

6. Measure in meters the distance from the zero dot to the chosen end dot. Record this distance in Table 2. Record the number of dots to this end point in Table 2.
7. Repeat Steps 5 and 6 twice more for a total of three trials.

EXPERIMENT 5.1 Newton's Second Law

Observations and Data
Table 1

	Value
Period of timer (s)	
Mass of laboratory cart (kg)	
Mass needed to equalize friction of cart (kg)	

Table 2

Trial	Accelerating force (N)	Distance (m)	Number of dots	Time (s)
1				
2				
3				

Table 3

Trial	Acceleration (m/s²)	Total mass (kg)	$(m)(a)$ (N)
1			
2			
3			

Analysis

1. Determine the time by multiplying the number of dots by the timer period. For example, 30 dots and a timer period of 1/60 s (30 dots × 1/60 s/dot) will yield the time value of 0.5 s. Record the times for the three trials in Table 2.

2. Calculate the acceleration of the entire system using the values for distance and time from Table 2. Show your calculations for all trials. Record the acceleration value for each trial in Table 3.

3. Are your acceleration values less than, equal to, or greater than g? Are these the values you would have predicted? Explain.

4. The total mass that was accelerated is equal to the mass of the cart, tape, mass and string, the small masses needed to equalize friction, and the 1000-g mass. Calculate the total mass of your system and record this value in Table 3.

5. Calculate the product of the total mass and the acceleration for each trial. Record these values in Table 3.

6. Compare the results for the product $(m)(a)$ to the accelerating force. Find the relative error using the accelerating force as the reference value.

7. Using your data, calculate the frictional force.

8. Why was it important to neutralize the effect of frictional force acting on the system?

Application

At a specific engine rpm, an automobile engine provides a constant force that is applied to the automobile. If the car is traveling on a horizontal surface, does the car accelerate when this force is applied? Explain.

EXPERIMENT

5.2 Friction

Purpose

Investigate friction and measure the coefficients of friction.

Concept and Skill Check

An object placed on an inclined plane may or may not slide. If the object is at rest, the force of friction is opposing the tendency of the object to slide down the plane. When the plane has been tilted at a certain angle θ with the horizontal, the object begins to slide down the inclined plane. If the object slides down the inclined plane at a constant speed, then the force of friction F_f is equal to the force down the plane $F_{\parallel}$. The force down the plane is the same as the component of the object's weight parallel to the plane, as shown in the figure. The parallel component of weight is described by $F_{\parallel} = F_w \sin \theta$, where F_w is the weight of the object. The perpendicular component of weight is described by $F_{\perp} = F_w \cos \theta$. When sliding just begins and the object is moving at a constant speed, the coefficient of friction μ is given by

$$\mu = \frac{F_f}{F_{\perp}} = \frac{F_{\parallel}}{F_{\perp}} = \frac{F_w \sin \theta}{F_w \cos \theta} = \tan \theta.$$

Materials

spring scale (with capacity sufficient to
    measure the weight of the object)
object: book, chalkboard eraser,
    2-by-4 block, or similar object
flat board
string (1 m)
masking tape
protractor

Procedure

1. Select an object and a flat board for this experiment. Describe the object and the surface of the board in Table 1.
2. Tape the string to the end of the object. Hang the object by the string from the spring scale. Measure the weight of the object. Record this value in Table 2.
3. Place the flat board on a horizontal surface. Hold the spring scale and, with the string held parallel to the level board, pull the object along the board at a constant speed. With the spring scale, measure the amount of force required to keep the object moving at a uniform rate. Repeat this procedure several times, average your results, and record this value in Table 2 as the force of sliding friction between the surface of the board and the surface of the object.
4. Detach the string from the object. Place the object on the flat board. Slowly lift one end of the board. Continue increasing the angle of the board with the horizontal until the object starts to slide. Use the protractor to measure this angle. Record the value of this angle in Table 3 as the angle for static friction. The tangent of this angle is the coefficient of static friction.

5.2 Friction

5. Move the object to one end of the board. Again, slowly lift this end of the board while your lab partner lightly taps the object. Adjust the angle of the board until the object slides at a constant speed after it has received an initial light tap. Use the protractor to measure this angle and record it in Table 3 as the angle for sliding friction. The tangent of this angle is the coefficient of sliding friction.
6. Repeat the experiment with a different object so that each lab partner has data to analyze.

Observations and Data
Table 1

	Description
Object	
Surface	

Table 2

Weight of object (N)				
	1	2	3	Average
Force of sliding friction (N)				

Table 3

Motion	Angle (degrees)	$\mu = \tan \theta$
Static		
Sliding		

Analysis

1. From the data in Table 3, calculate the coefficients of static and sliding friction for the object used. Record these values in Table 3.

5.2 Friction

2. Explain any difference between the values for the coefficients of static and sliding friction.

3. Using the data in Table 2, calculate the coefficient of sliding friction. Show your work.

4. Are your values for $\mu_{sliding}$ from Questions 1 and 3 equal? Explain any differences.

5. A brick is positioned first with its largest surface in contact with an inclined plane. The plane is tilted at an angle to the horizontal until the brick just begins to slide, and the angle, θ, of the plane with the horizontal is measured. Then the brick is turned on one of its narrow edges, the plane is tilted, and θ is again measured. Predict whether there will be a difference in these measured angles. Explain your answer in terms of the equation for the force of friction. Is the coefficient of static friction affected by the area of contact between the surfaces?

6. A brick is placed on an inclined plane, which is tilted at an angle to the horizontal until the brick just begins to slide. The angle, θ, of the plane with respect to the horizontal is measured. Then the brick is wrapped in waxed paper and placed on a plane. The plane is tilted, and θ is again measured. Predict whether there will be a difference in these measured angles. Explain.

5.2 Friction

7. From your answers to the previous two questions, determine the factors that influence the force of friction.

Application

While looking for a set of new tires for your car, you find an advertisement that offers two brands of tires, brand **X** and brand **Y**, at the same price. Brand **X** has a coefficient of friction on dry pavement of 0.90 and on wet pavement of 0.15. Brand **Y** has a coefficient of friction on dry pavement of 0.88 and on wet pavement of 0.45. If you live in an area with high levels of precipitation, which tire would give you better service? Explain.

Extension

Using another object, measure its weight and the force necessary to pull it along a horizontal surface at a constant speed. Record the information in a data table similar to Table 2. Calculate the coefficient of sliding friction. Since $\mu = \tan \theta$, find the angle θ. Estimate the angle at which sliding at a constant speed would begin. Using this as your prediction, slowly raise the flat board while lightly tapping the object. Record the angle at which the object begins sliding at a constant speed. Compare your prediction to your experimental results.

EXPERIMENT 6.1 Addition of Force Vectors

Purpose

Apply the laws of vector addition to resolve forces in equilibrium.

Concept and Skill Check

When two or more forces act at the same time on an object and their vector sum is zero, the object is in equilibrium. Each of the arrangements shown in Figure 1 illustrates three concurrent forces acting on point **P**. Since point **P** is not moving, these three forces are producing no net force on point **P**, and the diagrammed systems are in equilibrium. In this experiment, you will determine the vector sum of two of the concurrent forces, called the resultant, and investigate the relationship of the resultant to the third force.

(a)

String

Ringstand

(b)

Figure 1. The apparatus used to measure forces varies slightly. Your apparatus will probably be similar to one of these.

Materials

Method 1—force table and 3 spring scales
Method 2—2 spring scales, 2 ringstands, cross support, and 500-g mass

metric ruler
heavy string
pencil

protractor
paper

Procedure

Your teacher will demonstrate the apparatus you will be using—either Method 1 or Method 2.
Method 1
1. Set up the apparatus as indicated in Figure 1a. Check each spring scale to be sure that the needle points to zero when no load is attached. Attach the spring scales to the force table so that each scale registers a force at approximately mid-range.
2. Place a piece of paper beneath the spring scale arrangement. Using a sharp pencil, mark several points along the line (the string) of action of each force.
3. Remove the paper and, using the points that you marked, construct lines **A**, **B**, and **C**, each representing the direction of force action for scales *A*, *B*, and *C*.
4. Record the reading of each spring scale next to its corresponding line, as shown in Figure 2a.

6.1 Addition of Force Vectors

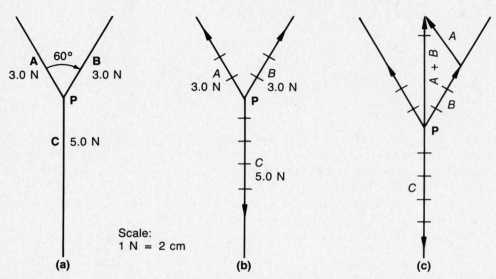

Figure 2. Be careful to draw each vector in its original direction and magnitude when you move it during the addition process.

5. Select a suitable number scale, such as 1 N = 2 cm, and record your scale near line **C**. Construct vectors, of proper scaled length, along lines **A**, **B**, and **C** to represent each force. If the spring scales are not calibrated in newtons, take the readings in grams or kilograms and convert these measurements to newtons by multiplying the mass readings in kilograms by 9.8 m/s^2. Figure 2b shows how these force vectors are scaled.

6. Add vector A to vector B by drawing A parallel to itself but with its tail at the head of B (the head-to-tail method), as shown in Figure 2c.

7. Draw a vector representing the vector sum of $A + B$, the resultant.

8. Repeat Steps 1 through 7 so that each laboratory partner has a set of data to analyze.

Method 2

1. Set up the apparatus as indicated in Figure 1b. With a protractor, measure each of the three angles at the intersection of the three strings.

2. Using these angle measurements, construct a diagram on paper of the forces acting on point **P** by drawing three lines to represent the lines of action of the three forces. Label the lines **A**, **B**, and **C**, as shown in Figure 2a.

3. Record the values of the two spring-scale readings and the weight in newtons of the 500-g mass next to lines **A**, **B**, and **C** on your paper. If the scales give readings in mass, convert the mass readings in kilograms, to weight in newtons by multiplying the mass by 9.8 m/s^2.

4. Select a suitable number scale and record your scale near line **C**. Using your scale, construct vectors along lines **A**, **B**, and **C** to represent the forces acting along each line of force, as shown in Figure 2b.

5. Add vector A to vector B by reproducing A parallel to itself but with its tail at the head of B (the head-to-tail method), as shown in Figure 2c.

6. Draw a vector representing the vector sum $A + B$, the resultant.

7. Repeat Steps 1 through 6 so that each laboratory partner has a set of data to analyze.

Observations and Data

On a separate sheet of paper, draw the vectors obtained from your experimental procedure. Follow the form shown in Figure 2.

6.1 Addition of Force Vectors

Analysis

1. What was the number scale you selected for your model? Compute the resultant using your number scale.

2. Compare the magnitude and direction of the computed resultant force of $A + B$ with the measured or known magnitude of force C. Explain your findings. Calculate the relative error in the magnitudes using force C as the reference value.

3. On a separate sheet of paper, reconstruct vectors A, B, and C and add them. Do this by placing a piece of paper over your first diagram and tracing the vectors. Place the tail of B at the head of A, and then place the tail of C at the head of B (the head-to-tail method). Label your vectors.

4. Explain the results of the graphical addition of $A + B + C$, which you performed as requested in Question 3.

5. Suppose that you had added B to C. What result would you expect?

6. What result would you expect if you added C to A?

7. On the same sheet you used for Question 3, add your three vectors in the order $C + B + A$. What result do you obtain?

Addition of Force Vectors

Application

A sky diver jumps from a plane and, after falling for 11 seconds, reaches a terminal velocity (constant speed) of 250 km/h. Changing her body configuration, she then accelerates to a different terminal velocity of 320 km/h. Finally, after releasing her parachute, she again accelerates and reaches a final terminal velocity of 15 km/h. Explain how it is possible to obtain the different terminal velocities.

Extension

Using a different method, repeat the investigation, setting the angle between *A* and *B* at some angle other than 90°. Solve for *C* both mathematically and graphically.

EXPERIMENT
6.2 : # Physics 500

Purpose

Understand the forces that act on moving vehicles.

Concept and Skill Check

When you prepare for your driver's license test, you will study the rules of the road and safe operating practices for motor vehicles. But you probably will not consider Newton's laws of motion during your preparation. In this investigation, you will observe how velocity, road surface, friction, and highway shape affect the motion of cars. You will test the hypothesis that a car moving around a banked curve can travel faster than one rounding an unbanked or flat curve. And you will gain an understanding of the physics of automobile driving. To complete this experiment, you must know how to draw vector components and resultants, as described in Chapter 6.

Materials

electric model race car set—several per classroom
electronic timer with photogates (optional)

Procedure

In order to answer the questions and make inferences, you should carefully observe and participate in the activities on each track. If your race set-up does not contain all of the features described by the procedure, your teacher may direct you to omit certain steps or to make inferences based on your other observations. If one of the tracks has an electronic lap timer with photocell gates, be sure to race one lap and record your results as directed by your teacher.

1. Set up the race-car tracks and make sure you include banked and flat curves, straightaways, loops, speed bumps, and hills to represent a road with varying contours and directions. One such set-up is shown in Figure 1.

Figure 1. An example of a Physics 500 track.

2. Trace the diagrams of cars on an outward-banked curve and on an inward-banked curve like those shown in Figure 2a and 2b. Draw and label the force vectors acting on each car, including friction, F_f, weight of the car, F_W, component of weight acting parallel to the highway, $F_{\parallel}$, component of weight acting perpendicular to the highway, $F_{\perp}$, accelerating force from the engine, F_a, and force from braking, F_b.

3. Observe the motion of a car on the portion of the track with speed bumps. Observe the motion of a car at different velocities as it travels over a speed bump.
4. Observe the cars as they travel at different velocities through a loop. Operate a car at low velocity through the loop. Draw a diagram of a loop with one car positioned at the bottom of the loop, one at about half-way up (or down) the loop, and one at the top of the loop, such as the one shown in Figure 3. Draw and label the vector F_W and the instantaneous velocity, v, for each car at each of the three locations.
5. Observe the motion of a car when it is quickly changing lanes.
6. Observe the motion of a car as it travels through a curved section of track that is banked and a curved section that is flat. Operate the car at different velocities as you take it through the same curved sections of track.

Observations and Data

Outward-banked curve
(a)

Inward-banked curve
(b)

Figure 2.

Figure 3.

Physics
500

Analysis

1. Look at the diagrams you made for Step 2. Describe the forces acting on a car as it rounds a curve and compare the effect of these forces as the vehicle moves through a flat curve, an inward-banked curve, and an outward-banked curve. You may need to make some inferences in order to provide a complete description of all these forces.

2. Summarize your observations of the car as it moves over the speed bump at different velocities.

3. If the car travels slowly through the loop, what happens? What keeps the car on the track as it travels through the loop?

4. What effect do rapid lane changes have on your ability to control the car?

5. At a constant velocity, is it easier to travel through a curve that is flat, inward banked, or outward banked? What is the purpose of an inward-banked curve?

Application

At a county or state fair, you may have seen motorcyclists riding on the inside of a cylindrical-shaped track or the inside of a spherical-shaped room. What allows the motorcyclists to ride in a manner that seems to defy the law of gravity?

Extension

A spare section of curved track can be moistened with water or lightly sprayed with silicone. Select one car to run on this track and do not use it on any other tracks. This section of track will model as an icy road surface or one covered with wet leaves. Observe how the car behaves as it travels at a high rate of speed and moves onto this section of track.

EXPERIMENT 7.1 : Projectile Motion

Purpose

Investigate the path of a projectile and verify equations of projectile motion.

Concept and Skill Check

An object that is launched into the air and then comes under the influence of gravity moves in two dimensions and is called a projectile. If the frictional force due to air resistance is disregarded, the horizontal component of velocity will remain constant during the projectile's entire path. The vertical component of velocity is the same as the motion of an object in free fall. The force due to gravity accelerates the projectile downward at the rate of 9.8 m/s^2. The equation for vertical displacement of an object falling with constant acceleration, g, is described by the following:

$$y = v_y t + \frac{1}{2} g t^2,$$

where y is the vertical displacement, v_y is the initial vertical velocity, t is the elapsed time, and g is the acceleration due to gravity. The equation for the horizontal displacement of an object is described by the following:

$$x = v_x t,$$

where x is the horizontal displacement, v_x is the initial horizontal velocity, and t is the elapsed time.

In the apparatus shown in Figure 1, a steel ball is projected horizontally from the bottom of the raised ruler and rolls down an inclined plane (the board or tray) across the paper. The acceleration of the steel ball is the component of the acceleration of gravity that acts parallel to the direction of the inclined plane. The projectile's horizontal velocity remains nearly constant since the frictional effects of the steel ball on the smooth paper are negligible.

Figure 1. The path of the steel ball will be marked on the lined paper in a pattern similar to the one shown by the dashed line above.

Materials

steel ball	board or tray	textbook support
1 sheet lined paper	grooved metric ruler	block support
masking tape	1 sheet carbon paper	

7.1 Projectile Motion

Procedure

1. Set up the apparatus as shown in Figure 1. Lay the lined paper on the board or tray. Position it so that the groove in the raised ruler is perpendicular to the vertical lines and tape the corners of the paper to the board. Adjust the height of the ruler so that the steel ball will begin its path across the paper at the upper left-hand corner and travel most of the way across the paper. Secure the ruler and block with tape when the ball rolls the proper distance. Practice placing the sphere at different heights on the raised ruler until you have found the best location for releasing the steel ball and obtaining the desired result.

2. Place the carbon paper over the lined sheet with the carbon side down and tape the top corners to hold it in place. As the steel ball moves across the carbon paper, it will trace its path on the lined paper.

3. Roll the steel ball down the grooved ruler, allowing the ball to move across the carbon paper. Lift the carbon paper and check to see that the carbon paper left a trace of the ball's path. Remove the carbon paper and the lined paper from the board. With a pencil, retrace the ball's path if it is difficult to see.

4. Because the horizontal velocity of the ball was constant, it took the ball the same time to travel each of the horizontal distances between adjacent vertical lines on the paper. Therefore, each width of a section on the paper can represent successive intervals of equal time. Draw a horizontal line, as shown in Figure 2, across the paper from the point where the projectile's path starts to the opposite side of the paper. Label this line **AB**, as indicated in Figure 2. Beginning at the first vertical line where the ball's path is visible, label this line 0. Number each successive vertical line across the paper as 1, 2, 3, 4, and so on.

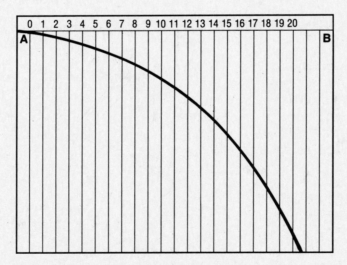

Figure 2. Draw line AB so that point A is where the path of the projectile crosses the first vertical line.

5. Measure in centimeters the vertical distance along each line from the horizontal line **AB** to the path of the ball. Record each of these distances in Table 1.

6. Determine the distance the ball traveled down the incline during each time interval. Using the values for vertical distance, subtract the length on the previous vertical line from the length on the current vertical line to determine the distance the ball traveled. The distance the ball traveled during each interval represents its average vertical velocity. Record each value for average vertical velocity in Table 1.

7.1 Projectile Motion

Observations and Data
Table 1

Time interval number	Total vertical distance (m)	Average vertical velocity (cm/interval)
0		
1		
2		
3		
4		
5		
6		
7		
8		
9		
10		
11		
12		
13		
14		
15		
16		
17		
18		
19		
20		

7.1 Projectile Motion

Analysis

1. Plot a graph of vertical distance versus time, with vertical distance on the y-axis and time on the x-axis.
2. What does this graph show about projectile motion?

3. What other data do you have that show the path of the steel ball in a form consistent with the shape of your graphed line from Question 1? Explain.

4. Plot a graph of vertical velocity versus time, with vertical velocity on the y-axis and time on the x-axis.
5. What does this graph indicate about projectile motion?

6. Does the line on this graph demonstrate projectile motion? Explain.

Application

A rifleman raises his gun and aims it at a tin can target on a shelf in the shooting range. If the bore of the gun is pointed straight at the can, under what conditions will the bullet hit the tin can?

EXPERIMENT
7.2
Range of a Projectile

Purpose

Predict where a horizontally projected object will land.

Concept and Skill Check

If an object moves in only one dimension, it is easy to describe the location of that object and to predict its final position when it comes to rest. On a calm day, an apple falls vertically from a tree limb to the ground below. However, a golf ball hit from the tee, a football thrown over the defensive line to a downfield receiver, and bullets fired from a gun move in two dimensions. Such objects, called projectiles, have horizontal and vertical components of motion that are independent of each other. The independence of vertical and horizontal motion is used to determine the location and the time of fall of projected objects. All projectiles described above had an initial vertical velocity at an angle above the horizontal. To simplify analysis of the motion of the projectile in this experiment, the steel ball will be launched horizontally; therefore, the initial vertical velocity, v_y, will be zero.

If you know the velocity, v_x, of a steel ball launched horizontally from a table and the ball's initial height, y, above the floor, the equations of projectile motion can be used to predict where the steel ball will land. Recall that the horizontal displacement or range, x, of an object with horizontal velocity, v_x, at time, t, is

$$x = v_x t.$$

The equation describing vertical displacement is that of a body falling with constant acceleration:

$$y = v_y t + \frac{1}{2} g t^2.$$

But if $v_y = 0$, then $y = \frac{1}{2} g t^2$.

The steel ball's fall time can be computed from the equation for vertical motion by solving for t:

$$t = \sqrt{\frac{2y}{g}},$$

where g is the acceleration due to gravity and y is the vertical height the projectile falls. The range of the projectile, x, can now be computed. In this experiment, you will try to predict the range of a projectile launched with a certain horizontal velocity.

Materials

2 50-cm pieces of U-shaped channel (track)	ringstand-support clamp	stopwatch or electronic timing apparatus with 2
steel ball	meter stick	photogates and lights
masking tape	string (1 m)	paper cup
ringstand	washer	

Procedure

1. Set up the apparatus as shown in the figure on the next page. Construct horizontal and inclined ramps on the table top, using the U-channel, ringstand, support clamps, and masking tape. At the end of the track, use the string to suspend a washer from the edge of the table to the floor.

NAME _____

Figure 1.

Align the end of the horizontal ramp with the edge of the table. Make a few test rolls, but catch the ball as it rolls off the table. The steel ball should stay in the U-shaped channels when you roll it down the inclined ramp. If the steel ball jumps out of the channel at the junction of the two channel pieces, then lower the support clamp and try again.

2. Set up the electronic timing apparatus with photogates along a section of the horizontal channel. Place the photogates 0.20 m apart. Record the distance as d in Table 1. If you are using a stopwatch, measure a 0.20-m interval along the horizontal channel. Use two small pieces of tape to mark the beginning and the end of the interval. Record the interval distance as d in Table 1.

3. Select a point on the incline where you will release the ball. Mark this location with a small piece of tape.

4. In order to determine the ball's horizontal velocity, you must measure the time it takes for the ball to travel the known distance, d, along the horizontal channel. Release the ball from the tape mark on the ramp. Using either the stopwatch or the electronic timer, measure the time it takes for the ball to roll past the tape marks or photogates. Catch the ball as it rolls off the table. Record the time, t, in Table 1. Roll the ball twice more, releasing it for each trial from the same location on the ramp. Record these times in Table 1.

5. Place the steel ball on the channel at the edge of the table. Measure the vertical distance, in meters, from the bottom of the ball to the floor. Record this distance, y, on the line provided under Table 1.

Observations and Data
Table 1

Trial	Distance (m)	Time (s)
1		
2		
3		
Average		

Vertical distance, y, _____ m

EXPERIMENT
7.2 : Range of a
: Projectile

Analysis

1. Calculate the average time for the three trials. Write this value in Table 1. Compute the horizontal velocity, v_x, using $v_x = \Delta d/\Delta t$.

2. Calculate the time, t, that the ball will be falling from the table, using your value for y.

3. Calculate the horizontal distance, x, that the ball should travel, using your values for v_x and t from Questions 1 and 2.

4. Measure the distance, x, in a straight line from the horizontal channel, starting where the washer touches the floor. Place a small piece of tape at this location. Place the paper cup with the front edge of the cup over the tape and the back side of the cup toward the table. Roll the steel ball from the same height on the inclined ramp from which it was released earlier. This time, let the ball roll off the table. Where does it land?

5. Does this experiment support the premise that the horizontal and vertical components of motion are not affected by each other? Explain.

6. If a very light, but fairly large, sponge ball, or a ping-pong ball, were rolled down the ramp would you expect the same result? Explain.

7.2 Range of a Projectile

Application

A diver achieves a horizontal velocity of 3.75 m/s from a diving platform located 6.0 m above the water. How far from the edge of the platform will the diver be when she hits the water?

Extension

1. The horizontal range, x, of a projectile launched at an angle, θ_i, with the horizontal at an initial velocity, v_i, can be determined by use of the following:

$$x = \frac{v_i^2}{g} \sin 2\,\theta_i.$$

Prove that x has a maximum value when $\theta_i = 45°$. Give some examples. Recall that $\sin 2\,\theta = 2 \sin \theta \cos \theta$.

2. Find the horizontal range of a baseball that leaves the bat at an angle of 63° with the horizontal with an initial velocity of 160 km/h. Disregard air resistance. Show all your calculations.

Kepler's
Laws

Purpose

Plot a planetary orbit and apply Kepler's Laws.

Concept and Skill Check

The motion of the planets has intrigued astronomers since they first gazed at the stars, moon, and planets filling the evening sky. But the old ideas of eccentrics and equants (combinations of circular motions) did not provide an accurate accounting of planetary movements. Johannes Kepler adopted the Copernican theory that Earth revolves around the sun (heliocentric, or sun-centered, view) and closely examined Tycho Brahe's meticulously recorded observations on Mars' orbit. With these data, he concluded that Mars' orbit was not circular and that there was no point around which the motion was uniform. When elliptical orbits were accepted, all the discrepancies found in the old theories of planetary motion were eliminated. From his studies, Kepler derived three laws that apply to the behavior of every satellite or planet orbiting another massive body.

1. The paths of the planets are ellipses, with the center of the sun at one focus.
2. An imaginary line from the sun to a planet sweeps out equal areas in equal time intervals, as shown in Figure 1.
3. The ratio of the squares of the periods of any two planets revolving about the sun is equal to the ratio of the cubes of their respective average distances from the sun. Mathematically, this relationship can be expressed as

$$\frac{T_a^2}{T_b^2} = \frac{r_a^3}{r_b^3}.$$

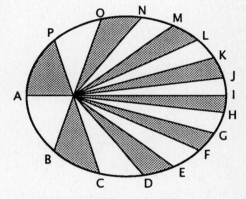

Figure 1. Kepler's law of areas.

In this experiment, you will use heliocentric data tables to plot the positions of Mercury on polar graph paper. Then you will draw Mercury's orbit. The distance from the sun, the radius vector, is compared to Earth's average distance from the sun, which is defined as 1 astronomical unit or 1 AU. The angle, or longitude, between the planet and a reference point in space is measured from the zero degree point, or vernal equinox.

Materials

polar graph paper   sharp pencil   metric ruler

Procedure

1. Orient your polar graph paper so that the zero degree point is on your right as you view the graph paper. The sun is located at the center of the paper. Label the sun without covering the center mark. Move about the center in a counter-clockwise direction as you measure and mark the longitude.
2. Select an appropriate scale to represent the values for the radius vectors of Mercury's positions. Since Mercury is closer to the sun than is Earth, the value of the radius vector will always be less than 1 AU. In this step, then, each concentric circle could represent one-tenth of an AU.

Kepler's Laws

NAME ————————————————————————————————

3. Table 1 provides the heliocentric positions of Mercury over a period of several months. Select the set of data for October 1 and locate the given longitude on the polar graph paper. Measure out along the longitude line an appropriate distance, in your scale, for the radius vector for this date. Make a small dot at this point to represent Mercury's distance from the sun. Write the date next to this point.
4. Repeat the procedure, plotting all given longitudes and associated radius vectors.
5. After plotting all the data, carefully connect the points of Mercury's positions and sketch the orbit of Mercury.

Observations and Data
Table 1

	Some Heliocentric Positions for Mercury for O^h Dynamical Time[*]				
Date	Radius vector (AU)	Longitude (degrees)	Date	Radius vector (AU)	Longitude (degrees)
Oct. 1, 1990	0.319	114	Nov. 16	0.458	280
3	0.327	126	18	0.452	285
5	0.336	137	20	0.447	291
7	0.347	147	22	0.440	297
9	0.358	157	24	0.432	304
11	0.369	166	26	0.423	310
13	0.381	175	28	0.413	317
15	0.392	183	30	0.403	325
17	0.403	191	Dec. 2	0.392	332
19	0.413	198	4	0.380	340
21	0.423	205	6	0.369	349
23	0.432	211	8	0.357	358
25	0.440	217	10	0.346	8
27	0.447	223	12	0.335	18
29	0.453	229	14	0.326	29
31	0.458	235	16	0.318	41
Nov. 2	0.462	241	18	0.312	53
4	0.465	246	20	0.309	65
6	0.466	251	22	0.307	78
8	0.467	257	24	0.309	90
10	0.466	262	26	0.312	102
12	0.464	268	28	0.319	114
14	0.462	273	30	0.327	126

[*]Adapted from *The Astronomical Almanac for the Year 1990*, U.S. Government Printing Office, Washington, D.C., 20402, p. E9.

8.1 Kepler's Laws

NAME ——————————————————————————

Analysis

1. Does your graph of Mercury's orbit support Kepler's law of orbits?

2. Draw a line from the sun to Mercury's position on December 20. Draw a second line from the sun to Mercury's position on December 30. The two lines and Mercury's orbit describe an area swept by an imaginary line between Mercury and the sun during the ten-day interval of time. Lightly shade this area. Over a small portion of an ellipse, the area can be approximated by assuming the ellipse is similar to a circle. The equation that describes this value is

$$\text{area} = (\theta/360°)\pi r^2,$$

where r is the average radius for the orbit.

Determine θ by finding the difference in degrees between December 20 and December 30. Measure the radius at a point midway in the orbit between the two dates. Calculate the area in AUs for this ten-day period of time.

3. Select two additional ten-day periods of time at points distant from the interval in Question 2 and shade these areas. Calculate the area in AUs for each of these ten-day periods.

4. Find the average area for the three periods of time from Questions 2 and 3. Calculate the relative error between each area and the average. Does Kepler's law of areas apply to your graph?

8.1 Kepler's Laws

5. Calculate the average radius for Mercury's orbit. This can be done by averaging all the radius vectors or, more simply, by averaging the longest and shortest radii that occur along the major axis. The major axis is shown in Figure 2. Recall that the sun is at one focus; the other focus is located at a point that is the same distance from the center of the ellipse as the sun, but in the opposite direction.

Figure 2. The major axis passes through the two foci (F and F') and the center of the ellipse. The value *ea* determines the location of the foci; *e* is the eccentricity of the orbit. If *e* = 0, the orbit is a circle, and the foci merge at one, central point.

From Table 1, find the longest radius vector. Then, align a metric ruler so that it describes a straight line passing through the point on the orbit that represents the longest radius vector and through the center of the sun to a point opposite on the orbit. Find the shortest radius vector by reading the longitude at this opposite point and consulting Table 1 for the corresponding radius vector. Average these two radius vector values. Using the values for Earth's average radius (1.0 AU), Earth's period (365.25 days), and your calculated average radius of Mercury's orbit, apply Kepler's third law to find the period of Mercury. Show your calculations.

6. Refer again to the graph of Mercury's orbit that you plotted. Count the number of days required for Mercury to complete one orbit of the sun; recall that this orbital time is the period of Mercury. Is there a difference in the two values (from Questions 5 and 6) for the period of Mercury? Calculate the relative difference in these two values. Are the results from your graph consistent with Kepler's law of periods?

8.1 Kepler's Laws

Application

There has been some discussion about a hypothetical planet **X** that is on the opposite side of the sun from Earth and that has an average radius of 1.0 AU. If this planet exists, what is its period? Show your calculations.

Extension

Using the data in Table 2, plot the radius vectors and corresponding longitudes for Mars. Does the orbit you drew support Kepler's law of ellipses? Select three different areas and find the area per day for each of these. Does Kepler's law of areas apply to your model of Mars?

Table 2

Some Heliocentric Positions for Mars for O^h Dynamical Time*						
Date	Radius vector (AU)	Longitude (degrees)		Date	Radius vector (AU)	Longitude (degrees)
Jan. 1, 1990	1.548	231		July 12	1.382	343
17	1.527	239		28	1.387	353
Feb. 2	1.507	247		Aug. 13	1.395	3
18	1.486	256		29	1.406	13
Mar. 6	1.466	265		Sept 14	1.420	23
22	1.446	274		30	1.436	32
Apr. 7	1.429	283		Oct. 16	1.455	42
23	1.413	293		Nov. 1	1.474	51
May 9	1.401	303		17	1.495	60
25	1.391	313		Dec. 3	1.516	68
June 10	1.384	323		19	1.537	76
26	1.381	333		Jan. 4, 1991	1.557	84

*Adapted from *The Astronomical Almanac for the Year 1990*, U.S. Government Printing Office, Washington, D.C., 20402, p. E12.

8.1 Kepler's Laws

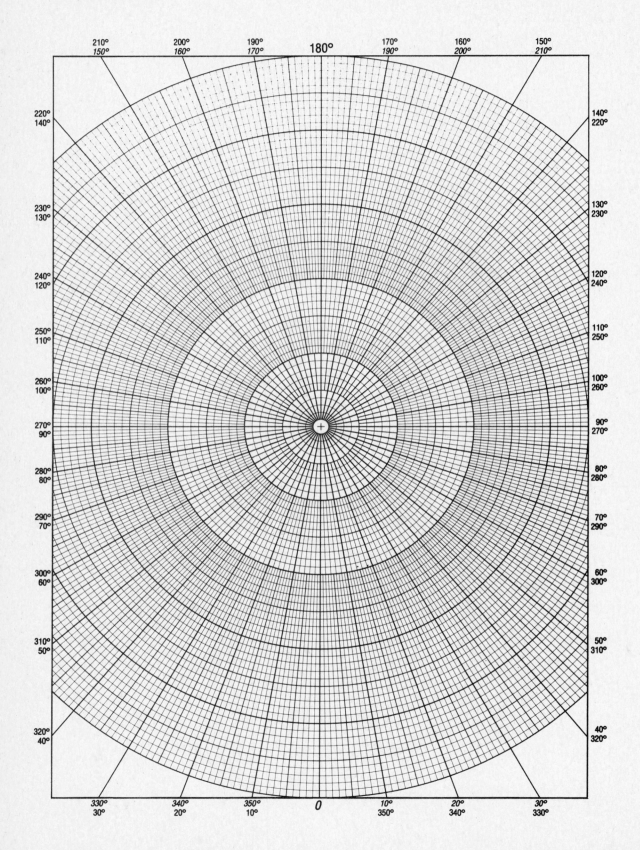

EXPERIMENT
9.1 : Conservation of Momentum

Purpose

Investigate the conservation of momentum for a collision in two dimensions.

Concept and Skill Check

Recall that the law of conservation of momentum states: The momentum of any closed, isolated system does not change. This law is true regardless of the number of objects or the directions of the objects before and after they collide. When there is a collision in two dimensions, the sum of the momentum components in the horizontal direction before the collision equals the sum of the momentum components in the horizontal direction after the collision, and, likewise, the sum of the momentum components in the vertical direction before the collision equals the sum of the momentum components in the vertical direction after the collision.

In this investigation, a steel ball rolls down an incline and collides with another steel ball of equal mass that is at rest. The force of gravity accelerates each steel ball vertically at an equal rate, and they strike the floor at the same time. The horizontal distance that each ball travels during the time of fall is the distance from a point on the floor just below the initial position of the target ball to the point where it lands. These horizontal distances can be measured directly along the floor.

When steel balls of equal mass are used for the incident ball (m) and the target ball (m'), the mass of each can be designated one mass unit ($m = m' = 1$). Since the time required for each ball to reach the floor is the same, this interval can be designated one time unit ($t = t' = 1$). Recall that $v = \Delta d/\Delta t$; but if $\Delta t = 1$, then $v = \Delta d$. Thus, the horizontal velocity of a steel ball during this time interval is equal to the horizontal distance it travels. This same horizontal distance can also represent the momentum of each ball because $p = mv$, but since $m = 1$, $p = v$. Therefore, the momentum vector for each ball can be represented by its horizontal distance and direction as measured on the floor.

Materials

2 steel balls of equal mass
C-clamp
apparatus for a collision in two dimensions
meter stick
4 sheets carbon paper
4 sheets tracing paper
masking tape
string (1.5 m)
washer

Procedure

1. Assemble the apparatus as shown in Figure 1. If your apparatus does not have an attached plumb line, a washer on a string suspended from the apparatus can serve as a plumb line. The set screw at the bottom of the inclined ramp has a small depression in

— Incident ball
— Target ball
— Set screw
— Plumb line
Paper over carbon paper

Figure 1.

its top to hold the target ball. Adjust the depression in the set screw so that it is positioned about one radius of the steel ball away from the bottom of the inclined ramp. Roll a steel ball down the inclined ramp and observe the ball as it travels over the set screw. Adjust the set screw so that the steel ball is just able to pass over it.

2. Tape four pieces of carbon paper together to form one large sheet of carbon paper. Tape four pieces of tracing paper together to form one large sheet of tracing paper. Set the carbon paper on the floor, with the carbon side up, and place the tracing paper over it. Arrange the center of one edge of the paper so that it is located just below the plumb line. Tape the paper in place on the floor. The spot just below the plumb line should be marked 0.

3. If your inclined ramp has an adjustable slider, move it about two-thirds of the distance up the incline and secure it. Otherwise, use a piece of tape to mark a position at this same point on the incline. Without placing a target ball on the set screw, roll a steel ball from the marked position on the incline and let it fall onto the paper. Roll the incident ball four more times from the same location on the incline; circle and label the cluster of points on the paper where the initial incident ball lands.

4. Adjust the position of the set screw so that the incident ball will collide with the target ball at an angle of approximately $45°$, as shown in Figure 2. Make sure that the two balls are at the same height above the floor at the time of collision.

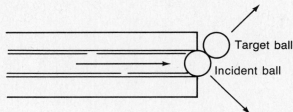

Figure 2. Adjust the position of the target ball so that the two steel balls are deflected at an angle.

5. Place the target ball on the set screw and release the incident ball from the marked position on the incline. Try five collisions between the incident and target balls, making sure that you release the incident ball each time from the same location on the incline. Circle and label the clusters of points where the incident and the target balls hit the paper.

6. Draw a vector from the point 0, under the plumb line, to a spot in the center of the initial incident cluster of points. This vector represents the initial momentum of the incident ball. Label this vector $p_{initial}$. Measure the magnitude of the initial momentum vector and record this value in Table 1.

(a)

(b)

Figure 3. (a) Move the vectors in a parallel manner until they begin at a point 0. (b) Then add the momentum of the incident ball to the momentum of the target ball.

7. Draw a vector from the point 0 to a spot in the center of the cluster of points where the target ball landed, as shown in Figure 3. Label this vector p_{target}. Measure its magnitude and record this value in Table 1.

EXPERIMENT 9.1 Conservation of Momentum

8. Draw a third vector from the point 0 to a spot in the center of the cluster of points where the incident ball landed. Label this vector $p_{incident}$. Measure its magnitude and record this value in Table 1.

Observations and Data

Table 1

Magnitude of Vectors		
$p_{initial}$ (cm)	p_{target} (cm)	$p_{incident}$ (cm)

Analysis

1. Add the magnitudes of p_{target} and $p_{incident}$. Do they equal $p_{initial}$? Explain.

2. Add the vector representing the momentum of the target ball to the vector representing that of the incident ball to determine the total momentum after the collision. Label this vector p_{final}.

3. Measure the magnitude of p_{final}. Compare the initial momentum to the final momentum. Explain your results.

4. Make a generalization about the direction of p_{final} and $p_{initial}$.

9.1 Conservation of Momentum

Application

While playing baseball with your friends, your hands begin to sting after you catch several fast balls. What method of catching the ball might prevent this stinging sensation?

Extension

1. If the incident ball, *a*, had hit two target balls, *b* and *c*, at an angle, predict what would have happened to the total momentum of the system after the collision. Explain your answer and write an equation that proves your answer.

2. In this experiment, you found that the velocity vectors formed a closed triangle (ideally). When an incident ball, *a*, collides at an angle with a target ball, *b*, of equal mass that is initially at rest, the two balls always move off at right angles to each other after the collision. Use a familiar equation for a right triangle to show that this statement is true. *Hint:* Since the collision is elastic, kinetic energy is conserved and

$$\frac{1}{2}\,mv_a^2 = \frac{1}{2}\,mv_a'^2 + \frac{1}{2}\,mv_b^2.$$

EXPERIMENT

9.2 : Angular Momentum

Purpose

Investigate torques and angular momentum.

Concept and Skill Check

Newton's second law applies to rotational motion as well as to linear motion. The rotational analog of $F = ma$ is $\tau = I\alpha$, where τ is the torque, the force applied to an object rotating about a fixed axis; I is the rotational inertia of the object; and α is the angular acceleration. The rotational inertia of an object is the resistance of that body to changes in its angular velocity. Rotational inertia involves the mass of a rotating object and the distribution of its mass, or its shape.

Like other linear values, linear momentum has an angular equivalent. Recall in linear motion that momentum is equal to mv. If the rotational equivalents of m and v are substituted, then the angular momentum, L, is given by

$$L = I\omega, \text{ where } \omega \text{ is the angular velocity.}$$

If we look at the change in angular momentum over a period of time, the equation can be written as

$$\Delta L / \Delta t = I(\Delta\omega/\Delta t).$$

Since $\alpha = \Delta\omega/\Delta t$, $\tau = I\alpha = I(\Delta\omega/\Delta t)$. Substituting $\Delta L/\Delta t$ for the $I(\Delta\omega/\Delta t)$ yields

$$\tau = \Delta L/\Delta t = \text{ change in angular momentum/time interval.}$$

Note that if the torque is zero, then ΔL must also be zero. If there is no change in the angular momentum over a period of time, it must be conserved. If there are no net external torques acting on an object, the angular momentum, $I\omega$, is a constant. While I and ω can change, their product must remain constant. This relationship can be written as

$$I_1\omega_1 = I_2\omega_2.$$

For example, if an object is rotating at a given velocity about a fixed axis, its rotational inertia must increase if its angular velocity decreases and vice versa. Angular momentum is a vector quantity, and its direction is along the axis of rotation perpendicular to the plane formed by ω and r, where r is the object's radius of rotation.

Materials

gyroscopic bicycle wheel   rotating stool or rotating platform   2 3-kg masses

Procedure

Use caution while performing the following activities. If you become dizzy or nauseated, you may lose your balance and fall off the stool or platform.

1. Sit on a rotating stool, or stand on a rotating platform, and hold a large mass in each hand. Extend your arms and have your lab partner give you a gentle spin. Observe what happens as you pull your arms inward. Record your observations in Item 1 of Observations and Data.
2. Hold only one side of the bicycle wheel shaft. Slowly tilt the wheel upward (the wheel should not be rotating). What happens? Record your observations in Item 2 of Observations and Data. Hold the gyroscopic bicycle wheel by the shaft. Have your lab partner give the wheel a strong spin. Now hold only one side of the shaft, as shown in Figure 1. Slowly tilt the shaft upward.

What happens? Record your observations in Item 3 of Observations and Data. Quickly tilt the shaft upward or downward. What happens? Record your observations in Item 3.

(a)   (b)

Figure 1. (a) **The angular momentum vector extends outward along the shaft from the axle of a spinning gyroscopic bicycle wheel.** (b) **When the shaft is tilted in time Δt, the angular momentum changes by ΔL.**

3. While sitting on the rotating stool, or standing on the rotating platform, hold the gyroscopic bicycle wheel shaft with both hands, as shown in Figure 2. Have your lab partner spin the wheel. Slowly rotate the wheel to the right by raising your left hand and lowering your right hand. Observe what happens. Record your observations in Item 4.

4. Change positions with your lab partner so that each student has a set of observations.

Observations and Data

1. Observations of student holding masses on spinning stool or platform:

Figure 2. The effect of tilting a rotating wheel will be observed.

2. Observations of effects of tilting the shaft of a stationary wheel upward:

9.2 Angular Momentum

3. Observations of effects of tilting the shaft of a rotating wheel upward:

4. Observations of effects of rotating the spinning wheel:

Analysis

1. According to the observations you recorded in Item 1, is your angular momentum conserved? Explain, using the law of conservation of momentum.

2. Under what conditions could the angular momentum of the closed, isolated student-stool-masses system change? Describe one such condition.

3. Compare the effects of tilting the shaft of a stationary wheel and of a rotating wheel. Using your observations in Item 2, Item 3, and the relationship between torque and angular momentum, explain the result of your attempt to change the angular momentum of the rotating wheel.

4. Using your observations in Item 4, explain what happened in terms of the law of conservation of momentum.

Application

If a uniformly filled cylinder, such as a solid wood cylinder, and a hollow cylinder or hoop, such as a can with clay pressed on the inside edge, are rolled down an inclined plane, would you expect them to reach the bottom at the same time? Try it. Explain your observations in terms of rotational inertia.

Extension

1. Describe in detail the changes in rotational inertia and the rate of rotation of a diver after he leaves the springboard as he perfoms a one-and-a-half forward-somersault dive. Is the diver's angular momentum conserved throughout the dive?

2. A child stands on a swing and pumps it, setting the swing in motion. Explain why the child and the swing do not represent a closed, isolated system.

EXPERIMENT

10.1 : Pulleys

Purpose

Find the mechanical advantage and the efficiency of several different pulley systems.

Concept and Skill Check

Pulleys are simple machines that can be used to change the direction of a force, to reduce the force needed to move a load through a distance, or to increase the speed at which the load is moving, but that do not change the amount of work done. However, if the required effort force is reduced, the distance the load moves is decreased in proportion to the distance the force moves. Pulley systems may contain a single pulley or a combination of fixed and movable pulleys.

In an ideal machine, one lacking friction, all the energy is transferred, and the work input of the system equals the work output. The work input equals the force times the distance that the force moves, $F_e d_e$. The work output equals the output force (load) times the distance it is moved, $F_r d_r$. The ideal mechanical advantage, IMA, of the pulley system can be found by dividing the distance the force moves by the distance the load moves. Thus $IMA = d_e/d_r$. The ideal machine has a 100% efficiency. In the real world, however, the measured efficiencies are less than 100%. Efficiency is found by the following:

$$\text{Efficiency} = \frac{\text{Work output}}{\text{Work input}} \times 100\%.$$

Materials

2 single pulleys   spring scale   string (2 m)
2 double pulleys   pulley support   meter stick
set of hooked metric masses

Procedure

1. Set up the single fixed pulley system, as shown in Figure 1a.

(a)   **(b)**   **(c)**   **(d)**

Figure 1. In (a), (c), and (d), the spring scale's weight acts as part of the force raising the load. Therefore, the scale must be used upside down so that it will register its own weight.

10.1 Pulleys

2. Select a mass that can be measured on your spring scale. Record the value of its mass in Table 1. Determine the weight, in newtons, of the mass to be raised by multiplying its mass in kilograms by the acceleration due to gravity. Recall that $W = mg$.
3. Carefully raise the mass by pulling on the spring scale. Measure the height, in meters, that the mass is lifted. Record this value in Table 1. Calculate the work output of the mass by multiplying its weight by the height it was raised. Record this value in Table 2.
4. Using the spring scale, raise the mass to the same height it was raised in Step 3. Ask your lab partner to read, directly from the spring scale, the force, in newtons, required to lift the mass. (If your spring scale is calibrated in grams, rather than newtons, calculate the force by multiplying the reading expressed in kilograms by the acceleration due to gravity.) Record this value in Table 1 as the force of spring scale. As you are lifting the load with the spring scale, pull upward at a slow, steady rate, using the minimum amount of force necessary to move the load. Any excess force will accelerate the mass and cause an error in your calculations.
5. Measure the distance, in meters, through which the force acted to lift the load to the height it was raised. Record this value in Table 1 as the distance, d, through which the force acts. Determine the work input in raising the mass by multiplying the force reading from the spring scale by the distance through which the force acted. Record the value for the work input in Table 2.
6. Repeat Steps 2 through 5 for a different load.
7. Repeat Steps 2 through 6 for each of the different pulley arrangements in Figures 1b, 1c, and 1d. Be sure to include the mass of the lower pulley(s) as part of the mass raised.
8. Count the number of lifting strands of string used to support the weight or load for each arrangement, (a) through (d). Record these values in Table 2.

Observations and Data
Table 1

Pulley arrange-ment	Mass raised (kg)	Weight (W) of mass (N)	Height (h) mass is raised (m)	Force (F) of spring scale (N)	Distance (d) through which force acts (m)
(a)					
(b)					
(c)					
(d)					

10.1 Pulleys

Table 2

Pulley arrangement	Work output (Wh) (J)	Work input (Fd) (J)	IMA (d_e/d_r)	MA Number of lifting strands	Efficiency %
(a)					
(b)					
(c)					
(d)					

Analysis

1. Find the efficiency of each system. Enter the results in Table 2. What are some possible reasons that the efficiency is never 100%.

2. Calculate the ideal mechanical advantage, IMA, for each arrangement by dividing d_e by d_r. Enter the results in Table 2. What happens to the force, F, as the mechanical advantage gets larger?

3. How does increasing the load affect the ideal mechanical advantage and efficiency of a pulley system?

4. How does increasing the number of pulleys affect the ideal mechanical advantage and efficiency of a pulley system?

5. The mechanical advantage may also be determined from the number of strands of string supporting the weight or load. Compare the calculated *IMA* from Question 2 with the number of strands of string you counted. Do the two results agree?

6. Explain why the following statement is false: A machine reduces the amount of work you have to do. Tell what a machine actually does.

Application

In the space provided below, sketch a pulley system that can be used to lift a boat from its trailer to the rafters of a garage, such that the effort force would move a distance of 60 m while the load will move 10 m.

EXPERIMENT
10.2 : Torques

Purpose

Investigate torque by finding the resultant of a number of forces.

Concept and Skill Check

There is a very good reason for placing a door knob as far as possible from the hinges of the door. When you have to open a heavy door, you must apply a force. But where you apply that force and in what direction you push or pull determine how easily that door will rotate open. You have learned that forces produce motion in a straight line, but they also tend to produce rotation if some point of a rigid body is fixed so as to constitute an axis. The turning movement caused by one or more forces acting on a body that is free to rotate about an axis is known as torque, τ, and is defined as the product of the vector quantities force, F, and lever arm, r. The lever arm is the perpendicular distance from the axis of rotation to a line drawn in the direction of the force. Thus, the further this line is from the axis, the more effective is the force that causes rotation. And since work, W, is the product of force and the distance through which the force acts, the work done during the angle of rotational displacement, θ, is $W = (F)(r\Delta\theta)$. But $Fr = \tau$; therefore, $W = \tau\,\theta$.

In this experiment, two parallel forces, the two spring balances, will balance the downward force of the hanging mass, as shown in the figure. The two parallel forces will tend to cause rotation because each is exerted over a specific distance, the lever arm, from the third force, the weight of the hanging mass. This latter force is located at what will be described as the pivot, point **B** in the figure. This fixed point **B** constitutes the axis of rotation.

The force at point **A** acts over a distance **AB** and produces a clockwise torque (a negative value). The force at point **C** acts over a distance **BC** and produces a counterclockwise torque (a positive value). The sum of these two torques may cause the meter stick to rotate in either a clockwise or

10.2 Torques

counterclockwise direction about the axis. If the sum of all the clockwise torques about the axis and the sum of all the counterclockwise torques about the same axis equal zero, the meter stick will balance and there will be no rotation. In this experiment, when the two parallel forces are balanced by the third force, the sum of all torques will equal zero, and the system will be in rotational equilibrium.

Materials

meter stick   3 meter-stick clamps   masking tape
2 spring balances, 5-N capacity or larger   500-g hooked mass

Procedure

1. Set up the apparatus as shown in the figure, omitting at this time the hanging mass. The two spring balances can either be hung from supports on the laboratory table or taped with masking tape so they are hanging over the edge of the table. Be sure that the spring scale mechanisms are able to move freely.
2. For the first trial, center one clamp at the 5-cm mark on the meter stick (point **A**) and center the other clamp at the 95-cm mark (point **C**), as shown in the figure.
3. Observe the force readings on the spring scales. Record these values in Table 1 as the original readings.
4. Hang a 500-g mass (4.9 N) from the clamp at point **B**, located at the center of the meter stick. Observe the scale readings at points **A** and **C** when the apparatus is in equilibrium. Record these values in Table 1 as the final readings.
5. The real reading of each spring scale is the difference between the final reading and the original reading. The real reading is the component of the force due to the hanging mass at point **B**. Calculate the real reading for each scale and record these values in Table 1.
6. Measure and record the distances **AB** and **BC** in Table 2.
7. The clockwise torque is equal to the product of the real reading for spring scale *a* and the distance **AB**. The counterclockwise torque is equal to the product of the real reading for spring scale *c* and the distance **BC**. Calculate the clockwise and counterclockwise torques and record these values in Table 2.
8. Repeat Steps 2 through 7 for Trials 2 and 3, moving the clamp at point **A** to two different positions on the meter stick.

Observations and Data
Table 1

	Balance *a*			Balance *c*		
Trial	Original reading (N)	Final reading (N)	Real reading (N)	Original reading (N)	Final reading (N)	Real reading (N)
1						
2						
3						

10.2 Torques

Table 2

Trial	Distance **AB** (m)	Distance **BC** (m)	Clockwise torque (N · m)	Counterclockwise torque (N · m)
1				
2				
3				

Analysis

1. Since the system in each trial was in equilibrium, what conditions had been met?

2. Compare the amount of force exerted (real reading) to the lever arm distance over which the forces were exerted.

3. Compare the absolute values of the clockwise and counterclockwise torques for each trial. In making your comparison, find the relative percent difference between the two values.

$$\% \text{ difference } = \frac{|\text{counterclockwise torque}| - |\text{clockwise torque}|}{|\text{counterclockwise torque}|} \times 100\%$$

4. What relationship should exist between the counterclockwise torque and the clockwise torque if the system is in equilibrium?

5. When the systems in your trials were in equilibrium, how much work was done? Explain your answer.

Application

The technique for measuring forces that was used in this experiment can be applied to determine the forces exerted by the piers of a bridge. However, in this instance, the forces are reversed. The two pier supports (replacing the two spring scales) will exert an upward force, and the person standing on the bridge (replacing the hanging mass) will exert a downward force on the bridge. Calculate the force exerted by each pier (F_1 and F_2) of a 5.0-m footbridge of 100.0-kg mass, evenly distributed, when a 55-kg person stands 2 m from one end of the bridge. In the space provided below, show all your calculations.

EXPERIMENT
11.1 : Conservation of Energy

Purpose
Verify the law of conservation of energy with an inclined plane.

Concept and Skill Check

In the absence of friction, the work done to pull an object up an inclined plane is equal to the work done to lift it straight up to the same height. The change in gravitational potential energy of an object caused by raising it to a given height is independent of the path through which the object is moved to reach that height.

When an object is lifted straight up, work is done only against gravity. The work done is equivalent to the increase in the gravitational potential energy of the object, *mgh*. In order to move the object up a plane, work must be done against gravity and friction. Therefore, to compare the work required to raise the object to the same height but over different paths, you must calculate the work done pulling the object up the plane in such a way as to remove from the comparison the work done against friction.

Materials

inclined plane
smooth wood block with hook
  in one end

spring scale (calibrated in newtons)
meter stick

string (1 m)
silicone spray

Procedure

1. Weigh the block of wood and enter this value in newtons on the line provided above Table 1. If your scale reads in grams, convert the reading to kilograms and multiply by 9.80 m/s² to find the weight in newtons.

2. Clean and spray with silicone the surfaces of the plane and block to make them as smooth as possible.

3. Set the plane at an angle, θ, so that the block will just slide down without being pushed. Measure the length, d, and the height, h, of the high end of the plane, as shown in Figure 1, and record these values in Table 1.

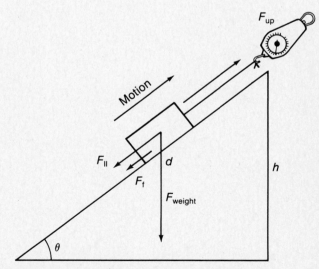

Figure 1. Be careful to pull the block in a direction parallel to the plane.

11.1 Conservation of Energy

4. Hook the spring scale to the block and pull the block up the plane at constant velocity. While the block is moving at constant velocity, have your lab partner read the applied force on the scale. Record the value in Table 1 as F_{up}. The force you applied, F_{up}, is the equilibrant of the component of the block's weight parallel to the plane, $F_{\parallel}$, plus the force of friction, F_f, described by

$$F_{up} = (F_{\parallel} + F_f).$$

5. Place the block at the top of the incline with the spring scale attached to the hook by a piece of string. Let the block slide down the plane at constant velocity and have your lab partner read and record in Table 1 the force, F_{down}. The frictional force has the same magnitude as before, but is exerted in the opposite direction. Thus, the force you exert is the equilibrant of the parallel component of the weight minus the frictional force described by

$$F_{down} = (F_{\parallel} - F_f).$$

6. Repeat Steps 3 through 5 twice more using different angles θ. Keep the height constant in all the trials. Each time you change the angle, θ, measure the length of the plane, d, to the point at which the surface of the plane is at height, h, from the table, as shown in Figure 2. Note that as the angle becomes larger, the length of the plane becomes shorter.

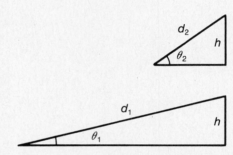

Figure 2. Vary the length, d, but retain the same height, h, of the plane for Step 6.

Observations and Data

Weight of the block _____ N

Table 1

Trial	Length, d (m)	Height, h (m)	F_{up} (N)	F_{down} (N)
1				
2				
3				

11.1 Conservation of Energy

Table 2

Trial	$F_\parallel$ (N)	Work done without friction, $F_\parallel d$ (J)	Potential energy mgh (J)	Work input $F_{up}d$ (J)
1				
2				
3				

Analysis

1. Add the two equations for F_{up} and F_{down} from Steps 4 and 5 and solve for $F_\parallel$.

2. Calculate the value of $F_\parallel$ for each trial and enter these values in Table 2.

3. For each trial, calculate and record in Table 2 the work done to pull the block up a frictionless plane. Use the calculated $F_\parallel$ and the length of the plane to solve $W = F_\parallel d$.

4. Calculate and record the potential energy, mgh, of the block at height h.

5. Compare the work required to pull the block up the plane set at various angles with the work required to lift the block straight up. Is energy conserved?

Application

A 60.0-kg student skis down an icy, frictionless hill with a vertical drop of 10.0 m. Explain how the law of conservation of energy applies to this situation and calculate how fast she will be going when she reaches the bottom of the hill.

Extension

Calculate the angle, θ, for each trial. Using your calculated angle, calculate the theoretical values for $F_{\parallel}$. Explain any differences between these theoretical values and those you obtained in Table 2.

EXPERIMENT
12.1 : Specific Heat

Purpose

Use the law of conservation of energy to calculate the specific heat of a metal.

Concept and Skill Check

One of several physical properties of a substance is the amount of energy that it will absorb per unit mass. This property is called specific heat, C_s. The specific heat of a material is the amount of energy, measured in joules, needed to raise the temperature of one kilogram of the material one Celsius degree (Kelvin).

A calorimeter is a device that can be used in the laboratory to measure the specific heat of a substance. The polystyrene cup, used as a calorimeter, insulates the water-metal system from the environment, while absorbing a negligible amount of heat. Since energy always flows from a hotter object to a cooler one and the total energy of a closed, isolated system always remains constant, the heat energy, Q, lost by one part of the system is gained by the other:

$$Q_{\text{lost by the metal}} = Q_{\text{gained by the water}}.$$

In this experiment, you will determine the specific heat of two different metals. The metal is heated to a known temperature and placed in the calorimeter containing a known mass of water at a measured temperature. The final temperature of the water and material in the calorimeter is then measured. Given the specific heat of water (4180 J/kg · K) and the temperature change of the water, you can calculate the heat gained by the water (heat lost by the metal) as follows:

$$Q_{\text{gained by the water}} = (m_{\text{water}})(\Delta T_{\text{water}})(4180 \text{ J/kg} \cdot \text{K}).$$

Since the heat lost by the metal is found by

$$Q_{\text{lost by the metal}} = (m_{\text{metal}})(\Delta T_{\text{metal}})(C_{\text{metal}}),$$

the specific heat of the metal can be calculated as follows:

$$C_{\text{metal}} = \frac{Q_{\text{gained by the water}}}{(m_{\text{metal}})(\Delta T_{\text{metal}})}.$$

Materials

string (60 cm)	hot plate (or burner with ringstand,	balance
safety goggles	ring, and wire screen)	specific heat set (brass,
250-mL beaker	tap water	aluminum, iron, lead,
polystyrene cup	thermometer	copper, etc.)

Procedure

1. Safety goggles must be worn for this laboratory activity. CAUTION: *Be careful when handling hot glassware, metals, or hot water.* Fill a 250-mL beaker about half full of water. Place the beaker of water on a hot plate (or a ringstand with a wire screen) and begin heating it.

2. While waiting for the water to boil, measure and record in Table 1 the mass of the metals you are using and the mass of the polystyrene cup.

3. Attach a 30-cm piece of string to each metal sample. Lower one of the metal samples, by the string, into the boiling water, as shown in the figure on the next page. Leave the metal in the boiling water for at least five minutes.

12.1

Specific Heat

Thermometer

Polystyrene cup calorimeter

Hot plate

The calorimeter is used to measure heat exchange by means of temperature changes.

4. Fill the polystyrene cup half full of room temperature water. Measure and record in Table 1 the total mass of the water and the cup.
5. Measure and record in Table 1 the temperature of the room temperature water in the polystyrene cup and the boiling water in the beaker. The temperature of the boiling water is also the temperature of the hot metal.
6. Carefully remove the metal from the boiling water and quickly lower it into the room temperature water in the polystyrene cup.
7. Gently stir the water in the polystyrene cup for several minutes with the thermometer. CAUTION: *Thermometers are easily broken. If you are using a mercury thermometer and it breaks, notify your teacher immediately. Mercury is a poisonous liquid and vapor.* When the water reaches a constant temperature, record this value in Table 1 as the final temperature of the system.
8. Remove the metal sample and repeat Steps 3 through 7 with another metal sample.

Observations and Data

Table 1

	Trial 1	Trial 2
Type of metal		
Mass of calorimeter cup (kg)		
Mass of calorimeter cup and water (kg)		
Mass of metal (kg)		
Initial temperature of room temperature water (°C)		
Temperature of hot metal (°C)		
Final temperature of metal and water (°C)		

Specific Heat

NAME —————————————————————————

Table 2

	Trial 1	Trial 2
Mass of room temperature water (kg)		
ΔT metal (°C)		
ΔT room temperature water (°C)		

Analysis

1. For each trial, calculate the mass of the room temperature water, the change in temperature of the metal, and the change in temperature of the water in the polystyrene cup. Record these values in Table 2.

2. For each trial, calculate the heat gained by the water (heat lost by the metal).

3. For each trial, calculate the specific heat of the metal. For each metal sample, use the value for heat gained by the water that you calculated in Question 2.

4. For each trial, use the values for specific heat of substances found in Table C:1 of Appendix C to calculate the relative error between your value for specific heat and the accepted value for the metal sample.

5. If you had some discrepancies in your values for specific heat of the metal samples, suggest possible sources of uncertainty in your measurements that may have contributed to the difference.

Application

The specific heat of a material can be used to identify it. For example, a 100.0-g sample of a substance is heated to 100.0°C and placed into a calorimeter cup (having a negligible amount of heat absorption) containing 150.0 g of water at 25°C. The sample raises the temperature of the water to 32.1°C. Use the values in Table C:1 in the Appendix, to identify the substance.

Extension

Obtain a sample of an unknown metal from your teacher. Use the procedure described in this laboratory activity to identify it by the value of its specific heat.

EXPERIMENT 13.1 Archimedes' Principle

Purpose

Investigate Archimedes' principle and measure the buoyant force of a fluid.

Concept and Skill Check

Archimedes' principle states that an object wholly or partially immersed in a fluid is buoyed up by a net force equal to the weight of the fluid that it displaces, $F_{buoyant} = F_{weight\ of\ fluid\ displaced}$. Recall that $F_{weight\ of\ fluid\ displaced} = \rho_{fluid} V_{fluid\ displaced}\, g$, where ρ = density. When an object with a density less than that of the fluid is submerged, it will sink only until it displaces a volume of fluid with a weight equal to the weight of the object. At this time, the object is floating underwater, equilibrium exists, and $\rho_{fluid} V_{fluid\ displaced} = \rho_{object} V_{object}$.

If the density of an object is greater than that of the fluid, an upward buoyant force from the pressure of the fluid will act on the object, but the magnitude of the buoyant force will be too small to balance the downward weight force of the denser material. While the object will sink, its apparent weight decreases by an amount equivalent to the buoyant force.

In this experiment, you will investigate the buoyant force of water acting on an object. Recall that 1 mL of water has a mass of 1 g and a weight of 0.01 N. The buoyant force acting on the object is determined by finding the difference between the weight of the object in air and the weight of the object when it is immersed in water and is given by the following equation:

$$F_{buoyant} = F_{weight\ of\ mass\ in\ air} - F_{weight\ of\ mass\ in\ water}.$$

Materials

500-mL beaker	500-g hooked mass	polystyrene cup
spring scale, 5-N capacity or greater	100-g hooked mass	paper towel

Procedure

1. Pour cool tap water into the 500-mL beaker to the 300-mL mark. Carefully read the volume from the gradations on the beaker and record this value in Table 1.
2. Hang the 500-g mass from the spring scale. Measure the weight of the mass in air and record this value in Table 1.
3. Immerse the 500-g mass, suspended from the spring scale, in the water, as shown in the figure. Do not let the mass rest on the bottom of the beaker or touch the sides of the beaker and keep it suspended from the spring scale. Measure the weight of the immersed mass and record this value in Table 1.
4. Measure the volume of the water with the mass immersed. Record the new volume reading in Table 1. Remove the 500-g mass from the beaker and set it aside.
5. Measure and record in Table 2 the volume of water in the beaker. Place the 100-g mass in the beaker of water. Measure and record in Table 2 the volume of the water in the beaker with the mass immersed.
6. The polystyrene cup will serve as a "boat." Remove the mass from the water, dry it with a paper towel, and place it in the polystyrene cup. Float the cup in the beaker of water. Measure and record in Table 2 the new volume of water.

Measure the weight of a mass submerged in water.

EXPERIMENT
13.1 Archimedes' Principle

Observations and Data
Table 1

Weight of 500-g mass in air	
Weight of 500-g mass immersed in water	
Volume of water in beaker	
Volume of water in beaker with 500-g mass immersed	

Table 2

Volume of water in beaker	
Volume of water with 100-g mass immersed	
Volume of water with 100-g mass in polystyrene cup	

Analysis

1. Calculate the buoyant force of water acting on the 500-g mass.

2. Using the values from Table 1, calculate the volume of water displaced by the 500-g mass. Calculate the weight of the water displaced. Compare the weight of the volume of water displaced with the buoyant force acting on the immersed object that you calculated in Question 1. If the values are different, describe sources of error to account for this difference.

3. What happened to the water level in the beaker when the 100-g mass was placed in the polystyrene cup (boat)? Propose an explanation, which includes density, for any difference in volume you found in Steps 5 and 6.

Application

Tim and Sally are floating on an inflatable raft in a swimming pool. What happens to the water level in the pool if both fall off the raft and into the water?

EXPERIMENT
14.1 Ripple Tank Waves

Purpose

Use a ripple tank to investigate wave properties of reflection, refraction, diffraction, and interference.

Concept and Skill Check

A ripple tank provides an ideal medium for observing the behavior of waves. The ripple tank projects images of waves in the water onto the paper screen below the tank. Just as you have probably observed in a swimming pool, light shining through water waves is seen as a pattern of bright lines and dark lines separated by gray areas. The water acts as a series of lenses, bending the light that passes through it. In the ripple tank, the wave crests focus the light from the light source and produce bright lines on the paper. Troughs in the ripple tank waves cause the light to diverge and produce dark lines. Areas of no disturbance project a uniform gray shade. Dampers placed along the sides of the tank help to prevent reflected waves from interfering with observations.

In this experiment, you will investigate a number of wave properties, including reflection, refraction, diffraction, and interference. The law of reflection states that the angle of incidence is equal to the angle of reflection. Waves undergoing a change in speed and direction as they pass from one medium to another are demonstrating refraction. The spreading of waves around the edge of a barrier or a small obstacle exemplifies diffraction. The result of the superposition of two or more waves is interference, which can be either constructive or destructive. You will generate waves in a ripple tank and observe the effects on wave behavior of different shapes and orientations of barriers.

Materials

ripple tank	meter stick	12 washers or pennies for
light source	protractor	glass supports
dowel rod (30 cm long,	large sheets plain white	two-point-source wave
2 cm diameter)	paper	generator
3 wood or paraffin blocks	eyedropper	0–12 VDC variable power
metal strip (parabolic) or	flat glass plate	supply for wave generator
rubber hose		

Figure 1.

Procedure

Set up the ripple tank as shown in Figure 1. Add water to a depth of 5–8 mm. Check the depth at all four corners to be sure the tank is level. Turn on the light source. While creating small disturbances with a pencil, adjust the light source so that clear images of waves are produced on the paper screen.
CAUTION: *Do not touch any electrical components if your hands are wet.*

14.1 Ripple Tank Waves

Reflection

1. Roll the dowel rod back and forth gently to generate straight pulses at one end of the tank. Place a straight barrier at the opposite end of the tank and send incident pulses toward it so that they strike the barrier head-on (angle of incidence = 0°). Observe and record in Item 1 of Table 1 a description of what happens to the pulses as they strike the barrier. Change the angle of the barrier with respect to the incoming pulse. Generate pulses and record your observations in Item 1 of Table 1. Remember that the behavior of pulses is the same as the behavior of waves. In the space provided in Item 2 of Table 1, sketch incoming pulses (waves) striking the barrier at an angle and show the reflected pulses.

2. Use your protractor to measure the angle at which incoming pulses approach the barrier. The angle of incidence (i) is the angle the wave front makes with the normal (N), which is perpendicular to the barrier at the point where the wave meets the barrier. Observe the reflected pulses. The angle between the reflected pulses and the normal is the angle of reflection (r). In Item 3 of Table 1, compare the relationship, provided by your data, between the angle of incidence and the angle of reflection.

3. Replace the straight barrier with a parabolic strip, arranged so that the open side of the curve is toward the dowel rod, as shown in Figure 2. Send straight pulses toward the curved barrier. Describe in Item 4 of Table 1 the shape of the reflected pulses.

Figure 2. Straight waves approaching a curved barrier.

4. Locate the point, or focus, where the reflected pulses come together. Using an eyedropper, let small drops of water fall at that point or, using your finger, gently tap the water at the focus. Note that there are two wave fronts, one that moves outward from the focus and one that moves toward the curved barrier and is reflected. Describe in Item 5 of Table 1 the reflection of a circular wave originating at the focus of the concave barrier.

Refraction

1. Place a glass plate in the center of the tank and to one side, as shown in Figure 3a in Table 2. Support the plate with washers, as necessary, to provide an area of shallow water.

2. Send straight pulses toward the glass plate. Carefully observe the pulses at the shallow-water boundary. In Figure 3a in Table 2, sketch the patterns you observe as the waves move through the shallow medium. Rotate the glass plate so that one corner is pointed toward the incident straight waves, as shown in Figure 3b in Table 2. Send a series of straight pulses toward the glass plate. In Figure 3b, sketch the patterns you observe as the waves encounter the shallow medium at an angle. Remove the glass plate and washers.

Diffraction

1. Arrange two wood or paraffin blocks, as shown in Figure 4. Generate a series of straight pulses and observe the diffraction of the incident waves as they pass through the opening. While generating waves at a constant rate, make the opening progressively smaller. Sketch in Item 1 of Table 3 two different widths of the incident barrier opening, one large and one small, showing diffraction of the incident waves.

Figure 4. Arrangement of blocks for observing diffraction.

Ripple Tank Waves

2. Increase the rate of wave generation. Recall that the effect of an increased frequency is a decreased wavelength. Observe what happens when the width of the opening is varied. Record your observations in Item 2 of Table 3. Remove the blocks from the tank.

Interference

1. Place the two-point-source generator in the tank near one end. Attach the variable power supply to the generator. Turn on the power supply to a low voltage setting so that the point sources produce a continuous series of circular waves of long wavelength. The superposition of waves from the two sources should produce an interference pattern in the tank. Nodal lines, lines of no disturbance where troughs and crests come together simultaneously, should be visible. Antinodal lines, where two troughs or two crests come together simultaneously, should also be visible between the nodal lines. Sketch the wave pattern in Item 1 of Table 4. Label the nodal and antinodal lines.

2. Increase the generator frequency and observe how the interference pattern changes. Sketch the new pattern in Item 2 of Table 4. Observe what happens to the pattern and number of nodal lines as the generator frequency is varied.

Observations and Data

Reflection

Table 1

1. Observations of straight pulses striking a straight barrier at 0° and at another angle:

2. Sketch of incoming pulses and reflected pulses:

3. Statement of the relationship between the angle of incidence and the angle of reflection:

4. Description of the shape of the reflected pulse from a concave surface:

5. Description of the reflection of circular waves originating at the focus:

Refraction
Table 2

Observations of refraction of straight waves:

(a)   **(b)**

Figure 3. Orientations of glass plate for observing refraction of straight waves.

Diffraction
Table 3

1. Observations of diffraction:
   a. large opening   b. small opening

2. Observations of diffraction with decreased wavelength:

Ripple Tank Waves

NAME ————————————————————

Interference

Table 4

1. Interference pattern:	2. Interference pattern (higher frequency than that used for Item 1):

Analysis

1. Using your observations of reflected waves, make a generalization about the angle of incidence and the angle of reflection from a straight barrier.

2. What happens to the velocity, wavelength, and frequency of a water wave as it is refracted at the boundary between the deep and shallow water?

3. How does wave diffraction change as the width of the opening is changed?

4. As the wavelength decreases, what happens to wave diffraction?

5. How does the interference pattern change as the wavelength is changed? How does a decrease in wavelength affect the interference pattern?

6. Predict the pattern of waves produced by a double-slit barrier.

7. Put your index finger and thumb together, so that they nearly touch. Hold them in front of a bright, incandescent light bulb. Look through the tiny opening. What explanation can you provide for the vertical lines you observe?

Applications

1. How can ocean waves help locate underwater reefs or sandbars?

2. How can you apply the law of reflection to sports like platform tennis, racquet ball, and pool?

Extension

Place three wood or paraffin blocks in the tank to create two openings (a double slit), as shown in Figure 5. Use the straight-wave generator (dowel) to send waves toward the openings. Sketch your observations. How does this result compare with your prediction in Question 6?

Figure 5. Arrangement of blocks for observing interference.

EXPERIMENT

14.2

Velocity, Wavelength, and Frequency in Ripple Tanks

Purpose

Investigate the relationship between wavelength, frequency, and velocity of waves.

Concept and Skill Check

The velocity in a given medium of all waves of the same kind is the same. The velocity of a periodic wave can be calculated from the equation

$$v = f\lambda,$$

where v is the velocity of the wave in the medium, f is the frequency of the wave, and λ is the wavelength of the wave. In Experiment 14.1, you found that the velocity of a wave changes only when the wave enters a different medium. Since the velocity remains constant, an increase in the frequency will result in a decrease in the wavelength. Likewise, a decrease in the frequency will result in an increase in the wavelength.

In this laboratory activity, you will measure the frequency and wavelength of water waves and use that information to determine the velocity of the moving waves. Since the ripple tank images on the screen are magnified, measurements of the wavelength on the screen must be adjusted for the magnification.

Materials

ripple tank	stopwatch or watch	large sheets plain white
light source	with second hand	paper
point-source wave generator	meter stick	masking tape
0–12 VDC variable power supply	stroboscope	two rulers
for wave generator		

Figure 1.

EXPERIMENT 14.2 Velocity, Wavelength, and Frequency in Ripple Tanks

NAME ———————————

Procedure

1. Set up the ripple tank, as shown in Figure 1. Place 5–8 mm of water in the tank. Measure the depth at each corner and adjust the tank until it is level. Place the wave generator into the ripple tank so that one point source touches the water. Turn the other point source upward so that it does not hit the water. Attach the power supply to the wave generator. Turn on the light source and the power supply for the wave generator. Adjust the power supply so that the wave generator produces clear images of radiating circles on the paper screen below the ripple tank. Do not change the adjustment on the power supply while following Steps 1 through 7. Doing so will change your data partway through the lab activity. CAUTION: *Do not operate the generator at a high rate of speed or damage to the generator may result. Do not touch electrical components if your hands are wet.*

2. Cover all but every third slit in the stroboscope with masking tape. This should leave four slits open at regular intervals. If not, select a different spacing for your stroboscope so that the intervals between open slits are identical. Hold the stroboscope in one hand with the shaft pointed toward your face. Put a finger of your other hand in the hole of the stroboscope and rotate the stroboscope disc at a constant rate. Through the stroboscope, observe the wave pattern on the paper screen. Vary the rate of rotation of the stroboscope until the waves appear to stand still.

3. While you are observing the "stopped" waves with the stroboscope, have your partner place the two rulers parallel (along a tangent) to the "stopped" waves and five wavelengths apart on the paper, as shown in Figure 2. Since your lab partner sees the waves constantly moving, you will have to direct the placement of the rulers. Measure in meters the width of five wavelengths and record this value in Table 1. Calculate the observed wavelength by dividing the distance between the rulers by five. Record in Table 3 this value for one wavelength.

Figure 2. Place rulers so that they are tangent to the circular waves and separated by five wavelengths.

4. Measure the length of a ruler, pencil, or block. Place it in the ripple tank and measure the length of the shadow it casts on your paper screen. Record the measurement in Table 2. Find the ratio of the length of the object's shadow to the actual length of the object and record this value in Table 2. This ratio is the magnification factor for the ripple tank. Divide the observed wavelength by the magnification to determine the corrected wavelength and record this value in Table 3 and in Table 4.

5. To measure the frequency of the waves, the rate of rotation of the stroboscope must be determined. Make a dark mark on one piece of tape on the stroboscope. While you are observing the "stopped" waves with the stroboscope, have your partner watch this mark and measure with the stopwatch the time for ten revolutions. Record the time for ten revolutions in Table 1. Divide this time by ten to determine the time for one revolution and record this value in Table 1.

Velocity, Wavelength, and Frequency in Ripple Tanks

NAME ——————————————

6. The frequency of the waves, in Hertz, is determined by dividing the number of open slits (which should be four) by the time for one revolution of the stroboscope. Calculate the frequency and record this value in Table 4.
7. Multiply the frequency by the corrected wavelength to determine the velocity and record this value in Table 4.
8. Repeat Steps 3 through 7 for two additional trials at different rates of wave generation.

Observations and Data

Table 1

Trial	Width of five wavelengths (m)	Time for ten revolutions (s)	Time for one revolution (s)
1			
2			
3			

Table 2

Length of object (cm)	Length of shadow (cm)	Magnification ratio (length of shadow/length of object)

Table 3

Trial	Observed wavelength (m)	Corrected wavelength (m)
1		
2		
3		

Table 4

Trial	Frequency (Hz)	Wavelength (m)	Velocity (m/s)
1			
2			
3			

Analysis

1. Which physical quantity did you vary in each trial? Which physical quantity responded to the manipulation?

Velocity, Wavelength, and Frequency in Ripple Tanks

2. Using your results from Table 4, compare the velocities of the water waves at different frequencies.

3. Does this laboratory activity support the rule that the velocity of a wave in a given medium is constant?

Applications

1. Is the relationship, $v = f\lambda$, different from the equation for velocity you used earlier in kinematics, where $v = \Delta d/\Delta t$? Explain.

2. A wave of wavelength 3.5 m has a velocity of 217 m/s. Find (a) the frequency and (b) the period of this wave.

EXPERIMENT
15.1 : The Sound Level of a Portable Radio or Tape Player

Purpose
Measure the sound level of a portable radio or tape player.

Concept and Skill Check

The human ear is sensitive to a wide range in the intensity of sound. The intensity of a sound at the threshold of pain is 1×10^{12} times greater than that of the faintest, detectible sound. However, the ear does not perceive sounds at the threshold of pain to be 1×10^{12} times louder than a barely audible tone. Loudness, as measured by the human ear, is not directly proportional to the intensity of a sound wave. Instead, a sound with ten times the intensity of another sound will be perceived as twice as loud. A practical unit for measuring the relative intensity of a sound level (β) is the decibel (dB), defined as

$$\beta = (10 \text{ dB}) \log \frac{I}{I_o},$$

where I is the intensity at sound level β and I_o is a standard reference intensity near the lower limit of human hearing, which corresponds to a sound level of 0 dB. A sound at the threshold of pain corresponds to a sound level of 120 dB.

Table 1 shows a comparison of intensity ratios and their sound level equivalents in decibels. Note that when the intensity doubles, the sound level increases by only 3 dB. If the intensity of a sound is multiplied by ten, the sound level increases by 10 dB, but if the intensity is multiplied by 100, the sound level increases by 20 dB.

Table 1

I/I_o	dB
2	3
3	5
5	7
10	10
20	13
32	15
100	20
1000	30

Table 2

Sound level (dB)	Exposure per day (h)
90	8
92	6
95	4
97	3
100	2
102	1.5
105	1
110	0.5

Prolonged exposure to loud sounds can damage your hearing; the longer the exposure, the greater is the extent of damage. Federal regulations state that workers cannot be exposed to sound levels of more than 90 dB during an eight-hour day. Table 2 shows a comparison of sound levels and the limit of exposure per day to avoid permanent damage to hearing.

In this laboratory activity, you will use a sound level meter, such as the one shown in the figure, to measure the sound level of a portable radio or tape player.

EXPERIMENT
15.1 The Sound Level of a Portable Radio or Tape Player

NAME —————————

Materials

portable radio or tape player, with earphones
cassette tape of music

masking tape
sound level meter

white correction fluid
graph paper

Procedure

1. Inspect the volume control of your radio or tape player to determine if it has numerical settings. If it does not, use the white correction fluid to make eight to ten equally spaced marks on the control dial, beginning at the off position.
2. Tune the portable radio to a station that is playing music or insert a cassette tape of your choice into the tape player.
3. Be sure you understand how to use and take readings from the sound level meter. If you do not, ask your teacher for instructions.
4. Use masking tape to attach the headphones to the sound level meter, placing the sound level meter microphone against one earpiece of the headphones.
5. Turn on the radio or tape player and the sound level meter. Measure the sound level at each increment on the volume control. Record the sound level data in Table 3. Repeat the procedure for other portable radios or players. In Table 3 record these data as additional trials.
6. Turn the volume control to a low setting. Remove the headphones from the sound meter and put them on your head. Tune into some music you enjoy and adjust the volume setting until you have reached the amplitude that you typically prefer. Record this volume setting in Table 4. Estimate the number of hours, in a given day, that you listen to music at this level. Record this value in Table 4.

Observations and Data
Table 3

Setting	Sound Level (dB)			Setting	Sound Level (dB)		
	Trial 1	Trial 2	Trial 3		Trial 1	Trial 2	Trial 3
0				6			
1				7			
2				8			
3				9			
4				10			
5							

15.1 The Sound Level of a Portable Radio or Tape Player

NAME ————————————————

Table 4

Volume setting for listening	
Estimate of time at preferred volume setting	

Analysis

1. Make a graph of sound level (*y*-axis) versus volume setting (*x*-axis). Is there any recognizable relationship existing between the measured sound level and the corresponding volume setting? Explain.

2. Use your graph to determine what sound level corresponds to your preferred listening volume setting.

3. Refer to Table 2 to determine the maximum time you should be listening to music at your preferred volume level. What is this value?

4. Is your portable radio or tape player potentially dangerous for your hearing? Explain.

The Sound Level of a Portable Radio or Tape Player

NAME —————————————

Applications

1. Jack's hearing test revealed that he needed a sound level of 20 dB to detect sounds at 2000 Hz. Sam's hearing test revealed that he needed a sound level of 40 dB to detect sounds at the same frequency. If the normal sound level for testing is 15 dB, how much greater than normal were the sound intensities Jack and Sam needed to detect sound?

2. The sound level of a rock group is 110 dB, while that of normal conversation at 1 m is 60 dB. Find the ratio of their intensities. Show all your calculations.

Extension

1. In open space, the intensity of sound varies inversely with the square of the distance from the source, $I \propto \frac{1}{r^2}$. Predict what happens to sound levels in an enclosed room. Explain your answer.

2. A student is considering a new stereo system for his room and thinks he needs a 150-W amplifier producing 100 W of power. He has asked you to determine if this is a good choice. To help this student, you must find (a) the possible intensity of the sound from this system at a distance $r = 2.5$ m from the source and (b) the corresponding sound level. Use the equation

$$I = \frac{P}{4\pi r^2}$$

where P is the power in watts and I is the intensity measured in W/m². $I_o = 10^{-12}$ W/m². Show all your calculations. Is this a wise choice for the student? Explain.

3. If this student has one speaker producing 100 dB of sound and he places a second speaker of the same capacity next to it, what is the new sound level at 1 m from the speakers?

EXPERIMENT
15.2
Resonance in an Open Tube

Purpose
Demonstrate resonance in an open tube and determine the velocity of sound in air.

Concept and Skill Check
Standing longitudinal waves are formed in air columns in open pipes (tubes) as well as closed pipes. Air rushes in and out of the pipe as the molecules of air inside the tube are disturbed by the vibrating tuning fork. A wave reflected at the end of the open tube can interfere with an incident wave to reinforce or to nullify the latter's effect. At the nodes, destructive interference occurs, while at the antinodes, constructive interference occurs, characterized by an increase in the amplitude of the vibrations. This increased amplitude is called resonance.

At the fundamental harmonic of an open tube, there is a pressure node at each end, with one pressure antinode between. The length, l, of the tube corresponds to approximately one-half of the wavelength, λ, of the sound, or $l = \lambda/2$. The effective length of the air column in a resonating open tube must be increased by a factor that relates to the diameter, d, of the tube. Thus, the wavelength is given by

$$\lambda = 2(l + 0.8d).$$

In this experiment, you will apply the principle of resonance to determine the velocity of sound in air. You will use a tuning fork of known frequency, f, to find the length of an open tube at which the air column resonates. From this result, you can find the wavelength of the sound with the equation given above. Then you will use the equation, $v = f\lambda$, to find the velocity, v, of sound in air.

To test your experimental results, you will perform another calculation. The velocity of sound in air increases as the temperature increases. The velocity of sound in air is 331.5 m/s at 0°C + 0.59 m/s per degree Celsius above 0°C. You will record the room temperature and determine the accepted value for the velocity of sound in air at the measured room temperature.

Materials
adjustable open pipe (tube),
    0.25–1.4 m long
tuning fork hammer
2 tuning forks, with frequencies
    between 126 Hz and 512 Hz
thermometer
meter stick

Procedure
1. Select an adjustable open tube. Figure 1 is a graph showing the approximate relationship between the length and the resonant frequency of an open tube of 4.8-cm diameter at room temperature. Using the information from Figure 1, select a tuning fork that corresponds to the range of your tube's length.

Open Tube Length vs Frequency

Figure 1. Approximate length of a resonating, open tube of 4.8-cm diameter at room temperature. Graph produced using the Lab Partner™ graphing program.

EXPERIMENT 15.2 Resonance in an Open Tube

NAME _____

2. Record in Table 1 the frequency of your tuning fork.
3. Measure and record in Table 1 the diameter of your adjustable open tube.
4. Strike the tuning fork with the tuning fork hammer. While you hold the tuning fork close to, but not touching the tube, as shown in Figure 2, have your lab partner slowly adjust the length of the tube until both partners hear the loudest sound.
5. Measure the length of the tube that produces the loudest, resonant sound. Record in Table 1 the measured length of the resonant tube.
6. The length of the air column must be increased by 0.8 times the diameter of the tube to correct for the amount of air vibrating outside the tube. Calculate 0.8d and add this length to the measured length of the tube to determine L, where $L = l + 0.8d$. Record in Table 2 the value of L.

Figure 2. Hold the tuning fork close to, but not touching, the open tube. Adjust the length of the tube to produce the loudest sound.

7. Calculate the wavelength and record this value in Table 2.
8. Record in Table 3 the room temperature in °C. Calculate the velocity correction for temperature by multiplying (0.59 m/s/°C)(the room temperature in °C). Enter this correction in Table 3. Calculate the accepted velocity of sound in air by adding 331.5 m/s to the velocity correction. Record in Table 3 the accepted velocity of sound.
9. Repeat the process using a tuning fork of different frequency. Record your data and calculations in the appropriate tables.

Observations and Data

Table 1

Trial	Frequency (Hz)	Pipe diameter (m)	Measured length of pipe (m)
1			
2			

Table 2

Trial	Corrected length (L) of air column (m)	Wavelength $\lambda = 2L$ (m)
1		
2		

EXPERIMENT 15.2 Resonance in an Open Tube

NAME ———————————————————————

Table 3

Trial	Air temperature (°C)	Velocity correction for temperature (m/s)	Accepted velocity of sound (m/s)
1			
2			

Analysis

1. Using $v = f\lambda$, determine the velocity of sound in air for each trial.

2. Calculate the relative error between the velocity of sound determined in Question 1 and the accepted value from Table 3.

3. What effect might steam have on the resonant frequency of the tube?

4. Does an open tube resonate at another length? Test your hypothesis.

EXPERIMENT
15.2 Resonance in an Open Tube

Application

A 3.0-m long, 0.15-m diameter open organ pipe resonates when air at 20.0°C is blown against its opening. What is the frequency of the note produced?

16.1 Light Days

Purpose
Study and describe the properties of light.

Concept and Skill Check
Recall that visible light is the region of the electromagnetic spectrum that stimulates the retina of the human eye. The wavelengths of light that your eyes can detect range from about 400 nm (violet) to 700 nm (red), a range that represents only a small portion of the entire spectrum. The human eye varies in its ability to perceive different wavelengths of the visible spectrum. A graph of the relative sensitivity of the human eye at different wavelengths shows that the eye is most sensitive to light at the center of the visible range, 555 nm. Light of this wavelength corresponds to what is sensed as a yellow-green color. Does this explain why some emergency vehicles are painted yellow-green and school buses are painted yellow? In this introduction to light, you will make qualitative observations of various light phenomena.

Materials
Numbers in parentheses indicate the lab station where equipment is set up.

film with single slit (1)
film with double slit (1)
diffraction grating (1, 8)
rubber bands (1, 5, 6, 19)
10 incandescent light bulbs (40 W or smaller), with sockets and cords (1, 5, 6, 7, 13, 19)
4 pieces red filter material (1, 5, 6, 19)
2 concave lenses (2, 24)
2 convex lenses (2, 24)
Newton's rings apparatus (3)
Newton's color disc (4)
3 pieces each: blue, green, and yellow filter material (5, 6, 19)
500-g mass (5)
paper screen (5)
fiber optic rod or fiber optic sculpture (7)

strobe light (8)
2 spectroscopes (8, 13)
transmission hologram with colored filter (9)
slide projector, for transmission of hologram light source (9)
He-Ne laser (10, 11, 12)
plane mirror (10)
flashlight (11)
semicircular plastic dish (12)
4 polarizing filters (14, 21, 22)
clear plastic box (14)
white paper
paint brush (15)
red, blue, green, and yellow paints (15)
optic mirage apparatus (16)

reflector, from a light or bicycle (17)
white light hologram (18)
red, blue, green, yellow, and orange paper (19)
orange filter (19)
kaleidoscope (20)
liquid crystal display, such as a calculator (21)
Iceland spar calcite crystal (22)
spotlight or car headlight (23)
light ray box (24)
4 light ray boxes or projectors (25)
red, blue, green, and yellow plastic filters for light ray boxes or projectors (25)

Procedure
A number of different setups have been installed at stations throughout the lab. As you perform the requested activities at each station, record your observations, make sketches of the setups, and answer the questions. You may be asked to draw upon your knowledge of the properties of waves to explain what you are observing. Take comprehensive notes and make careful

EXPERIMENT
16.1 Light Days

NAME ————————————————————

observations. Many of the setups in this experiment will be the basis for in-depth, quantitative studies found in later experiments. CAUTION: *Observe safety precautions when using electrical equipment and never look directly into an operating laser or laser beam.*

Observations and Data

Lab Stations

1. Light Through a Slit: Observe an unfrosted incandescent light bulb through a single slit, a double slit, and a diffraction grating. Hold the films by their edges. Record your observations. Place a red filter over the light bulb and secure it with a rubber band. Record your observations of red light viewed through the slits and the diffraction grating.

2. Lenses—Converging and Diverging: Look through each type of lens at some writing or a familiar object. Make your observations while you are close to the object, and then when you have moved some distance away. Sketch your observations.

3. Newton's Rings: Observe this phenomenon. Sketch what you see. What causes this effect? Have you seen anything that looks similar to this?

4. Newton's Color Disc: Describe the colors on the disc and their pattern. Spin the disc as fast as possible, using daylight as the light source. What do you see?

Figure 1. Arrangement of materials for Step 5 to produce shadows.

5. Shadows: In a dark location, place a 500-g mass (the object) a few centimeters from a paper screen. Place two lights about 40 cm from the object and about 20 cm apart, so that two adjacent shadows are created on the screen, as shown in the figure. Completely cover one light with a red filter. Observe, sketch, and label the colors of the shadows. Remove the red filter and repeat your observations and sketches with a yellow, a green, and a blue filter.

   a. Red filter   b. Yellow filter

   c. Green filter   d. Blue filter

6. Colored Lights: Why do these lights, covered with red, blue, green, and yellow filter material, appear to be colored instead of white?

7. Fiber Optics: Hold a fiber optic rod (or sculpture) in front of a light source. What do you observe about light in the fiber optic rod? Is light transmitted, reflected, or absorbed?

8. Strobe: Look through a spectroscope (or a diffraction grating) at a flashing strobe light. Record your observations.

9. Transmission Hologram: Observe a transmission hologram. Stand about one meter behind the hologram with the colored (monochromatic) light source shining through it. How does this image compare to ordinary photographs? Explain what causes this effect.

10. Plane Mirror: CAUTION: *Be sure that the laser light is not reflected into anyone's eyes.* Clap two chalk-filled erasers together or spray a fine mist of water into the air above the laser beam. Observe the incident and reflected rays of laser light that are reflected from a plane mirror.

11. Operating Laser: Direct the laser beam across the classroom. Compare the size of the beam's diameter at a point next to the laser and the diameter at a point on the far side of the room. How does the beam divergence compare with that of another type of light source, such as a flashlight?

12. Bending Light: Shine the laser beam into the flat side of a semicircular-shaped plastic dish filled with water. Record your observations of the beam's path as it travels through the water at different angles of incidence.

13. Spectroscope: Observe an incandescent light bulb through a spectroscope. Draw your observations. Now look through a spectroscope at a fluorescent light bulb in the hallway or elsewhere. Compare your observations and describe any differences. What could account for the different patterns you observed?

14. Polarizing Filters: These filters polarize light passing through them into one plane of vibration. While looking at an object through both filters, rotate one of the filters. Describe what happens. Place a clear plastic box between the filters. Look at the corners of the box. Rotate one of the filters as before. Suggest an explanation for your observations.

15. Pigment Color: Mix some paint pigments on a sheet of white paper. What colors can you produce using combinations of blue, yellow, red, and green pigments?

16. Optic Mirage: Where does the object appear? Can the image be projected onto a sheet of paper? Compare the sizes of the object and of the image.

17. Reflectors: Draw a reflector and show how light strikes and reflects from its surface.

18. White Light Hologram: Observe this hologram and compare it to the transmission hologram in Step 9. Describe the image.

19. Colored Light on Colored Paper: Place a colored filter over the light and observe the effect on different colors of paper. Repeat this procedure for all colored filters. Record your observations in Table 1 below.

Table 1

Color of paper in white light	Color of paper when incident light is				
	red	orange	yellow	green	blue
red					
orange					
yellow					
green					
blue					

20. Kaleidoscope: Look into this instrument and draw some of the patterns you observe. What causes the symmetry in the patterns?

21. Liquid Crystals: Observe a liquid crystal display, such as a calculator, through a polarizing lens. Rotate the lens. What happens? Explain.

22. Iceland Spar: Place this calcite crystal over some writing. Draw your observations. Place a polarizing filter over the crystal and rotate the filter while observing the images. Record your observations and provide a possible explanation.

23. Spotlight: Draw a diagram of this spotlight. The small filament should be shown in the proper position. Is the location of the filament with respect to the mirror important? Explain.

24. Light Ray Projector: Observe and draw diagrams showing how light rays, from the light ray box, are affected as they pass through a convex lens and a concave lens.
    a. Concave   b. Convex

25. Colors of Light: Using a variety of colored filters, project the colored light onto a white screen, so that the colors mix. Observe the results of various combinations. Record your observations in Table 2 below.

Table 2

Mixture of lights	Observed color of mixture
red + blue	
red + green	
red + yellow	
green + yellow	
green + blue	
blue + green + yellow	
red + blue + green	
red + blue + yellow	

a. Which mixtures of lights produce white light?

b. What are the three primary colors of light that together produce white light?

1.   2.   3.

c. A complementary color is the color that, when mixed with a primary color, will produce white light. These can be found by mixing two colors of light.

The complementary color for primary color 1 is _____.

The complementary color for primary color 2 is _____.

The complementary color for primary color 3 is _____.

Applications

1. Look at the color adjustment controls on a color television set. You will find "intensity," which controls the amount of red, and "tint," which adjusts the amount of green or blue in the picture. Explain how the amount of yellow in the picture can be adjusted.

2. In dim light, all colored objects appear to be shades of gray. Explain.

3. A woman considering the purchase of a dress in a clothing store asks the salesclerk if she might take the merchandise to a window to view it in "natural" light. Explain why she is making such a request.

EXPERIMENT

16.2

Polarized Light

Purpose

Analyze light and describe uses for polarized light.

Concept and Skill Check

While at the beach or swimming pool you probably noticed the bright reflection of light from the water. If you were wearing polarized sunglasses, the glare from reflected sunlight should have been reduced. Light reflected from the water's surface is partially polarized by the reflection effect.

Only transverse waves can be polarized, or made to vibrate in one plane. Since light travels in transverse waves, it can be polarized by absorption, reflection, or scattering from shiny objects or materials. Light is also polarized when it is passed through certain materials. If you rotate a polarizing filter while observing a light beam, the light intensity may vary from dark to light. Light waves affected in this manner are polarized. If light observed through the rotating filter does not change in intensity, it is unpolarized. In this activity, you will use polarizing filters, as shown in Figure 1, to observe and analyze light from various sources to determine if it is polarized.

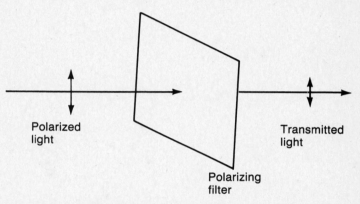

Figure 1. Polarized light varies in intensity when it is viewed through a rotating polarizing filter.

Materials

2 polarizing discs or sheets
Iceland spar calcite crystal
clear plastic object, such as a box, protractor, or plexiglass rod

light bulb with socket and cord
plane mirror

glass plate
protractor (optional)
ruler (optional)

Procedure

1. Hold one polarizing filter between a light source and your eyes. Rotate the polarizing filter through 360°. Observe the intensity of light as the filter is rotated. Record your observations in Table 1.
2. Repeat Step 1, adding a second filter. Observe what happens to the intensity of light as the filter closer to the light source is rotated. Record your observations in Table 1.
3. Repeat Step 2 and this time rotate the polarizing filter closer to your eye. Record your observations in Table 1.
4. Place an Iceland spar calcite crystal over a written word. Draw what you see in Table 2.
5. Hold one polarizing filter over the Iceland spar crystal. Observe the word as in Step 4 while you rotate the filter through 360°. Record your observations in Table 2.

16.2 Polarized Light

6. While rotating one polarizing filter, observe light reflected from a plane mirror. Record your observations of light intensity in Table 3.
7. While rotating one polarizing filter, observe light reflected from a glass plate. Then observe light reflected from a shiny table top. Record your observations of light intensity in Table 3.
8. Place a piece of plastic between two polarizing filters. While rotating one of the filters, observe patterns and colors in the plastic. Apply stress to the plastic by pushing on one side. Observe what happens to the patterns and colors as stress is applied and released. Record your observations in Table 4.

Observations and Data
Table 1

Observations of light source with 1 polarizing filter	
Observations of light source with 2 polarizing filters, rotating the filter closer to the light	
Observations of light source with 2 polarizing filters, rotating the filter closer to your eye	

Table 2

Drawing of a word viewed through Iceland spar	
Observations of a word viewed through Iceland spar, with one rotating polarizing filter	

Table 3

Observations of light reflected from plane mirror	
Observations of light reflected from glass plate	
Observations of light reflected from shiny table top	

16.2 Polarized Light

NAME —————————————————————

Table 4

Observations of plastic	Unstressed	Stressed

Analysis

1. Is light from a light bulb polarized? Explain.

2. What happens to the intensity of light viewed through two polarizing filters as one filter is rotated? Does it matter which filter is rotated? Explain. How far must one filter be rotated for transmitted light to go from maximum to minimum brightness?

3. Describe the light images viewed through the Iceland spar crystal. What is a possible explanation for this phenomenon?

4. Is light reflected from a plane mirror polarized? Explain.

5. Is light reflected from a glass plate or shiny laboratory surface polarized? Explain.

6. Describe the appearance of the unstressed plastic placed between two polarizing filters. What happened as stress was applied to the plastic?

16.2 Polarized Light

Applications

1. Describe an orientation of polarizing material on cars that would enable drivers to use their high-beam lights at all times.

2. How might engineers use polarized light and the elastic property of plastic to design better and safer products?

Extension

Use a single polarizing filter to observe light reflected from a glass plate. Examine various angles of reflection until the reflected light is entirely eliminated, as shown in Figure 2. With your protractor, measure this angle, θ_p. When unpolarized light strikes a smooth surface and is partially reflected, the light is partially, completely, or not polarized, depending on the angle of incidence. The angle of incidence at which the reflected light is completely polarized is called the polarizing angle. The law of reflection states that the angle of incidence and the angle of reflection are equal. An expression relating the polarizing angle, θ_p, to the index of refraction, n, of the reflecting surface is the following:

$$n = \tan \theta_p,$$

which is called Brewster's law.

Using the measured angle of reflection, calculate the index of refraction for the glass plate. After completing your calculations for the index of refraction of glass, substitute a beaker of water and measure the angle of incidence at which reflected light is completely polarized. Calculate the index of refraction of water.

Figure 2. Estimate the angle of reflection by sighting parallel to a ruler.

17.1 Reflection of Light

Purpose
Use the law of reflection to locate the image formed by a plane mirror.

Concept and Skill Check
When a light ray strikes a reflecting surface, the angle of reflection is equal to the angle of incidence. Both angles are measured from the normal, an imaginary line perpendicular to the surface at the point where the ray is reflected. In this laboratory activity, you will investigate and measure light rays reflected from the smooth, flat surface of a plane mirror in order to determine the apparent location of an image. This type of reflection is called regular reflection. The image of an object viewed in a plane mirror is a virtual image. By tracing the direction of the incident rays of light, you will be able to construct a ray diagram that locates the image formed by a plane mirror.

Materials
thin plane mirror	2 straight pins or	4 thumbtacks or pieces of
small wooden block	dissecting pins	masking tape
metric ruler	rubber band	He-Ne Laser
protractor	cork board (or cardboard)	glass plate (optional)
2 sheets blank paper	thick plane mirror	small blocks of wood (optional)

Procedure

A. The Law of Reflection
1. Attach a sheet of paper to the cork board with the tacks or tape. Draw a line, **ML**, across the width of the paper. Attach the small block of wood to the back of the mirror with a rubber band, so that the mirror is perpendicular to the surface of the paper. Center the silvered surface (normally the back side) of the mirror along the line, **ML**, as shown in Figure 1.
2. About 4 cm in front of the mirror, make a dot on the paper with a pencil and label it point **P**. Place a pin, representing the object, upright at point **P**.

Figure 1. Arrangement of materials for Part A.

3. Place your ruler on the paper about 5 cm to the left of the pin. Sight along the edge of the ruler at the image of the pin in the mirror. When the edge of the ruler is lined up on the image, draw a line along it toward, but not touching, the mirror. Label this line **A**.
4. Move the ruler another 3 or 4 cm to the left and sight along it at the image of the pin in the mirror. Draw a line along the edge of the ruler toward, but not touching, the mirror. Label it line **B**.

17.1 Reflection of Light

5. Remove the pin and the mirror from the paper. Extend lines **A** and **B** to line **ML**. Using dotted lines, extend each of these lines beyond line **ML** until they intersect. Label the point of intersection point **I**. This is the position of the image. Measure the object distance from point **P** to line **ML** and the image distance from point **I** to line **ML**. Record these distances in Table 1.

6. Draw a line from point **P** to point **X**, where line **A** meets line **ML**, as shown in Figure 2. Using your protractor, construct a normal at this point and measure the angle of incidence, i_1, and the angle of reflection, r_1. Record the values of these angles in Table 1. In a similar manner, draw line **PY** from point **P** to point **Y** where line **B** meets line **ML**. Construct the normal at point **Y**. Measure the angle of incidence, i_2,

Figure 2. Sight along the ruler at the pin's image.

and the angle of reflection, r_2. Record the values of these angles in Table 1. A line such as **PXA** or **PYB** is the path followed by a ray of light as it is transmitted from the pin (object) to the mirror, and reflected from the mirror to your eye. Drawing many such rays enables you to locate and recognize images in a mirror.

B. Image Formation

1. Draw a line, **ML**, across the width of another sheet of paper. Draw an object triangle in front of the line, as shown in Figure 3, and label the vertices **A**, **B**, and **C**. Attach the paper to the cork board and place the mirror and block along line **ML**, as you did in Part A.

2. Place a pin in vertex **A**. Sight twice along the ruler to obtain two different sketched lines from the location of the pin at vertex **A** to line **ML**, as you did in Part A. Label these lines **A₁** and **A₂**.

3. Remove the pin from vertex **A** and place it at vertex **B**. Again, sight along the ruler to obtain two lines from the location of the pin at **B** to **ML** and label these lines **B₁** and **B₂**.

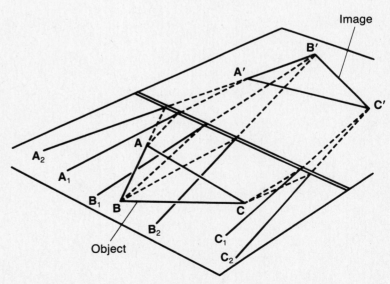

Figure 3. Describe the front-back and right-left orientation of the image with respect to the object.

4. Remove the pin from vertex **B** and place it at vertex **C**. Repeat the procedure and draw lines **C₁** and **C₂**.

5. Remove the mirror and the pin. Extend the pairs of lines, **A₁** and **A₂**, **B₁** and **B₂**, and **C₁** and **C₂**, beyond the mirror and locate points **A′**, **B′**, and **C′**, as shown in Figure 3. Construct the image of the triangle. Measure and record in Table 2, the distances from points **A**, **B**, **C**, **A′**, **B′**, and **C′** perpendicular to the mirror line **ML**.

C. Laser Light Reflection

CAUTION: *Do not look directly at the laser beam or its reflection.*

1. Arrange your thin plane mirror so that the laser beam strikes it at an angle of incidence of about 60° from the normal. Reflect the laser beam onto the ceiling. In Table 3, draw your observations of the reflected image. Repeat the process using a clean, thick plane mirror (rear surfaced). In Table 3, record your observations of the reflected image.

2. With the room lights off, spray a fine mist of water in the air (or clap two chalk-filled erasers) over the reflected beam. In Table 3 record your observations.

Observations and Data

Table 1

Object distance	
Image distance	
Angle of incidence, i_1, **PXN**	
Angle of reflection, r_1, **AXN**	
Angle of incidence, i_2, **PYN′**	
Angle of reflection, r_2, **BYN′**	

Table 2

Point	Distance to mirror line (cm)
A	
B	
C	
A′	
B′	
C′	

17.1 Reflection of Light

Table 3

Drawing of reflected laser light from thin plane mirror	
Drawing of reflected laser light from thick plane mirror	
Observation of reflected laser beams	

Analysis

1. Using your observations from Table 1, what can you conclude about the angle of incidence and the angle of reflection?

2. How far behind a plane mirror is the image of an object that is located in front of the mirror?

Reflection of Light

3. Using your observations from Table 2, compare the size and orientation of your constructed image with those of the triangle object.

4. From your observations in this experiment, summarize the general characteristics of images formed by plane mirrors.

5. Why do you think the image formed by a plane mirror is called virtual rather than real?

6. When you used the thick plane mirror, which reflected spot of the laser beam was brightest? Suggest a possible explanation for the bright beam.

7. Provide an explanation to account for the difference in patterns of the reflected laser beam from the thin and thick plane mirrors. Draw a diagram that demonstrates the pattern of laser light reflected from a thick plane mirror and your explanation for this result.

EXPERIMENT 17.1 Reflection of Light

Application

In many department stores, large plane mirrors have been placed high on walls or on projections from ceilings. These may be one-way mirrors that are designed to allow one-way surveillance of the store. From one side, this surface looks like a mirror, but from the other side, the activities of the shoppers can be observed. Suggest how this type of mirror works.

Extension

Use small blocks of wood or a stand to set a piece of plate glass vertically on a line, **ML**, drawn on a sheet of paper that is attached to a cork board. The glass must be perpendicular to the paper, and you must be able to sight through the middle portion of the glass. Place one pin upright in front of the plate glass. Place a second pin upright in back of the plate glass at a point where the reflected image from the plate glass seems to be, as you sight through the glass. View the image at different angles and adjust the second pin slightly until this pin behind the plate glass is always at the position of the image, regardless of the viewing angle. Measure the distance from the object pin to the mirror line, **ML**, and compare it to the distance from the second pin to **ML**.

EXPERIMENT 17.2 Snell's Law

Purpose

Determine the index of refraction of glass using Snell's law.

Concept and Skill Check

Light travels at different speeds in different media. As light rays pass at an angle from one medium to another, they are refracted or bent at the boundary between the two media. If a light ray enters an optically more dense medium at an angle, it is bent toward the normal. If a light ray enters an optically less dense medium, it is bent away from the normal. This change in direction or bending of light at the boundary at two media is called refraction.

The index of refraction of a substance, n_s, is the ratio of the speed of light in a vacuum, c, to its speed in the substance, v_s:

$$n_s = \frac{c}{v_s}.$$

All indices of refraction are greater than one, because light always travels slower in media other than a vacuum.

The index of refraction is also obtained from Snell's law, which states: a ray of light bends in such a way that the ratio of the sine of the angle of incidence to the sine of the angle of refraction is a constant. Snell's law can be written:

$$n = \frac{\sin \theta_i}{\sin \theta_r}.$$

For any light ray traveling between media, Snell's law, in a more general form, can be written as

$$n_i \sin \theta_i = n_r \sin \theta_r,$$

where n_i is the index of refraction of the incident medium and n_r is the index of refraction of the second medium. The angle of incidence is θ_i, and the angle of refraction is θ_r.

In this investigation, you will construct ray diagrams to analyze the path of light as it passes through plate glass. For each angle of incidence, you will measure the angle of refraction to find the index of refraction of plate glass.

Materials

glass plate	100-mL sample bottle of	100-mL sample bottle of
metric ruler	mineral oil or oil of	olive oil (optional)
protractor	wintergreen (optional)	100-mL sample bottle of
sheet plain white paper	100-mL sample bottle of	cinnamon oil (optional)
small samples of glass, garnet,	clove oil (optional)	tweezers (optional)
tourmaline, beryl, topaz,	100-mL sample bottle of	
and quartz (optional)	water (optional)	

Procedure

1. Place the glass plate in the center of a sheet of plain white paper. Use a pencil to trace an outline of the plate.
2. Remove the glass plate and construct a normal **N₁B** at the top left of the outline, as shown in Figure 1 on the next page.

Figure 1. Construct normals N_1 and N_2 to the surface of the glass at C and D, respectively.

Figure 2. Sight through the glass block and align the ruler with line AB.

3. Use your ruler and protractor to draw a heavy line **AB** at an angle of 30° with the normal. Angle **ABN₁** is the angle of incidence, θ_i.
4. Replace the glass plate over the outline on the paper. With your eyes on a level with the glass plate, sight along the edge of the glass plate opposite the line **AB** until you locate the heavy line through the glass as shown in Figure 2. Sight your ruler at the line until its edge appears to be a continuation of the line. Draw the line **CD** as shown in Figure 1.
5. Remove the glass plate and draw another line **CB** connecting lines **CD** and **AB**. Extend the normal **N₁B** through the rectangle, forming a new line **N₁CN₁′**.
6. Use a protractor to measure angle **CBN₁′**. This is the angle of refraction, θ_r. Record the value of this angle in Table 1. Consult the table of trigonometric functions in Appendix A to find the sines corresponding to the measured angles of incidence and refraction. Record these values in Table 1. Determine the ratio of $\sin \theta_i / \sin \theta_r$ and record this value in Table 1 as the index of refraction, n.
7. Construct a normal **N₂** at point **C**. Measure angle **DCN₂**, which will be called $\theta_{r'}$, and record this value in Table 1.
8. Turn the paper over and repeat Steps 1 through 7, using an angle of incidence of 45°. Record all the data in Table 1. Again, determine the index of refraction from your data.

Observations and Data
Table 1

θ_i	θ_r	$\sin \theta_i$	$\sin \theta_r$	$\theta_{r'}$	Index of refraction, n
30°					
45°					

Analysis

1. Is there good agreement between the two values for the index of refraction of plate glass?

2. According to your diagrams, are light rays refracted away from or toward the normal as they pass at an angle from an optically less dense medium into an optically more dense medium?

3. According to your diagrams, are light rays refracted away from or toward the normal as they pass from an optically more dense medium into an optically less dense medium?

4. Compare θ_i and $\theta_{r'}$. Is the measure of $\theta_{r'}$ what you should expect? Explain.

5. Use your results to determine the approximate speed of light as it travels through glass. By what percent is the speed of light traveling in a vacuum faster than the speed of light traveling in glass?

Snell's Law

Application

Will light be refracted more while passing from air into water or while passing from water into glass? Explain.

Extension

Gemologists can identify an unknown gem by measuring its index of refraction, specific to each type of gemstone. The gemologist places the unknown gem in a series of liquids with known indices of refraction. When the gem becomes nearly invisible in a liquid, the gemologist concludes that the gem has an index of refraction corresponding to that of the liquid in which it is immersed. With this information, the gemologist consults a reference giving the indices of refraction of gemstones to identify the unknown gem. The following lists the indices of refraction of some liquids and materials.

Liquid	n	Material	n
water	1.34	glass	1.48–1.7
olive oil	1.47	quartz	1.54
mineral oil	1.48	beryl	1.58
oil of wintergreen	1.48	topaz	1.62
clove oil	1.54	tourmaline	1.63
cinnamon oil	1.60	garnet	1.75

Use these liquids to identify the unknown materials your teacher will give you. With tweezers, carefully place each sample material alternately into each bottle of liquid. Observe the material and the behavior of light as it passes through the liquid and the material. Before immersing the sample in the next bottle of liquid, rinse it off in water and dry it gently to prevent contamination of the oils. When the material seems to disappear, record the index of refraction for the liquid and use this value to identify the material.

EXPERIMENT
18.1 Concave and Convex Mirrors

Purpose

Investigate positions and characteristics of images produced by curved mirrors.

Concept and Skill Check

Spherical mirrors are portions of spheres one side of which is silvered and serves as a reflecting surface. If the inner side is the reflecting surface, the mirror is a concave mirror. If the outer side is the reflecting surface, the mirror is a convex mirror.

The center of the sphere of which the mirror is a portion is called the center of curvature (**C**) of the mirror. An imaginary line perpendicular to the center or vertex of the mirror (**A**) and that also passes through the center of curvature is called the principal axis of the mirror. The point halfway between **C** and **A** is called the focal point (**F**) of the mirror. The distance from the focal point **F** to the center of the mirror **A** is called the focal length (f) of the mirror. The distance of the object from the mirror, d_o, and the distance of the image from the mirror, d_i, are related to the focal length by the mirror equation

$$\frac{1}{f} = \frac{1}{d_i} + \frac{1}{d_o}.$$

Figure 1 illustrates these relationships.

Concave mirrors produce real images, virtual images, or no images. Light rays actually pass through real images, which can be projected on a screen. Convex mirrors produce only virtual images. Virtual images appear to originate behind the mirror and cannot be projected onto a screen.

Light rays that approach a concave spherical mirror from a position close to the mirror and parallel with the principal axis will, upon reflection, converge at the focal point. If all the rays approaching a concave mirror are parallel with the principal axis, they will meet approximately at the focal point where they will form an image of the object from which the light rays come. In this experiment, you will be placing an object at various distances from curved mirrors and observing the location, size, and orientation of the images.

Figure 1. The center of curvature C is located at a distance of twice the focal length f from the center of the mirror, along the principal axis.

Materials

concave mirror	cardboard screen	masking tape
convex mirror	holders for mirror, screen,	metric ruler
2 meter sticks	and light source	light source

18.1 Concave and Convex Mirrors

Procedure

The laboratory room must be darkened so that images are easily observed. The electric light sources are sufficient to illuminate laboratory work areas while students set up equipment. One unshaded window should be available for student use.

A. Focal Length of Concave Mirrors

1. Arrange your mirror, meter stick, and screen, as shown in Figure 2. If the sun is visible, the focal length can be determined by projecting a focused image of the sun onto a screen and measuring the distance from the mirror's vertex to the screen. CAUTION: *Do not look directly at the sun since this can cause severe damage to your eyes.* An alternate method is to point the mirror at a distant object (more than ten meters away) and move the screen along the

Figure 2. The focal length of a mirror can be determined by projecting a focused image of the sun onto a screen.

meter stick until you obtain a sharp image of the distant object on the screen. The distance between the mirror and the screen is the approximate focal length of the mirror. Record in Table 1 the focal length of your mirror.

B. Concave Mirrors

1. The center of curvature of the mirror, **C**, is twice the focal length. Record this value in Table 1. Arrange the two meter sticks, mirror, light source, and screen, as shown in Figure 3. Use a piece of masking tape to hold the meter sticks in place.

2. Place the light source at a distance greater than **C** (beyond **C**) from the mirror. Measure the height of the light source and record this value in Table 1 as h_o. Move the screen back and forth along the meter stick until you obtain a sharp image of the light source. Determine the distance of the image from the mirror, d_i, by measuring from the mirror's vertex to the screen. Record in Table 2 your measurements of d_i, d_o, h_i, and your observations of the image.

Figure 3. Adjust the location of the screen until you obtain a clear, sharp image of the light source.

18.1 Concave and Convex Mirrors

3. Move the light source to the center of curvature, **C**. Move the screen back and forth to obtain a sharp image. Record in Table 2 your measurements of d_i, d_o, h_i and your observations of the image.

4. Move the light source to a position that is between **F** and **C**. Move the screen back and forth to obtain a sharp image. Record in Table 2 your measurement of d_i, d_o, h_i and your observations of the image.

5. Move the light source to a distance **F** from the mirror. Try to locate an image on the screen. Observe the light source in the mirror. Record your observations in Table 2.

6. Move the light source to a position between **F** and **A**. Try to locate an image on the screen. Observe the image in the mirror. Record your observations in Table 2.

C. Convex Mirrors

Place the convex mirror in the holder. Place the light source anywhere along the meter stick. Try to obtain an image on the screen. Observe the image in the mirror. Move the light source to two additional positions along the meter stick and try each time to produce an image on the screen. Observe the image in the mirror. Record your observations in Table 3.

Observations and Data

Table 1

Focal length of mirror, f	
Center of curvature of mirror, **C**	
Height of light source, h_o	

Table 2

Position of object	Beyond **C**	At **C**	Between **C** and **F**	At **F**	Between **F** and **A**
d_o					
d_i					
h_i					
Type of image: real, none, or virtual					
Direction of image: inverted or erect					

Table 3

Trial	Position of object	Position of image	Type of image: real or virtual	Image size compared to object size	Direction of image: inverted or erect
1					
2					
3					

18.1 Concave and Convex Mirrors

NAME ————————————————————

Analysis

1. Use your observations from Table 2 to summarize the characteristics of images formed by concave mirrors in each of the following situations.
   a. The object is located beyond the center of curvature.

   b. The object is located at the center of curvature.

   c. The object is located between the center of curvature and the focal point.

   d. The object is located at the focal point.

   e. The object is located between the focal point and the mirror.

2. Use your observations from Table 3 to summarize the characteristics of images formed by convex mirrors.

3. For each of the real images you observed, use the mirror equation to calculate f. Do your calculated values agree with each other?

4. Average the values of f that you calculated for Question 3 and compute the relative error between the average and the measured value for f recorded in Table 1.

Application

The apparatus shown in Figure 4 can project the image of an illuminated light bulb onto an empty socket. Describe how to orient a large, spherical mirror to reflect the illuminated light bulb in the box onto the socket on top of the box.

Illuminated
light bulb

Figure 4. Illusion apparatus for use with a concave mirror.

EXPERIMENT
18.2

Convex and Concave Lenses

Purpose

Observe the positions and characteristics of images produced by convex and concave lenses.

Concept and Skill Check

A convex or converging lens is thicker in the middle of the lens than at the edges of the lens. A concave or diverging lens is thinner in the middle than at the edges. The principal axis of the lens is an imaginary line perpendicular to the plane of the lens that passes through its midpoint. It extends from both sides of the lens. At some distance from the lens along the principal axis is the focal point (F) of the lens. Light rays that strike a convex lens parallel to the principal axis come together or converge at this point. The focal length of the lens depends on both the shape and the index of refraction of the lens material. As with mirrors, an important point designated $2F$ is at twice the focal length. If the lens is symmetrical, the focal point F and point $2F$ are located the same distances on either side of the lens, as shown in Figure 1.

Figure 1. Focal length, object distance, and image distance are measured from the lens along the principal axis.

A concave lens causes all incident parallel light rays to diverge. Rays approaching a concave lens parallel to the principal axis appear to intersect on the near side of the lens. Thus, the focal length of a concave lens is negative. Figure 2 shows the relationship of the incoming and refracted rays passing through a concave lens.

The distance from the center of the lens to the object is designated d_o, while the distance from the center of the lens to the image is designated d_i. The lens equation is

$$\frac{1}{f} = \frac{1}{d_i} + \frac{1}{d_o}.$$

In this activity, you will measure the focal length, f, of a convex lens and place an object at various distances from the lens to observe the location, size, and orientation of the images. Find the focal length of a concave

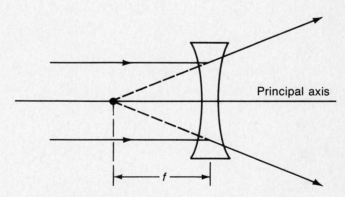

Figure 2. The focal length of a concave lens is negative. All light rays passing through a concave lens diverge.

lens by tracing diverging rays backwards to locate the focal point. Recall that real images can be projected onto a screen; virtual images cannot be projected.

18.2 Convex and Concave Lenses

Materials

double convex lens
concave lens
2 meter sticks
2 meter-stick supports

small cardboard screen
light source
holders for screen, light source,
    and lens

metric ruler
sunlight or He-Ne laser

Procedure

The laboratory room must be darkened so that images are easily observed. The electric light sources are sufficient to illuminate laboratory work areas while students set up equipment. One unshaded window should be available for student use.

A. Focal Length of a Convex Lens

1. To find the focal length of the convex lens, arrange your lens, meter stick, and screen, as shown in Figure 3. Point the lens at a distant object and move the screen back and forth until you obtain a clear, sharp image of the object on the screen. A darkened room makes the image much easier to observe. Record in Table 1 your measurement of the focal length. Compute the distance *2F* and record this value in Table 1.

B. Convex Lens

1. Arrange the apparatus as shown in Figure 4. Place the light source somewhere beyond *2F* on one side of the lens and place the screen on the opposite side of the lens. Move the screen back and forth until a clear, sharp image is formed on the screen. Record in Table 1 the height of the light source (object), h_o. Record in Table 2 your measurements of d_o, d_i, and h_i and your observations of the image.

Figure 3. The focal point of a convex lens if found by locating the image of a distance object.

2. Move the light source to *2F*. Move the screen back and forth until a clear, sharp image is formed on the screen. Record in Table 2 your measurements of d_o, d_i, and h_i and your observations of the image.

3. Move the light source to a location between *F* and *2F*. Move the screen back and forth until a clear, sharp image is formed on the screen. Record in Table 2 your measurements of d_o, d_i, and h_i and your observations of the image.

4. Move the light source to a distance *F* from the lens. Try to locate an image on the screen. Record your observations in Table 2.

Figure 4.

18.2 Convex and Concave Lenses

NAME —————————————————————————————

5. Move the light source to a position between *F* and the lens. Try to locate an image on the screen. Look through the lens at the light source and observe the image. Record your observations in Table 2.

C. Concave Lens

1. Place a concave lens in a lens holder and set it on the meter stick. Place a screen on one side of the lens. One of the following procedures can be used to determine the focal length.

Sunlight: Allow the parallel rays of the sun to strike the lens along the principal axis so that an image is formed on the screen. CAUTION: *Do not look directly at the sun since this can cause severe damage to your eyes.* The image should appear as a dark circle inside a larger, brighter circle. Place the screen close to the lens. Quickly measure the distance from the lens to the screen and the diameter of the bright circle. Record these data in Table 3. Move the screen and repeat the measurements for five additional sets of data.

He-Ne Laser: Shine a laser beam through the concave lens so that an image is formed on the screen. CAUTION: *Do not look directly at the laser source since this can cause severe damage to your eyes.* Measure the distance from the screen to the lens and the diameter of the circle of light projected onto the screen. Record these data in Table 3. Move the screen and repeat the measurements for five additional sets of data.

Observations and Data

Table 1

Focal length	
2F	
Height of light source, h_o	

Table 2

Position of object	Beyond 2F (cm)	At 2F (cm)	Between 2F and F (cm)	At F (cm)	Between F and lens (cm)
d_o					
d_i					
h_i					
Type of image: real, none, or virtual					
Direction of image: inverted or erect					

Convex and Concave Lenses

NAME —————————————————————

Table 3

Distance from lens (m)	Diameter of screen image (cm)

Analysis

1. Use the data from Table 2 to summarize the characteristics of images formed by convex lenses in each of the following situations.
   a. The object is located beyond *2F*.

   b. The object is located at *2F*.

   c. The object is located between *2F* and *F*.

   d. The object is located at *F*.

   e. The object is located between *F* and the lens.

Convex and
Concave Lenses

NAME ——————————————————————

2. For each of the real images you observed, calculate the focal length of the lens using the lens equation. Do your values agree with each other?

3. Average the values for *f* found in Question 2 and calculate the relative error between this average and the value for *f* from Table 1.

4. Plot a graph of the image diameter on the vertical axis versus the distance from the lens on the horizontal axis. Allow room along the horizontal axis for negative distances. The rays expanding from the lens appear to originate from the focal point. Draw a smooth line that best connects the data points and extend the line until it intersects the horizontal axis. The negative distance along the horizontal axis at the intersection represents the value of the focal length. What is the focal length you derived from your graph? If your lens package includes an accepted focal length, calculate the relative error for the focal length you determined.

18.2 Convex and Concave Lenses

NAME —————————————————————

Application

The following demonstration is best done when participants have removed their glasses or contact lenses. The relative direction of movement of reflected laser light with respect to an observer's moving head is a means to determine near- or farsightedness. In a darkened room, use a concave lens to expand the beam diameter of the laser so that a large spot is projected onto a screen. Observers should move their heads from side to side while looking at the spot. Each student should record the direction in which the reflected speckles of laser light appear to move and the direction in which his or her head is moving. Then ask observers to replace their glasses or contact lenses and to repeat the process and make their observations.

Extension

Use two identical, clear watch glasses and a small fish aquarium to investigate an air lens. Carefully glue the edges of the watch glasses together with epoxy cement or a silicone sealant so that the unit is watertight. Attach the air lens to the bottom of an empty fish aquarium with a lump of clay and arrange an object nearby, as shown in Figure 5. Observe the object through the lens and record your observations. Predict what will happen when the aquarium is filled with water such that light is passing from a more dense to a less dense medium as it passes through the air lens. Fill the aquarium with water and repeat your observations. Compare the two sets of observations. Explain your results. What should you expect if you used a concave air lens? Design and construct a concave air lens to test your hypothesis.

Figure 5.

EXPERIMENT
19.1

Double-Slit Interference

Purpose

Use a double slit to determine the wavelength of light.

Concept and Skill Check

As Thomas Young demonstrated in 1801, light falling on two closely spaced slits will pass through the slits and be diffracted. The spreading light from the two slits overlaps and produces an interference pattern, an alternating sequence of dark and light lines, on a screen. A bright band appears at the center of the screen. On either side of the central band, alternating bright and dark lines appear on the screen. Bright lines appear at points where constructive interference occurs, and dark lines appear where destructive interference occurs. The first bright line on either side of the central band is called the first-order line. This line is bright because, at this point on the screen, the path lengths of light waves arriving from each slit differ by one wavelength. The next line is the second-order line. Several lines are visible on either side of the central bright band. The equation that relates the wavelength of light, the separation of the slits, the distance from the central band to the first-order line, and the distance to the screen is

$$\lambda = xd/L.$$

The figure below shows this relationship.

Figure 1.

In this experiment, you will use an arrangement similar to that employed in Young's experiment to determine the wavelengths of several different colors of light. As the colored light is diffracted through a double slit, you will observe an interference pattern and will measure the distance between the central bright line and the first-order line. Other distances can be measured, and these values can be used to calculate the wavelength of light.

Materials

double slit
clear filament light with socket
red, yellow, and violet transparent
  filter material

rubber band
meter stick
metric ruler
magnifier with scale

masking tape
index cards, 5 × 7 inch
He-Ne laser (optional)

19.1 Double-Slit Interference

Procedure

1. Measure the slit separation of your double slit, using the magnifier and a graduated millimeter scale. If it is known, use the actual slit separation. Record in millimeters the width, d, in Table 2. This value will remain constant for all trials.
2. Place a red-colored filter over the light bulb and secure it with a rubber band. Turn on the light bulb. Turn off the classroom lights.
3. Stand 1 m from the light and observe the light bulb through the double slit. Record in Table 1 your observations of the light bands. Move several meters away from the light and repeat your observations, recording them in Table 1.
4. Move approximately 2–4 m from the light and mark the location with a small piece of tape. Measure the distance from the light bulb filament to the small piece of tape. Record the distance, L, in Table 2.
5. Make a dark line on a 5 × 7-inch index card. With your lab partner viewing the light through the double slit, place the card, as directed by your partner, so that the dark line is located over the central bright band, or light bulb filament.
6. While your lab partner observes the light bulb through the double slit, slowly move your pencil back and forth until your partner tells you that it is located over one of the first-order lines. Make a mark on the index card where the first-order line occurs. Measure the distance, x, from the central bright line to the first-order line. Record this value in Table 2.
7. Remove the red filter material from the light. Repeat Steps 4 through 6 with the other colored filters. Record your data in Table 2.

Observations and Data

Table 1

	Observations of Light
Close	
Far away	

Table 2

Color	d (mm)	x (m)	L (m)
Red			
Yellow			
Violet			

19.1 Double-Slit Interference

Analysis

1. Describe how the double-slit pattern changes as you move farther away from the light source.

2. Calculate the wavelength, in nm, for each of the colors. Show your work.

3. Which color of light will be diffracted most as it passes through the double slit? Explain.

4. Predict where the first-order line for infrared light of wavelength 1000 nm would be located. How does this location compare with the other first-order lines observed in this experiment?

5. Predict where the first-order line for ultraviolet light of wavelength 375 nm would be located. How does this location compare with the other first-order lines observed in this experiment?

19.1 Double-Slit Interference

Applications

1. A bright light, visible from 50.0 m away, produces an angle of 0.8° to the first-order line when viewed through a double slit having a width of 0.05 mm. What color is the light?

2. Blue-green light of wavelength 500 nm falls on two slits that are 0.0150 mm apart. A first-order line appears 14.7 mm from the central bright line. What is the distance between the slits and the screen? Show all your calculations.

3. The slit separation and the distance between the slits and the screen are the same as those in Question 2, but sodium light of wavelength 589 nm is used. What is the distance from the central line to the first-order line with this light? Show all your calculations.

Extension

Place a double slit over the front of a He-Ne laser. Project the interference pattern onto a screen. Measure L and x for the first-order line and calculate the separation of the double slit using the value 632.8 nm for the wavelength of the laser light.

EXPERIMENT
19.2 : White Light Holograms

Purpose

Create a white light hologram.

Concept and Skill Check

A unique and unusual application of lasers is in the production of holograms. Holograms are three-dimensional images or photographs produced by interference of coherent light. There are two primary types of holograms — reflection and transmission. Most of you have seen a white light, reflection hologram, such as those on cereal boxes, credit cards, or in magazines. Reflection holograms are created when laser light is directed through the film and reflected off the object back onto the film. The incident light and the reflected light create an interference pattern on the film.

Holograms with greater depth and clarity are transmission holograms. They are produced when a laser beam is split into two parts. One part of the beam reflects off the object being photographed and strikes the holographic film, while the other falls directly on the film. The two superimposed beams form an interference pattern, which is recorded on the film. The film picks up the intensity of the incident light and its phase relationship. When the developed film is viewed, it is illuminated by a coherent light beam of the same wavelength used to expose the film, and the viewer looks at the transmission hologram back along the direction of the beam's origination. In this experiment you will use a He-Ne laser to make a reflection hologram.

Materials

He-Ne Laser
small concave mirror or
 beam diverging lens
 (expander)
holographic film plates
 (or holographic film
 and two glass plates)
automobile inner tube
bicycle air pump
2 index cards,
 5 × 7 inches

holographic developer
 and bleach solution
plastic tongs
rubber gloves
green safe light
3 plastic or glass trays,
 4 × 4 inches
quarter or other shiny
 object to photograph
steel plate, 12 × 12 inches

helping hand project
 holder
12 disk magnets
stopwatch or watch with
 second hand
black paper or posterboard
front-surfaced mirror,
 4 × 6 inches (optional)
notebook-paper clips
 (optional)

Procedure

1. Follow your teacher's safety instructions for using photographic chemicals to develop your holographic image. CAUTION: *The compounds used to develop the film are poisonous and caustic. If you use any of these compounds, protect your eyes, skin, and clothing.*
2. To construct a vibration-isolation system, partially inflate the inner tube and place it on a stable lab table. Set the steel plate (or another massive piece of equipment) on the inner tube. This setup will minimize vibrations that can affect the quality of the hologram while the film is being exposed.
3. Place the small concave mirror in the helping hand. Place the helping hand on the steel plate, as shown in Figure 1 on the next page.
4. Place the laser on an adjacent table and direct the beam onto the mirror. CAUTION: *Do not look directly at the laser beam.* The reflected, expanded beam from the laser should be

White Light Holograms

Figure 1. Arrangement of mirror, helping hand, disk magnets, and objects on the steel plate for production of a reflection hologram.

directed toward the steel plate. Place the small green light nearby so that it is just possible to see the steel plate in the darkened room. Turn the room lights back on.

5. Trim a small index card to the size of your holographic film plate (a square, approximately 2½ × 2½ inches). Arrange the small disk magnets on the steel plate so that four columns horizontally support each corner of the trimmed index card (temporarily taking the place of the glass plate). Adjust the height of the magnet supports so that the index card is just above the objects being photographed. Adjust the helping hand so that the reflected beam illuminates the index card. Remove the index card.

6. Select one or more metallic, shiny objects. Arrange them within the illuminated area. Block the laser beam with a 5 × 7-inch index card. The index card will serve as a camera shutter.

7. Turn off the room lights. Carefully open the film container and remove one holographic film plate. Close and reseal the remaining film plates in the light-tight container. Place the glass plate on the magnet supports, with the emulsion side facing the objects. The emulsion side is slightly sticky and has a dull appearance. Do not touch the emulsion.

8. During exposure of the hologram, all students in the room should minimize movement to help reduce vibrations. While one lab partner removes the index-card shutter, the other partner should begin timing the exposure. Try an exposure time of 20 seconds or follow your teacher's instructions for timing. After the appropriate timing interval, replace the index-card shutter. Remove the film plate and take it to the teacher for developing. The room lights cannot be turned on until after the film has been developed and bleached. Photographic glass plates should have a goldish color after developing. Overexposed plates appear bluish, and underexposed plates appear reddish. Remove your objects from the steel plate.

9. Repeat Steps 6 through 8 for each lab group.

10. When your hologram is dry, hold it up to an overhead light or sunlight and look through it. CAUTION: *Never look directly into sunlight.* Record your observations in Table 1. Drying can be accelerated by directing warm air from a hair dryer, slide projector, or overhead projector onto the plate.

11. Place a black background against the glass. Hold your hologram in front of a bright white light, such as a slide projector, overhead projector, or sunlight. Look at the hologram and observe the reflected light. Record your observations in Table 1.

12. Wash your hands with soap and water before you leave the laboratory.

White Light Holograms

NAME ——————————————————————————————

Observations and Data
Table 1

Observations of Hologram
Looking through hologram:
Looking at reflection:

Analysis

1. Compare your observations of the hologram from Table 1. How do you account for the different observations?

2. Look at an ordinary photograph, such as one found in your textbook or a magazine. How does the hologram compare to the photograph?

3. The film used to produce the hologram was black and white film. How can the color, visible in the hologram, be produced?

White Light Holograms

NAME _____

Application

Explain the value of using holograms in money, credit cards, or images of rare coins.

Extension

Use the vertical arrangement shown in Figure 2 to make a transmission hologram. Place the helping hand with the mirror near the laser, so that the laser beam reflects off it and the expanded beam shines onto the table. An index card serves again as the shutter. Use some small, notebook-paper clips to hold the film perpendicular to the steel plate. This hologram must be viewed by looking through the hologram at the expanded laser beam. CAUTION: *Never look directly into the laser source or into an unexpanded beam.*

Figure 2. A downward view of the arrangement of mirror, object, and holographic plate with respect to the incoming laser beam for production of a transmission hologram.

Describe your transmission hologram and compare it to the white light reflection hologram.

EXPERIMENT
20.1 Investigating Static Electricity

Purpose
Investigate the behavior of static electricity.

Concept and Skill Check
Clothes removed from a clothes dryer usually cling to each other and spark or crackle with static electricity when they are separated. A fabric softener is usually added to prevent this static buildup. When two dissimilar materials are rubbed together, they can become charged. Objects can acquire static electric charges by either gaining or losing electrons. An object that gains electrons has a net negative charge and is said to be negatively charged. An object that loses electrons has a net positive charge and is said to be positively charged. Only those objects separated from a ground, or Earth, by an insulator will retain their charge for any length of time. Objects that are attached to a ground through a conductor will remain uncharged, since the charge travels into the ground and is quickly dissipated. Recall that a hard rubber rod rubbed with wool or fur will become negatively charged, while a glass rod rubbed with silk will become positively charged. In this experiment, you will charge objects and observe their interactions with other charged objects.

Materials

hard rubber rod or vinyl strip	wool pad or cat's fur	leaf or vane electroscope
glass rod	pith ball suspended from	Leyden jar
plastic wrap or acrylic rod	holder by silk thread	wire with alligator clip
silk pad		

Procedure
It is best to perform these activities on a cool, dry day. If it is a humid day, charged objects tend to lose their charge fairly rapidly, making it difficult to observe some phenomena. Perform each part of the experiment several times to be sure you have proper observations of the phenomena. You may have to rub the rods vigorously to charge them, particularly when you use the glass rods.

A. Negatively Charging a Pith Ball
1. Rub the hard rubber rod with the fur or wool pad to charge it. Bring the rod close to, but not touching, a suspended pith ball, as shown in Figure 1. Observe the behavior of the pith ball and record your observations in Table 1. Touch the pith ball with your finger to remove any charge it may have.
2. Charge the rubber rod again. Bring it close to the pith ball and allow it to touch the ball. Then bring the charged rod near the charged ball and observe the behavior of the ball. Record your observations in Table 1.

B. Positively Charging a Pith Ball
1. Rub the glass rod with a piece of silk to charge it. Bring the rod close to, but not touching, a sus-

Figure 1. Bring the charged rod near but not touching the uncharged pith ball.

Investigating Static Electricity

NAME ————————————————

pended pith ball. Observe the behavior of the pith ball and record your observations in Table 2. Touch the pith ball with your finger to remove any charge it may have.

2. Charge the glass rod again. Bring it close to the pith ball and allow it to touch the ball. Then bring the charged rod near the charged ball and observe the behavior of the pith ball. Record your observations in Table 2.

C. Charging an Electroscope by Conduction

1. Look at the vane electroscope or the leaf electroscope that you will be using and familiarize yourself with its response to static charges. A vane electroscope is shown in Figure 2. Charge the rubber rod with the fur or wool. Gently bring it in contact with the metal top of the vane or leaf electroscope. The electroscope is now negatively charged. Observe what changes take place in the electroscope. Record your observations in Table 3.

2. Recharge the rubber rod. Bring it near the charged electroscope top. Observe what happens to the leaves or vane. Record your observations in Table 3.

3. Recharge the electroscope with a negative charge from the rubber rod. Charge the glass rod and bring it near the top of the negatively-charged electroscope. Observe the electroscope deflection as the charged glass rod is moved close to and away from the electroscope. Record your observations in Table 3. Discharge the electroscope by momentarily touching the top of it with your finger.

4. Charge the plastic wrap or acrylic rod with a piece of silk. Touch the plastic material to the top of the electroscope to charge it. Set the plastic material aside. Charge the rubber rod and bring it near the electroscope while observing the deflection of the leaves or vane. Record your observations in Table 3. What type of charge is on the electroscope?

D. Charging an Electroscope by Induction

1. Select one of the rods and charge it. Bring it near, within 1–2 cm, but not touching the electroscope. Observe the leaves or vane. Record your observations in Table 4.

2. With the charged rod near the electroscope, momentarily touch the top of the electroscope with your finger. Remove your finger from the top of the electroscope, and then remove the charged rod. Observe the electroscope leaves or vane. Record your observations in Table 4.

3. Following the procedure from Part C, determine the type of charge on the electroscope. Record your observations in Table 4.

Clip   Wire   Clip

Vane electroscope   Leyden jar

Figure 2. The clip wire attaches the electroscope to the Leyden jar.

Investigating Static Electricity

E. Charging a Leyden Jar

1. Place a Leyden jar beside the electroscope.
2. Charge one of the rods and gently touch the electroscope to charge it. Repeat the procedure to place a fairly large charge on the electroscope and to cause a large deflection.
3. Discharge the electroscope by momentarily touching the top with your finger. Use the clip wire to attach the top of the electroscope to the top of the Leyden jar, as shown in Figure 2 on the previous page. Note that the Leyden jar is not grounded. Repeat Step 2 to charge the combination. Is there any difference in the ability of the electroscope to become charged? Record your observations in Table 5.

Observations and Data

Table 1
A. Negatively Charging a Pith Ball

Observations of pith ball with nearby charged rod:

Observations of pith ball after it has been touched with a charged rod:

Table 2
B. Positively Charging a Pith Ball

Observations of pith ball with nearby charged rod:

Observations of pith ball after it has been touched with a charged rod:

20.1 Investigating Static Electricity

Table 3
C. Charging an Electroscope by Conduction

Observations of uncharged electroscope when negatively-charged rod touches it:

_____

Observations of negatively-charged electroscope when negatively-charged rod is brought near:

_____

Observations of negatively-charged electroscope when positively-charged rod is brought near:

_____

Observations of deflection of leaves or vane when plastic material charges the electroscope and negatively-charged rod is brought near:

_____

Table 4
D. Charging an Electroscope by Induction

Observations of electroscope when charged rod is brought near:

_____

Table 4 (continued)

Observations of electroscope after touching with finger:

Observations to determine the type of charge:

Table 5
E. Charging a Leyden Jar

Observations of charging a Leyden jar-electroscope combination:

Analysis

1. Summarize your observations of negatively charging a pith ball (Part A).

2. Summarize your observations of positively charging a pith ball (Part B).

3. Compare the negative and positive charging of a pith ball.

4. Summarize your observations of charging the electroscope by conduction (Part C).

5. Using your data from Part C, explain why the leaves of the electroscope diverged or the vane deflected.

6. Using your data from Part C, explain why the leaves (vane) remained apart (deflected) when the charged rod was removed.

7. What type of charge did the plastic wrap/plastic rod produce? How can you prove this?

8. Why did the electroscope vane or leaves move in Part D?

9. Compared to that of the charged rod, what type of charge did the electroscope receive by induction?

10. What purpose did your finger serve when it touched the electroscope?

11. Compared to that of the charging body, what is the type of charge on an electroscope when it is charged by conduction? Induction?

12. In Part E, what effect did the Leyden jar have on the ability to charge the electroscope? What is your proof of this effect?

Application

Some long-playing records are packaged in a plastic dust cover. As the record is slid out of its cover, the record and cover rub together. What is the likely result of this action? What function do record cleaning systems perform?

EXPERIMENT 21.1 : The Capacitor

Purpose

Investigate the relationship of the flow of charge to time in a charging capacitor.

Concept and Skill Check

A capacitor is a device that stores electrical charge. An early form of a capacitor is the Leyden jar, which you worked with in Experiment 20.1. Capacitors are made of two conducting plates separated by air or another insulating material, often referred to as a dielectric. The capacitance, or capacity, of a capacitor is dependent upon the nature of the dielectric substance, the area of the plates, and the distance between the plates.

The figure below is a circuit diagram of a capacitor, a battery, a switch, a resistor, a voltmeter, and an ammeter to measure the flow of charge, connected in series. The resistor is a simple device that resists the flow of charge. The flow of electrical charge over a period of time is measured in units called amperes or amps; 1 coulomb/second = 1 ampere. When the switch is open, as shown in the figure, no charge flows from the battery. However, when the switch is closed, the battery supplies electrical energy to move positive charges to one plate of the capacitor and negative charges to the other. Charge accumulates on each plate of the capacitor, but no current flows through it since the center of the capacitor is an insulator. As charge accumulates in the capacitor, the potential difference increases between the two plates until it reaches the same potential difference as that of the battery. At this point, the system is in equilibrium, and no more charge flows to the capacitor. Capacitance is measured by placing a specific amount of charge on a capacitor and then measuring the resulting potential difference. The capacitance, C, is found by the following relationship

$$C = q/V,$$

where C is the capacitance in farads, q is the charge in coulombs, and V is the potential difference in volts.

In this experiment, you will charge a capacitor and measure the amount of current that flows to it over a period of time. Then you will determine the capacitance of the capacitor.

Materials

1000-µF capacitor
10-kΩ resistor
27-kΩ resistor
voltmeter
15-VDC source
    (battery or
    power supply)

DC ammeter, 0–1.0 mA
knife switch
connecting wire
stopwatch
    (or watch with
    second hand)

Procedure

1. Set up the circuit as shown in the figure. The ammeter, capacitor, and battery must be wired in the proper order. Look for the + and − markings on the circuit components. The positive plate of the capacitor must be wired to the positive terminal of the battery. If the connections

Carefully follow the circuit diagram as you wire the + and − connections.

The Capacitor

are reversed, the capacitor may be destroyed. Resistors have no + or − end. Record in Table 1 the battery voltage and the value of the capacitor.

2. With one lab partner timing and the other reading and recording the current values, close the knife switch and begin taking readings. At the instant the switch is closed, a large current will flow. Take a current reading every five seconds until the current is too small to measure. Estimate your ammeter readings as closely as possible. Record the readings in Table 2.

3. Open the knife switch. Using a spare piece of wire, connect both ends of the capacitor to discharge it.

4. Replace the 27-kΩ resistor with the 10-kΩ resistor.

5. Repeat Steps 1 through 3 with the 10-kΩ resistor. Record the readings in Table 2.

6. After all readings have been taken, dismantle the circuit. Be sure to disconnect all wires from the battery (or power supply).

Observations and Data

Table 1

Battery voltage	
Capacitance	

Table 2

Time (s)	27 kΩ Current (mA)	10 kΩ Current (mA)
0		
5		
10		
15		
20		
25		
30		
35		

Table 2 (continued)

Time (s)	27 kΩ Current (mA)	10 kΩ Current (mA)
40		
45		
50		
55		
60		
65		
70		
75		
80		
85		
90		

EXPERIMENT
21.1 The Capacitor

Analysis

1. Why did the current start at a maximum value and drop toward zero while the capacitor was charging?

2. Look at the data for the two different resistors. Explain the purpose of the resistor in the circuit.

3. Using the data in Table 1, plot two graphs for current as a function of time. Sketch in a smooth curve.

4. The area between the curve and the time axis represents the charge stored in the capacitor. Estimate the area under the curve by sketching in one or more triangles to approximate the area. Note that the current is in mA, so this should be converted to amps by using 1 mA = 1×10^{-3} A. What is the estimated charge for the capacitor with the 27-kΩ resistor and with the 10-kΩ resistor?

5. Calculate the capacitance of the capacitor, $C = q/V$, using the value for charge from Question 4 and the measured potential difference of the power source.

6. Compare the value determined in Question 5 with the manufacturer's stated value you recorded in Table 1. Electrolytic capacitors have large tolerances, frequently on the order of 50%, so there may be a sizeable difference. Find the relative error between the two values.

7. Predict what would happen if the circuit were set up without the resistor.

8. Which variables were manipulated and which remained constant during the experiment? Describe the current versus time curve.

Application

Describe how an *RC* circuit (a circuit that includes a resistor and a capacitor), capable of charging and discharging at a very specific and constant rate, could be applied for use in the home, an automobile, or an entertainment center.

Extension

Repeat the experiment with another capacitor obtained from your teacher or connect several capacitors in parallel. Capacitors connected in parallel have an effective value equal to the sum of the individual capacitors. The quantity *RC* is called the time constant for the circuit and has units of seconds, as long as *R* is measured in ohms and *C* is measured in farads. The time constant is the time required for the current to drop to 37% of its original value. Before you begin, check to see that the value of *RC* can be easily measured. Follow the same procedure as before and compare the results of the graph with your earlier results.

EXPERIMENT
22.1 : Ohm's Law

Purpose
Use Ohm's law to determine the values of resistors.

Concept and Skill Check
Ohm's law states that as long as the temperature of a resistor, R, does not change, the electric current, I, flowing in a circuit is directly proportional to the applied voltage, V, and inversely proportional to the resistance. The current, I, is given by

$$I = \frac{V}{R} \text{ ; thus } R = \frac{V}{I} \text{ .}$$

The resistance is measured in ohms (Ω), where $1\ \Omega = 1\ V/1\ A$. In this experiment, you will measure the applied voltage and the current passing through a resistor and use these data to determine the value of the resistance.

Materials
voltmeter, 0–5 VDC
power supply, 0–6 VDC
milliammeter, 0–50 mA

knife switch
connecting wires

resistors: 100 Ω, 150 Ω, and 220 Ω, with 0.5-W or 1.0-W rating

Procedure

1. Review Appendix D, "Rules for Using Meters." Study the scales on the meter faces until you can read them properly. Some meters may have more than one positive or negative terminal. Select the set of terminals corresponding to the voltage range you will be using, such that the meter will give readings in the middle of the scale. CAUTION: *Resistors can become hot if too high a voltage is applied to them. Do not touch resistors when current is supplied to the circuit.*

2. Study Figure 1 on the next page. Notice in Figure 1(a) the arrangement of the meters, resistor, and power supply. Compare the arrangement in Figure 1(a) with the schematic diagram of the same circuit in Figure 1(b). Select a 100-Ω resistor. Refer to the resistor color code in Appendix E to determine the corresponding values for the various color bands. Determine the tolerance range for the resistor and record this value in Table 1. Connect the circuit, knife switch open, as shown in Figure 1; use the 100-Ω resistor. Leave the knife switch open so that no current flows in the circuit until your teacher has checked your circuit and has given you permission to proceed to the next step.

3. To prevent the resistors from overheating, the knife switch should be closed only long enough to obtain readings of current and voltage. Close the switch and then adjust the voltage to about 1.5 V. If you are using a battery, there will be no adjustment of the potential difference. Quickly read the meters. Open the knife switch as soon as you complete the readings. Record these readings in Table 1.

4. Close the switch and adjust the voltage to a higher reading, such as 3.0 V. If you are using a battery, repeat Step 3, so that you have two sets of data for each resistor. Read the milliammeter current and the potential difference. Open the knife switch. Record these readings in Table 1. Convert the current from mA (milliamperes) to A (amperes) by dividing the current in mA by 1000, since 1 mA = 0.001 A. Record this converted value for current in A.

Ohm's Law

Figure 1. Be sure to connect the voltmeter in parallel with the resistor and the ammeter in series with the resistor. Note the + and − terminals of both meters in relation to the + and − terminals of the power supply. The circuit diagram for the apparatus is shown in (b).

5. Remove the 100-Ω resistor and replace it with the 150-Ω resistor. Starting with the lower voltage, repeat the procedure to obtain two sets of data for current and voltage.

6. Remove the 150-Ω resistor and replace it with the 220-Ω resistor. Starting with the lower voltage, repeat the procedure to obtain two sets of data for current and voltage.

Observations and Data
Table 1

Resistor	Printed value of resistor (Ω)	Tolerance range (+/− %)	Voltage (V)	Current (mA)	Current (A)	Resistance (Ω)
R_1						
R_2						
R_3						

Analysis

1. Use the data in Table 1 to calculate the resistance for each set of data, applying $R = \dfrac{V}{I}$, where V is in units of volts and I is in units of amperes. Record the resistances in Table 1.
2. Calculate the average of your two values for each resistor. Compare the printed values of the resistors you used with your averages of the calculated values. Determine the relative error for each resistor.

3. If your values were not within the tolerance range of the printed values, suggest some reasons for the discrepancy.

4. Describe the proper placement of an ammeter in a circuit.

5. Describe the proper placement of a voltmeter in a circuit.

6. State the relationship between the current flowing through a circuit and the voltage and resistance of the circuit.

EXPERIMENT 22.1 Ohm's Law

Application

A light bulb, after it has reached its operating temperature, has a potential difference of 120 V applied across it while 0.5 A of current passes through it. What is the resistance of the light bulb?

Extension

From your teacher obtain a resistor of unknown value. Connect the circuit components in proper order and take several voltage and current readings through this resistor. Plot a graph of voltage (y-axis) versus current (x-axis). Sketch in a smooth line that best fits all the data. Determine the resistance and calculate the slope of the line, using measurements of potential difference in volts and of current in amperes.

EXPERIMENT
22.2 Electrical Equivalent of Heat

Purpose
Observe the conservation of energy in a conversion of electrical energy to thermal energy.

Concept and Skill Check
The law of conservation of energy requires energy to change from one form to another without loss. This means that one joule of potential energy, when converted to electricity, should develop one joule of electrical energy. One joule of electrical energy, when converted to thermal energy, should produce one joule of thermal energy. Electrical power is $P = IV$ where I is the current in amperes, and V is the potential difference in volts. Electrical energy is power multiplied by time, so $E = Pt = IVt$, where E is the energy in joules, and t is the time in seconds. The thermal energy in water can be written as $Q_W = m_W C_W \Delta T_W$, where Q is the thermal energy in joules, m_W is the mass of the water, C_W is the specific heat of water, and ΔT_W is the temperature change of the water.

In this experiment, you will measure the amount of electrical energy converted into thermal energy by means of an electric heating coil (a resistor) immersed in water. At the same time, you will measure the amount of heat absorbed by a known mass of water. The polystyrene cup, used as a calorimeter, has a negligible specific heat and will not absorb thermal energy. Your results should indicate that the thermal energy transferred to the water is equal to the electrical energy expended in the coil.

To minimize the effect of heat loss to the atmosphere, it is best to warm the water to as many degrees above room temperature as it was below room temperature before heating started. Thus, if you start with water at 10°C and room temperature is 20°C, the final temperature of the water should be 30°C. In this way, any heat gained from the surroundings while the temperatures are below room temperature is likely to be offset by an equal heat loss while temperatures are higher than room temperature.

Materials

polystyrene cup	DC ammeter, 0–5 A	Celsius thermometer
power supply, 0–12 V	rheostat	balance
connecting wire	voltmeter, 0–10 VDC	stopwatch or watch with second hand

Procedure

1. Measure the mass of a polystyrene cup and record this value in Table 1. Record the room temperature in Table 1. Fill the cup about two-thirds full of cold water.
2. Measure the mass of the cup plus water. Record this value in Table 1. Calculate the mass of the water. Record this value in Table 1.
3. Set up the circuit, as shown in the figure on the next page. If you have an adjustable power supply, the rheostat is built in, rather than separate. Make sure the coil is immersed in the water. If it is not, add more water and repeat Step 2. After the teacher has checked your circuit, close the switch. Adjust the rheostat until the current flow is 2–3 A. Open the switch at once.
4. Stir the water gently with the thermometer. Read the initial temperature of the water. Record this value in Table 1.
5. Prepare to time your readings. Close the switch. At the end of each minute, read the ammeter and voltmeter readings and record these values in Table 2. Gently stir the water from time to time and, if necessary, adjust the rheostat to maintain a constant current flow.

Electrical Equivalent of Heat

NAME —————————————————————

Figure 1. **(a) The heating coil changes electric energy to heat energy that is transferred to the water. (b) Circuit diagram of the apparatus.**

6. Monitor the water temperature to determine when it is approximately as many degrees above room temperature as it was below room temperature at the beginning of the experiment. At the end of the next minute after this temperature is reached, open the switch.

7. Stir the water gently until a constant temperature is reached. Record the final temperature of the water in Table 1. Compute the change in temperature of the water. Record this value in Table 1.

8. Determine the average current and the average voltage. Record these values in Table 1.

Observations and Data
Table 1

Mass of polystyrene cup	
Mass of water and cup	
Mass of cold water	
Initial temperature of water	
Room temperature	
Final temperature of water	
Change in temperature of water	
Average current	
Average voltage	

22.2 Electrical Equivalent of Heat

NAME —————————————————

Table 2

Time (min)	Current (A)	Voltage (V)	Time (min)	Current (A)	Voltage (V)
1			9		
2			10		
3			11		
4			12		
5			13		
6			14		
7			15		
8					

Analysis

1. Determine the electrical energy expended in the resistance, using $E = IVt$.

2. Determine the heat absorbed by the water, using $Q_W = m_W C_W \Delta T_W$, where C_W is 4.18 J/g·C°.

3. Find the relative difference between the electrical energy expended and the thermal energy absorbed by the water. Use % difference = $(E - Q_W)(100\%)/E$.

4. Taking into account the apparatus you used, suggest why exact agreement was not obtained in Question 3. Consider the heating coil when providing this answer.

EXPERIMENT

22.2 Electrical Equivalent of Heat

NAME —————————————————

5. Was sufficient agreement obtained to indicate that, under ideal conditions, you would find exact agreement in the energy exchange? Explain.

6. What percent of the electrical energy was converted to thermal energy in the water?

7. A 100-W light bulb is about 16% efficient. How many joules of heat energy are dissipated by the bulb each second?

Applications

1. Think about using the conversion of gravitational potential energy to thermal energy in order to heat water for showers. Assume that 1.0 L of water (1.0 kg or 1000 g of water), initially at 12.7°C, falls over a 50.0-m waterfall. If all of the potential energy of the water is converted to kinetic energy as the water is falling, and the kinetic energy is converted into thermal energy when it reaches the bottom, what temperature difference exists between the bottom and the top of the waterfall? Will this be sufficient to produce a warm shower? Show all your calculations.

2. An electric immersion heating coil is used to bring 90.0 mL of water to a boil for a cup of tea. If the immersion heater is rated at 200 W, find the time needed to bring this amount of water, initially at 21°C, to the boiling point. Show all your calculations.

EXPERIMENT 23.1 : Series Resistance

Purpose

Investigate resistance and determine the equivalent resistance of resistances in series.

Concept and Skill Check

A series circuit consists of resistors connected with the voltage source in such a way that all current travels through each resistor in turn. The equivalent resistance, R, of a series circuit is the sum of the resistances of the individual resistors in the circuit.

$$R = R_1 + R_2 + R_3$$

The potential difference across the voltage source is equal to the sum of the voltage drops across each resistor.

$$V = V_1 + V_2 + V_3$$

The total current flowing in the circuit is most easily found by calculating the equivalent resistance and then using the equation

$$I = \frac{V}{R},$$

where I is the circuit current in amperes, R is the equivalent resistance of the circuit in ohms, and V is the voltage source in volts.

In this experiment, you will measure voltage drops across circuit resistances and apply Ohm's law to determine the equivalent circuit resistance.

Materials

DC power supply or dry cells	voltmeter, 0–5 VDC knife switch	68-Ω, 82-Ω, and 100-Ω resistors, 0.5 W or greater
8 connecting wires		milliammeter, 0–50 mA or 0–100 mA

Procedure

A. One Resistor

1. Refer to the resistor color code in Appendix E to determine the value of your resistors. Arrange the 100-Ω resistor in series with the ammeter, open switch, and voltage source, as shown in Figure 1(a) on the next page. Arrange the voltmeter in parallel with the resistor, as shown in the figure. Record the printed value for R_1 and its tolerance in Table 1. Have your teacher check the circuit before you proceed.
2. Close the switch and set the voltage source at 5 V. Read the ammeter. Open the switch as soon as your readings are complete. Do not leave the switch closed for more than a few seconds at a time. Record the meter readings in Table 1.

B. Two Resistors

1. Arrange a second resistor in series with the first, as shown in Figure 1(b). Record the printed values for the resistors and their tolerances in Table 2.
2. Close the switch and adjust the voltage as necessary to maintain 5 V. Read the ammeter. Open the switch. Record the meter readings in Table 2.

23.1 Series Resistance

(a) **(b)** **(c)**

Figure 1. Circuit diagram for measuring the current and voltage through (a) one resistor, (b) two resistors in series, and (c) three resistors in series.

C. Three Resistors

1. Arrange a third resistor in series with the first two, as shown in Figure 1(c). A diagram of the equipment is shown in Figure 2. Record the printed values for the resistors and their tolerances in Table 2.

Figure 2. The apparatus is connected for three resistors in series.

2. Close the switch and adjust the voltage as necessary to maintain 5 V. Read the ammeter. Open the switch. The voltmeter reading is $V_{1,2,3}$ across the three resistors. Record the meter readings in Table 3.

3. With the three resistors still in series, use the voltmeter to find the voltage drop across each resistor. Touch the lead wires of the voltmeter to each end of the resistor R_1. Close the switch and read the voltmeter. Record the meter reading for V_1 in Table 3.

4. Repeat Step 3 for R_2 and R_3 and record the voltage readings of V_2 and V_3 in Table 3.

EXPERIMENT 23.1 Series Resistance

Observations and Data

Table 1

	R_1 (Ω)	Ammeter reading (mA)	Voltmeter reading (V)
Tolerance (%)			

Table 2

	R_1 (Ω)	R_2 (Ω)	Ammeter reading (mA)	Voltmeter reading (V)
Tolerance (%)				

Table 3

	R_1 (Ω)	R_2 (Ω)	R_3 (Ω)	Ammeter reading (mA)	Voltmeter reading (V)			
					$V_{1,2,3}$	V_1	V_2	V_3
Tolerance (%)								

Analysis

1. Use the current and voltage data in Table 1 to calculate the measured value of resistance. Be sure to convert milliampere readings to amperes before you perform the calculations. Taking into account the tolerance, compare the printed value of the resistor with your measured value of R_1.

2. Use the current and voltage data in Table 2 to calculate the measured value of the equivalent resistance. The equivalent tolerance could be as large as the sum of the individual tolerances. Calculate the equivalent resistance by adding the printed values of $R_1 + R_2$. Taking into account the total tolerance, compare the calculated equivalent resistance with your measured equivalent resistance of $R_1 + R_2$.

3. Use the current and voltage $(V_{1,2,3})$ data in Table 3 to calculate the measured equivalent resistance. Calculate the equivalent resistance using the printed values for the resistors. Taking into account the total tolerance, compare the calculated equivalent resistance with your measured equivalent resistance of $R_1 + R_2 + R_3$.

4. When a circuit consists of resistors in series, how is the equivalent resistance determined?

5. Use your data in Table 3 to describe how the voltage drops across individual resistances are related to the total voltage drop in a series circuit.

6. What determines the total current in a series circuit?

Application

A set of miniature, decorative tree lights contains 50 individual light bulbs of equal resistance, wired in series, and is designed for 120-V operation. If the set uses 1.0 A of current, what is the resistance of an individual light bulb and what is the voltage drop across each light bulb?

EXPERIMENT
23.2
:
Parallel Resistance

Purpose

Measure current and voltage to determine the equivalent resistance of resistances in parallel.

Concept and Skill Check

When resistors are connected in parallel, each resistor provides a path for current to follow and, therefore, reduces the equivalent resistance to the current. In parallel circuits, each circuit element has the same applied potential difference. In Figure 1(c), for example, three resistors are connected in parallel across the voltage source. There are three paths by which the current can pass from junction a to junction b. More current will flow between these junctions with three resistors attached than would be the case if only one or two resistors connected them. The total current, I, is given by

$$I = I_1 + I_2 + I_3.$$

Each time an additional resistance is connected in parallel with other resistors, the equivalent resistance decreases. The equivalent resistance of resistors in parallel can be determined by

$$\frac{1}{R} = \frac{1}{R_1} + \frac{1}{R_2} + \frac{1}{R_3} + ...$$

In this experiment, you will take numerous current and voltage readings with resistors in parallel and apply Ohm's law to verify your results. It will be necessary for you to follow very closely the circuit diagrams of Figure 1. Although the diagrams show several meters in use at one time, you probably have been provided with only one ammeter and one voltmeter. In that case, you must move the meters from position to position until all readings are obtained. You can, for example, take the total current, I, and total voltage, V, readings, move the meters to positions I_1 and V_1, and so on, until you have all the required readings. Before applying Ohm's law, be sure to convert milliampere readings to amperes, where 1 mA = 0.001 A.

Figure 1. Circuit diagram for resistors connected in parallel. Be sure to note the positive and negative terminals of the voltmeter and ammeter in relation to the positive and negative terminals of the voltage source.

23.2 Parallel Resistance

Materials

DC power supply or dry cells
3 resistors, 150–330 Ω range, 0.5 W,
   such as 180 Ω, 220 Ω, and 330 Ω

connecting wires
knife switch
voltmeter, 0–5 V

milliammeter, 0–50 mA
   or 0–100 mA

Procedure

A. One Resistor

1. Set up the circuit as shown in Figure 1(a), using one of the resistors. Close the switch. Adjust the power supply to a set voltage on the voltmeter, such as 3.0 V. Read the current value on the ammeter. Open the switch. Record your readings in Table 1.

B. Two Resistors

1. Set up the circuit as indicated in Figure 1(b) by adding a second resistor. Close the switch and adjust the power supply as necessary to maintain the same voltage reading as in Part A. Read the current value on the ammeter. Open the switch. Record your readings in Table 2.
2. Move the meters as necessary to obtain the required readings of current and voltage. Record the readings in Table 2.

C. Three Resistors

1. Set up the circuit as shown in Figure 1(c) by adding the third resistor. Close the switch, adjust the power supply, and read the meters. Open the switch. Record the readings in Table 3.
2. Move the meters as necessary to obtain all required readings. Record the readings in Table 3.

Observations and Data

Table 1

	R_1 (Ω)	Ammeter reading (mA)	Voltmeter reading (V)
Tolerance (%)			

Table 2

	R_1 (Ω)	R_2 (Ω)	Ammeter reading (mA)			Voltmeter reading (V)		
			I	I_1	I_2	V	V_1	V_2
Tolerance (%)								

23.2 Parallel Resistance

NAME ────────────────────────────

Table 3

	R_1 (Ω)	R_2 (Ω)	R_3 (Ω)	Ammeter reading (mA)				Voltmeter reading (V)			
				I	I_1	I_2	I_3	V	V_1	V_2	V_3
Tolerance (%)											

Analysis

1. Use the readings from Table 1 to calculate the measured value for R_1, where $R_1 = \dfrac{V}{I}$. Is this within the tolerance expected for the printed value for R_1?

2. Use the readings from Table 2 to calculate the following values:

   a. the measured value for the equivalent resistance, R, where $R = \dfrac{V}{I}$.

   b. the measured current, $I_1 + I_2$.

   c. the measured resistance of R_1, where $R_1 = \dfrac{V_1}{I_1}$.

   d. the measured resistance of R_2, where $R_2 = \dfrac{V_2}{I_2}$.

   e. the calculated equivalent resistance, R, where $\dfrac{1}{R} = \dfrac{1}{R_1} + \dfrac{1}{R_2}$.

3. a. Compare the measured current sum, $I_1 + I_2$, to the measured current, I.

   b. Compare the calculated equivalent resistance to the measured equivalent resistance. Was the measured equivalent resistance within the tolerance range for the resistors?

4. Use the readings from Table 3 to calculate the following:

   a. the measured equivalent resistance, R, where $R = \dfrac{V}{I}$.

   b. the measured current, $I = I_1 + I_2 + I_3$.

   c. the measured resistance of R_1, where $R_1 = \dfrac{V_1}{I_1}$.

   d. the measured resistance of R_2, where $R_2 = \dfrac{V_2}{I_2}$.

   e. the measured resistance of R_3, where $R_3 = \dfrac{V_3}{I_3}$.

   f. the calculated equivalent resistance, R, where $\dfrac{1}{R} = \dfrac{1}{R_1} + \dfrac{1}{R_2} + \dfrac{1}{R_3}$.

5. a. Compare the value of I with the measured current sum, $I_1 + I_2 + I_3$.

   b. Compare the calculated equivalent resistance to the measured equivalent resistance. Was the measured equivalent resistance within the tolerance range for the resistors?

6. How does the current in the branches of a parallel circuit relate to the total current in the circuit?

7. How does the voltage drop across each branch of a parallel circuit relate to the voltage drop across the entire circuit?

8. As more resistors are added in parallel to an existing circuit, what happens to the total circuit current?

Application

Tom has a sensitive ammeter that requires only 1.000 mA of current to provide a full-scale reading. The resistance of the ammeter coil is 500.0 Ω. He wants to use the meter for a physics experiment that requires an ammeter capable of reading to 1.000 A. He has calculated that an equivalent resistance of 0.5000 Ω will produce the necessary voltage drop of 0.5000 V ($V = IR = 1.000 \times 10^{-3}$ A $\times$ 500.0 Ω), so that only 1.000 mA of current passes through the meter. What value of shunt resistor, a resistor placed in parallel with the meter, is needed?

Parallel Resistance

Extension

A unique cube of 100-Ω resistors, as shown in Figure 2, is attached to a 1.0-V battery. The circuit can be reduced to combinations of parallel and series resistances. Predict the equivalent resistance. What is the total current flowing from the battery? Obtain twelve 100-Ω resistors, construct the circuit, and test your prediction.

Figure 2. All resistors are 100 Ω. What is the equivalent resistance and the current moving through the circuit?

EXPERIMENT 24.1 : The Nature of Magnetism

Purpose

Explore the shape, direction, and interaction of magnetic fields.

Concept and Skill Check

Although many substances exhibit slight magnetic properties, only iron, cobalt, and nickel and their alloys make strong permanent magnets. Iron alloys are easily magnetized, while cobalt or nickel alloys are not. Magnets made of these substances or of their alloys are capable of attracting or repelling other magnets, both near and at a distance. If an object contains iron, cobalt, or nickel and a magnet is brought close to it, the magnet will cause, or induce, magnetism in the object and will then interact with it. Thus, a magnet can attract a nail that was not at first a magnet.

The concept of a force field is used to describe the force that one body exerts on another at a given distance. Just as gravitational and electric forces can be explained by gravitational and electric fields, magnetic forces can be explained in terms of a magnetic field around a magnet.

A compass is a small magnet free to pivot in a horizontal plane. The end of the magnet that points north is called the north (N) pole. The opposite end of the magnet is called the south (S) pole. The direction of the magnetic field lines is defined as the direction to which the north pole of a compass points when it is placed in a magnetic field. In this experiment, you will use a compass to investigate and map the magnetic field about a magnet.

Materials

2 bar magnets	sheet of paper	2 paper clips
small magnetic compass	iron nail	lodestone
iron filings		

Procedure

A. Pole Types

1. Hold the compass and allow its needle to come to rest. To verify that it does point north, set the compass on the table. Then pick up one of the bar magnets and bring its north pole near the compass. The north pole of the magnet should cause the compass needle to deflect so that the south pole of the compass points toward the north pole of the bar magnet. Verify that both bar magnets have the correct polar orientation. If the north pole of a bar magnet attracts the north pole of the compass, the magnet may be incorrectly magnetized. If this is the case, report the magnet's condition to your teacher. If both magnets have the correct orientation, then proceed with the experiment.

B. Magnetic Field Lines

1. Place a bar magnet on the table and cover it with a sheet of paper. Gently, and as uniformly as possible, sprinkle iron filings over the paper. Tap the paper lightly with your finger several times until the filings form a pattern. The iron filings have aligned themselves with the magnetic field.
2. On your paper, or in Part B of Observations and Data, sketch the pattern of the iron filings about the magnet.
3. Carefully pick up the sheet of paper and return the iron filings to the container.

EXPERIMENT 24.1 The Nature of Magnetism

C. Magnetic Field Lines Between Poles

1. Place both magnets on the table with the north pole of one magnet about 4 cm from the north pole of the other magnet. Lay the piece of paper over the magnets. Gently sprinkle some iron filings over the paper. Tap the paper lightly several times until the iron filings form definite lines. Sketch the magnetic-field-line pattern on your paper, or in Part C of Observations and Data, showing the polar orientation of the two magnets. Return the iron filings to the container.
2. Repeat Step 1 with the south pole of one magnet facing the north pole of the other magnet.

D. Direction of the Magnetic Field Lines

1. Trace the bar magnet onto your paper and label the north and south poles. Place the magnet over its traced shape. While referring to your sketch from Part B, slowly move the compass from one pole to the other along one of the magnetic field line arcs. On your paper, or in Part D of Observations and Data, draw arrows pointing in the direction of the north pole of the compass. Move the compass to different locations around the magnet and draw the direction of the magnetic field line at each location.

E. Lodestone Properties

1. Bring a lodestone near the paper clips. Record your observations in Part E of Observations and Data.
2. Bring a compass near the lodestone and move it around the lodestone. Record your observations.

F. Induced Magnetism

1. Test an iron nail for magnetism by touching it to the paper clips. Place the nail at one end of a bar magnet. Now bring the nail close to the paper clips while it is attached to the magnet. Record your observations in Part F of Observations and Data.
2. Bring the free end of the nail near your compass. Note that the free end of the nail has become a pole. Check its polarity compared to that of the end of the magnet to which it is attached. Record your observations.

Observations and Data

B. Magnetic Field Lines

24.1 The Nature of Magnetism

NAME _____

C. Magnetic Field Lines Between Poles

(a)

N   N

(b)

N   S

D. Direction of the Magnetic Field Lines

N   S

E. Lodestone Properties

Observations of lodestone:

F. Induced Magnetism

Observations of nail:

EXPERIMENT 24.1 The Nature of Magnetism

Analysis

1. At what points in the magnetic field about a magnet are the magnetic field lines most concentrated?

2. Describe the magnetic field lines between two like poles.

3. Describe the magnetic field lines between two unlike poles.

4. Describe the orientation of the compass needle relative to the magnet's poles in the magnetic field of a bar magnet.

5. Summarize the properties of a lodestone.

6. When a iron nail is attached to a magnet, how does the pole type at its free end compare with the pole type of the end of the magnet to which it is attached?

Application

Draw an Earth-shaped object on a sheet of paper and label the north and south poles. The interior of Earth can be thought of as a bar magnet with one pole of the magnet at Earth's north magnetic pole and one pole at the south magnetic pole. Sketch in a bar magnet and show the correct pole types for Earth. Sketch the magnetic field lines about Earth.

DATE

EXPERIMENT 24.2 : Principles of Electromagnetism

Purpose

Investigate the basic principles of electromagnetism.

Concept and Skill Check

While experimenting with electric currents in wires, Hans Christian Oersted discovered that a nearby compass needle is deflected when current passes through the wires. This deflection indicates the presence of a magnetic field around the wire. You have learned that a compass shows the direction of the magnetic field lines. Likewise, the direction of the magnetic field can be determined with the first right-hand rule: when the right thumb points in the direction of the conventional current, the fingers point in the direction of the magnetic field.

When an electric current flows through a loop of wire, a magnetic field appears around the loop. An electromagnet can be made by winding a current-carrying wire around a soft iron core. A wire looped several times forms a coil. The coil has a field like that of a permanent magnet. A coil of wire wrapped around a core is called a solenoid. The magnetic field lines around the wire windings are collected by the iron core. The result is a strong magnet.

In this experiment, you will investigate some of the basic principles of electromagnetism while working with current-carrying wires, wire loops, and an electromagnet.

Materials

compass	knife switch	paper
DC power supply, 0–5 A (or 3 dry cells)	ringstand	meter stick
ammeter, 0–5 A	ringstand clamp	masking tape
14–18 gauge wire, 1.5 m	iron filings	box of steel paper clips
large iron nail or other piece of iron for use as a magnet core	cardboard sheet, 8½ × 11 inches	

Procedure

A. The Field Around a Long, Straight Wire

1. Place the cardboard at the edge of the lab table. Arrange the wire so that it passes vertically through a hole in the center of the cardboard, as shown in Figure 1. Position the ringstand and clamp so that the wire can continue vertically up from the hole to the clamp. Bring the wire down the clamp and ringstand to the ammeter, and then to the positive terminal of the power supply.

Figure 1. Arrangement of equipment for Part A.

EXPERIMENT
24.2 Principles of Electromagnetism

The wire passing below the cardboard should pass vertically at least 10 cm below the cardboard before it is routed along the table to the knife switch and then to the negative terminal of the power supply. Observe the proper polarity of the power supply and the ammeter as you connect the wires.

2. Close the switch and set the current to 2–3 A. Open the knife switch. Place the compass next to the wire. CAUTION: *The wire may become hot if current is permitted to flow for very long. Close the switch only long enough to make your observations.* Move the compass about the wire to map the field. In Part A of Observations and Data, record your observations with a sketch of the field around the wire.

3. Reverse the connections at the power supply and ammeter so that the current will flow in the opposite direction. Close the switch and again map the field around the wire, using the compass to determine the direction of the magnetic field. Record your observations with a sketch of the field around the wire.

B. Strength of the Field

1. Place a piece of paper, containing a slit and a hole, on the cardboard with the wire at the center. Sprinkle some iron filings on the paper around the wire.

2. Close the switch and set the current to about 4 A. Gently tap the cardboard several times with your finger. Turn off the current. In Part B of Observations and Data, record your observations.

3. Tap the cardboard to disarrange the filings. Turn on the current and reduce it to 2.5 A. Gently tap the cardboard several times with your finger. Record your observations.

4. Tap the cardboard to disarrange the filings. Turn on the current and reduce it to 0.5 A. Gently tap the cardboard several times with your finger. Record your observations. Return the iron filings to the container.

C. The Field Around a Coil

1. Remove the long, straight wire from the cardboard. In the center of the wire, make three loops of wire around your hand so that a coil of wire with a diameter of approximately 10 cm is formed. Place several pieces of tape on the wire to keep the loops together.

2. Connect the coil to the power supply through the ammeter and knife switch. Close the knife switch and adjust the current to 2.5 A. Hold the wire coil in a vertical plane and bring the compass near the coil, moving it through and around the coil of wire. In Part C of Observations and Data, record your observations with a sketch of the magnetic field direction around the coil. Show the positive and negative connections of your coil.

D. An Electromagnet

1. Uncoil your large air-core loops. Wind loops of wire around the iron core until about half of the core is covered with wire. Connect the coil to the power supply, knife switch, and ammeter. Adjust the current so that 1.0 A of current flows in the coil. Bring the core near the box of paper clips and see how many paper clips the electromagnet can pick up. Open the switch and record your observations in Part D of Observations and Data.

2. Wind several more turns of wire on the iron core so that the number of turns is double that of Step 1. Close the switch and see how many paper clips the electromagnet can now pick up. Open the switch and record your observations.

3. Increase the current to 2.0 A and see how many paper clips the electromagnet can pick up. Record your observations.

4. Turn the current back on and, using the compass, determine the polarity of the electromagnet.

24.2 Principles of Electromagnetism

Observations and Data

A. The Field Around a Long, Straight Wire
Observations of direction of north pole:

B. Strength of the Field
Observations of magnetic field with different currents:

C. The Field Around a Coil
Observations of magnetic field around a coil of current-carrying wire:

D. An Electromagnet
1. Several loops of wire on iron core:

2. Double the number of loops:

3. Double the current:

EXPERIMENT

24.2 Principles of Electromagnetism

NAME ————————————————————

Analysis

1. How does the right-hand rule apply to the current in a long, straight wire?

2. What is the effect of increasing the current strength in a wire?

3. Draw the magnetic field direction and the polarities for the current-carrying coil shown in Figure 2.

Figure 2.

4. What three factors determine the strength of an electromagnet?

5. Explain the difference between a bar magnet and an electromagnet.

Application

List several solenoid applications that operate with either continuously applied or intermittently applied currents.

24.3 : Magnetic Field About a Coil

Purpose

Determine the quantitative relationship between magnetic induction and current in a solenoid.

Concept and Skill Check

The magnitude of the force, F, produced by a magnetic field on a current-carrying wire is given by the expression $F = BIL$, where B represents the magnetic field strength or the magnetic induction, I is the current in the wire, and L is the length of the wire that lies at right angles to the magnetic field. Solving for magnetic induction,

$$B = \frac{F}{IL}.$$

The unit of magnetic induction is the tesla, T, which is equivalent to one newton per ampere-meter, N/A · m. The tesla is defined in terms of the force on a section of straight wire one meter long, carrying one ampere of current.

A solenoid is a long coil of wire. When a current is passed through the coil, a uniform magnetic field develops inside it. A small length of wire that is part of a current balance will be placed inside the solenoid. This wire is part of a conducting strip that forms a loop and runs around the edge of the current balance. If a current passes through this strip inside the solenoid, the magnetic field around this loop will interact with the magnetic field of the solenoid. Because interactions between the fields on the sides of the loop and the coil's field oppose each other, it is only the field around the end of the loop, L, that interacts with the coil's field to develop a force on the balance. That force is perpendicular to the solenoid's magnetic field. L, then, is the length of the end of the loop and is measured from the centers of the side strips, as shown in Figure 1. With the current passing in the proper direction through the loop, there will be a net downward force on the part of the loop inside the solenoid, and the opposite end of the current balance will tilt upward.

Figure 1. The length of the current balance loop, L, is measured across the width of the end.

The magnitude of the net downward force on the balance inside the solenoid can be measured by adding small weights to the end of the balance outside the solenoid until the current balance is balanced. In this experiment, you will apply a constant current to the small length of wire and vary the current in the coil. Then you will find the force, F, required to balance the coil current to determine the strength of the solenoid's magnetic field, B.

Materials

air-core solenoid
current balance
2 ammeters, 0–5 A
DC power supply, 0–6 VDC,
   at 5 A

DC power supply, 0–6 VDC, at 1 A
   (or 1 power supply and
   2 rheostats—see Alternative
   Materials)
connecting wires

fine sandpaper
string
2 knife switches
balance

24.3 Magnetic Field About a Coil

NAME ――――――――――――――――――――――

Procedure

1. Measure the length, L, of the end of the loop on the current balance. Record this value, in meters, in Table 1. L does not change and will remain constant for all trials.

2. Arrange the equipment, as shown in Figure 2. The smaller-rated power supply, 1 A, is to be used for the loop circuit. The larger-capacity power supply is to be used for the coil circuit. (If you are using a single power supply and rheostats, your teacher will provide an alternate electrical diagram.) Pay careful attention to the polarity of the power supply and ammeters, so that they are properly attached. Clean the current balance supports and the pivots of the current balance with the fine sandpaper. Place the current balance inside the coil. It must be carefully balanced before any current is applied to the coil. There is usually an adjustment nut at the end of the balance for this purpose. If you are unable to balance the current balance with the adjustment nut, add small pieces of masking tape to the end to provide additional weight.

Figure 2. (a) The magnetic field is induced in the current balance. The force exerted by the magnetic field of the coil deflects the balance. (b) This is the circuit diagram for the setup shown in (a).

3. Make a final inspection of the wiring to be certain that the circuit is wired correctly. Have the teacher check your circuit.

4. Adjust the small power supply (or the rheostat) controlling the current in the loop until about 1 A flows through it.

5. Adjust the power supply (or rheostat) controlling the current in the coil until about 4 A flows through it.

6. The balance should be deflected upward (outside the coil). If it is deflected downward, turn off the power supply and reverse the two connections to the loop. Turn off the coil current.

7. Hang a piece of string on the end of the balance, by the adjustment nut. Turn the coil current up slowly until the current balance is level (balanced). When the balance is level, the downward force (weight) of the string equals the upward force due to the interaction of the magnetic fields inside the coil. Record the string length and the coil current in Table 1.

Magnetic Field About a Coil

NAME _____

8. While maintaining the loop current at 1 A, repeat the process in Step 7 with other lengths of string to obtain other values of coil current needed to balance the forces of the different string lengths. Do not exceed a coil current of 4.5 A, or the coil may overheat.

9. Find the mass in kg of a length of string. Divide the mass by the length in meters to obtain the mass per length, kg/m. Multiply this mass by 9.80 m/s² to determine the force per length, N/m. Record this value in Table 1. This value will remain constant for all trials. To determine the force for each trial, multiply the length of string from Table 1 by your value for force per length.

Observations and Data
Table 1

Trial	Length of wire, L (m)	Current in wire, I (A)	Current in coil, I_c (A)	Length of string (m)	Force per length of string (N/m)
1					
2					
3					
4					
5					

Table 2

Trial	Force (N)	Magnetic induction, B (T, N/A · m)
1		
2		
3		
4		
5		

24.3 Magnetic Field About a Coil

Analysis

1. Calculate the force for each trial by multiplying the length of string by the force per length of string. Record the values for force in Table 2.

2. Calculate the magnetic induction, B, inside the coil by using the equation $B = \dfrac{F}{IL}$. The force, F, is the force in newtons from Table 2, the current, I, is the current in the loop in amps, and L is the length of the end of the loop in meters. Show your work. Record the values of B in Table 2.

3. Plot a graph with the current in the coil, I_c, on the x-axis and the magnetic induction, B, on the y-axis. What does the curve of the graph indicate about the relationship between the magnetic induction and the current through the solenoid? Keep a copy of this graph if you will be doing Experiment 26.1, Mass of the Electron.

Application

How long must a 1.0-A current-carrying wire be to support a mass of 1.0 kg if the wire is oriented perpendicular to Earth's magnetic field with a field strength of 5.0×10^{-5} T? Does it seem reasonable to use Earth's magnetic field to lift things?

EXPERIMENT 25.1 : Electromagnetic Induction 1

Purpose

Observe the generation of an electric current when a wire cuts through a magnetic field.

Concept and Skill Check

In 1831, Michael Faraday discovered that when a conductor moves in a magnetic field in any direction other than parallel to the field, an electric current is induced in the conductor. The strongest current is generated when the conductor moves perpendicular to the magnetic field. This process of generating an electric current is called electromagnetic induction, and the current produced is called induced current. Current is produced only when there is relative motion between the conductor and the magnetic field; it does not matter which moves. In this experiment, you will use a moving magnetic field to induce a current in a stationary conductor.

Materials

galvanometer with zero in center of scale
1-turn coil of wire

25-turn coil of wire
100-turn coil of wire

2 bar magnets
connecting wires

Procedure

1. Attach the single loop of wire to the galvanometer, as shown in Figure 1. Thrust one of the bar magnets through the coil. Record your observations in Item 1 of Observations and Data.
2. Move the galvanometer connections to the 25-turn coil of wire. Thrust the magnet into the coil. Record your observations in Item 2 of Observations and Data.
3. Move the galvanometer connections to the 100-turn coil of wire. Thrust the magnet into the coil. Record your observations in Item 3 of Observations and Data.
4. With the galvanometer connected to the 100-turn coil of wire, thrust the north pole of the magnet into the coil. Observe the direction of movement of the galvanometer

Figure 1. Thrust the bar magnet through a single loop of wire.

needle. Pull the magnet out of the coil. Observe the direction of movement of the galvanometer needle. Thrust the south pole of the magnet into the coil. Pull it back out. Note the movement of the galvanometer needle. Record your observations in Item 4 of Observations and Data.
5. Place two bar magnets together to make a more powerful magnet. Thrust them into the 100-turn coil of wire. Observe the deflection of the galvanometer needle. Slowly pull the two magnets out of the coil. Try different rates of speed for pushing the magnets into and out of the coil and compare the deflections of the galvanometer needle. Record your observations in Item 5 of Observations and Data.

Electromagnetic
Induction 1

6. Place the magnets in the 100-turn coil. While the magnets are stationary, does the galvanometer needle deflect? Move the coil back and forth while the magnets are stationary. Observe the motion of the galvanometer needle. Record your observations in Item 6 of Observations and Data.

Observations and Data

1. Observations of needle deflection when magnet is thrust into single loop of wire:

2. Observations of needle deflection when magnet is thrust into 25-turn coil of wire:

3. Observations of needle deflection when magnet is thrust into 100-turn coil of wire:

4. Observations of needle deflection when magnet is thrust into and then pulled out of the coil:

5. Observations of needle deflection when two magnets are thrust into 100-turn coil and moved at different velocities:

6. Observations of needle deflection when magnets are stationary in 100-turn coil and when coil is moving:

Electromagnetic Induction 1

Analysis

1. In Step 4, why did the galvanometer needle deflect in one direction when the magnet went into the coil and in the opposite direction when the magnet was pulled back out?

2. Summarize the factors that affect the amount of current and *EMF* induced by a magnetic field.

3. In your textbook, the equation given for the electromotive force induced in a wire by a magnetic field is $EMF = Blv$, where B is magnetic induction, l is the length of the wire in the magnetic field, and v is the velocity of the wire with respect to the field. Explain how the results of this experiment substantiate this equation.

4. What happens when a conducting wire is held stationary in or is moved parallel to a magnetic field? Explain.

5. Compare the induced electric field generated in this experiment to the electric field caused by static charges.

Application

Figure 2 shows a diagram of a transformer. This device changes the AC voltage of the primary coil by inducing an increased or decreased *EMF* in the secondary coil. The value of the secondary voltage depends on the ratio of the number of turns of wire in the two coils. How is it possible for a magnetic field to move across the secondary coil and induce the *EMF*? Why does this device operate only on alternating, not direct, current?

Figure 2. A transformer contains two coils of insulated wire wound around an iron core.

Extension

1. The equation *EMF* = *Blv* applies only when the wire moves perpendicular to the magnetic field lines. A more general form of the equation would have to take into account movement at an angle to the magnetic field lines. Find the induced *EMF* of a wire 0.40 m long that moves through a magnetic field of magnetic strength 0.75×10^{-2} T at a speed of 5.0 m/s. The angle θ between *v* and *B* is 45°. Show the equation you will use to solve for *EMF* and show all your calculations.

2. Write a statement that describes the effect on *EMF* of the angle θ between *v* and *B*.

3. As a conducting loop rotates in an external magnetic field, the induced current alternately increases and decreases. Describe the output produced and predict the shape of a graph that plots current against time.

EXPERIMENT
25.2

Electromagnetic Induction 2

Purpose

Compare a generator and a simple motor.

Concept and Skill Check

Electromagnetic induction is the process of generating an electric current from the relative motion of a conductor in a magnetic field. The third right-hand rule is used to indicate the direction of the induced current. Hold your right hand flat with your thumb pointing in the direction in which the wire is moving and your fingers pointing in the direction of the magnetic field. The palm of your hand will point in the direction of the conventional (positive) current flow.

Michael Faraday invented the electric generator, which converts mechanical energy into electrical energy. It consists of a large number of wire loops wound about an iron core, called the armature, which is placed in a strong magnetic field. As the armature turns, the wire cuts through the magnetic field and an *EMF* is induced. The $EMF = Blv$, where B is magnetic induction, l is the length of wire rotating in the field, and v is the velocity with which the loops move through the magnetic field. An electric motor is the opposite of a generator. In an electric motor, the magnetic field of an electrical current, applied to the coil, turns the armature in a magnetic field. Alternately attracted and repelled by fixed magnets, the armature spins, using a magnetic force to convert electric energy to mechanical energy. In this experiment, you will investigate the relationship between a simple motor and a generator.

Materials

100-mL beaker or card- board tube to form coil
22-, 24-, 26-, or 28-gauge enameled magnet wire, (60 m)

galvanometer, with zero in center of scale (or 500-μA to 0 to 500-μA meter)
ringstand
2 ringstand clamps

masking or electrical tape
2 horseshoe magnets
fine sandpaper
connecting wires

Procedure

1. Wind two 120-turn coils of enam- eled magnet wire around a 100-mL beaker, a toilet-paper tube, or a paper-towel tube. Leave a 15-cm long wire lead at each end of the coil, coming out about 4 cm apart on the same side of the coil, as shown in Figure 1. After winding each coil, carefully slide it off the coil form and wrap several small pieces of tape around the coils so that they maintain their shape.

2. Carefully sand 1 cm of each end of the enameled wires to expose clean copper.

Figure 1. The leads should be about 15 cm long and about 4 cm apart on the coil. Use small pieces of tape to hold the coil together.

Electromagnetic Induction 2

NAME _____

3. Place a ringstand clamp on the ringstand approximately 20 cm above the bottom of the ringstand. Place the second clamp next to the first one, but pointing in the opposite direction. Hang the coils from the ringstand clamps, as shown in Figure 2, using a piece of tape to secure the wire leads to the clamps. Place the horseshoe magnets, as shown in Figure 2. Adjust the height of the ringstand clamps as required so that one bar of each horseshoe magnet is positioned in the center of each coil and projects several centimeters through the coil.

Figure 2. Arrangement of the two coils, ringstand, clamps, and two horseshoe magnets.

4. Attach one set of coil leads to the galvanometer with connecting wire. Swing this coil on the horseshoe magnet and observe the galvanometer needle. Swing the coil faster. Try adding a stronger magnet or put two magnets side by side with like poles together. Swing the coil again. Record your observations in Item 1 of Observations and Data.

5. Use the right-hand rule to determine the direction of current flow to the galvanometer when the first coil is pushed toward the magnet. Label the positive lead. Attach the galvanometer to the leads of the other coil. Swing this coil. Again use the right-hand rule to determine the current flow to the galvanometer when the second coil is pushed toward the magnet. Label the positive lead.

6. Disconnect the galvanometer. Swing one coil and observe its motion. With a connecting wire, connect the leads that you marked as positive. Connect the other two leads with a piece of connecting wire.

7. Start one coil swinging. Observe the entire system. Record your observations in Item 2 of Observations and Data. How does the speed of the swinging coil compare to its motion when it was not attached to any other components? Record your observations in Item 3.

8. Unhook one set of connecting wires and insert the galvanometer in series with the two coils. Start one coil swinging. Observe the galvanometer. Record your observations in Item 4.

Observations and Data

1. Observations of swinging coil on magnet:

2. Observations of swinging coil attached to other coil:

Electromagnetic Induction 2

3. Observations of unhooked swinging coil compared to its motion in the circuit:

4. Observations of system with galvanometer:

Analysis

1. Use your observations from Item 1 to summarize the factors that affect the strength of the induced current.

2. Use your observations from Item 2 to explain the motion of the coils.

Electromagnetic
Induction 2

3. Compare the rates of swinging of the coil that you observed in Steps 6 and 7. How can the difference be explained?

4. Which coil acts like a generator and which coil acts like a motor? Explain.

Application

When a load is applied to or increased on a generator, why is it more difficult to keep the generator turning? You may have felt this effect when you turned on bicycle lights powered by a pedal-driven generator.

EXPERIMENT 26.1 Mass of an Electron

Purpose
Determine the ratio of mass to charge of the electron and calculate the mass of an electron.

Concept and Skill Check

J. J. Thomson was the first to measure the ratio of charge to mass for the electron. He observed the deflection of a beam of electrons emitted from a cathode-ray tube through an area of combined electric and magnetic fields, at right angles to each other. In this experiment, the forces exerted by the electric and magnetic fields were perpendicular to the direction of motion of the electrons. A fixed electric field was applied and the magnetic field was adjusted until the beam of electrons traveled a straight path (zero deflection). By equating the forces due to the two fields, Thomson was able to calculate the charge to mass ratio.

In this experiment, you will follow a process similar to Thomson's to balance the forces on electrons and determine the ratio of mass to charge. You will be using a mass-of-the-electron apparatus—either the new 6E5-style tube or an older 6AF6G-style tube. Under a circular metal cap at the center of the tube is the cathode. Electrons emitted from the cathode are accelerated horizontally toward the large conical-shaped anode that nearly fills the top of the tube. The anode is coated with a fluorescent material that glows when electrons strike it. The newer 6E5-style tube has a single deflection pattern, while the older 6AF6G-style tube has a double deflection pattern.

In the absence of any external electric or magnetic fields, the electrons falling on the fluorescent anode produce the patterns shown in Figure 1(a). If you insert the tube into an air-core solenoid and allow a current to flow in the solenoid, the electrons are subjected to a constant magnetic field acting perpendicularly to their direction of motion. Since the electrons are moving at a fairly uniform speed, the situation can be described as that of a moving charged particle subjected to a constant force. As a result, the electrons move in the arc of a circle. The pattern observed will be similar to one of those shown in Figure 1(b). The radius of curvature of the electrons can be found by inserting a short dowel rod, or other circular-shaped object, into the coil and placing it over the tube, and then varying the coil current until the pattern matches the dowel rod curvature.

When an electron is acted upon by a magnetic force in a direction perpendicular to its motion, it must travel in the arc of a circle with radius r. To produce the circular motion, the centripetal force, which results in an acceleration v^2/r, is given by the equation

$$F_c = \frac{mv^2}{r}.$$

Figure 1. (a) The tube pattern in the absence of a magnetic field. (b) The tube pattern when a magnetic field deflects the electron beam.

Mass of an Electron

The force exerted by the magnetic field is equal to Bqv. When the two forces are equal,

$$Bqv = \frac{mv^2}{r}.$$

Manipulating and solving for v yields

$$v = \frac{Bqr}{m}$$

and, by squaring both sides,

$$v^2 = \frac{B^2q^2r^2}{m^2}.$$

The electrons are accelerated through a potential difference in the tube. The energy that each electron acquires as it is accelerated through a potential difference is qV, where q is the charge carried by an electron in coulombs, and V is the potential difference in volts. Since 1 V = 1 J/C, qV is expressed in joules. The energy acquired by the electron is in the form of kinetic energy $\frac{mv^2}{2}$. Thus,

$$qV = \frac{mv^2}{2}.$$

The velocity, v, is the velocity the electron acquires as it moves through a potential difference, V. If the particle then passes perpendicularly through a magnetic field, B, the velocity is the same v found from equating the electric and magnetic forces. Therefore, if we substitute for v^2,

$$qV = \frac{mv^2}{2} \text{ becomes}$$

$$qV = \frac{mB^2q^2r^2}{2m^2},$$

and, by rearranging terms,

$$\frac{m}{q} = \frac{B^2r^2}{2V}.$$

An electron carrying a charge, q, accelerated by a known voltage, V, entering a magnetic field of magnitude, B, will travel in a circular path of radius, r, which can be measured to determine the mass to charge ratio. In order to determine the magnetic induction, the graph of magnetic induction strength versus solenoid coil current from Experiment 24.3 is used. Since the charge, q, on an electron is a known value, 1.6×10^{-19} C, you can determine the mass of an electron, m, from the following

$$m = q\left(\frac{m}{q}\right),$$

where $\frac{m}{q}$ is the ratio you calculated earlier.

Materials

mass-of-the-electron apparatus (either 6E5- or 6AF6G-style tuning-eye tube)
DC power source, 0–5 A (or 6-VDC power supply and rheostat)

DC power source, 90–250 V
air-core solenoid (used in Experiment 24.3)
connecting wires

ammeter, 0–5 A
3 dowel rods, different diameters
voltmeter, 0–250 VDC

EXPERIMENT 26.1 Mass of an Electron

Procedure

1. Wire the mass-of-the-electron apparatus, as shown in Figure 2. Figure 2(a) shows the newer 6E5-style tube, while Figure 2(b) shows the older 6AF6G-style tube. Both tubes should be premounted and supplied with color-coded wires that match the figure. Have your teacher check your wiring.

Figure 2. (a) Circuit diagram for connecting the 6E5-style tube. (b) Circuit diagram for connecting the 6AFGG-style tube.

2. Turn on the low voltage filament power supply. Wait about 30 seconds before applying the high voltage plate supply. Set the plate voltage between 130–250 V. Inspect the resulting pattern. It should match one of the patterns shown in Figure 1(a).

3. Connect the air-core solenoid to the power source, as shown in Figure 3. CAUTION: *The tubes are fragile and can be easily broken.* Carefully place the coil over your tube. Turn on the power supply to the coil. Increase the current to 3–4 A. The tube pattern should now look like one of the patterns in Figure 1(b). Turn off the coil current.

Figure 3. Circuit diagram for connecting the air-core solenoid to the power source.

4. Carefully insert one of the dowel rods, or another round object such as a pencil, into the coil and allow the end of it to rest on the top of the tube. Adjust the coil current until the curvature of the deflected pattern approximates the dowel rod curvature. The pattern will not match the curvature exactly, but will be close.

5. Record in Table 1 the radius, r, of the dowel rod, the accelerating voltage, V, and the coil current, I, that causes the deflection.

6. Use your graph of magnetic induction versus solenoid coil current from Experiment 24.3, to find the magnetic induction, B, for the coil current, I. Record this value in Table 1.

7. Repeat Steps 4 through 6, making several more trials with dowel rods of other sizes. The accelerating voltage can be altered if you desire.

8. Record in Table 2 the known value, q, for the charge carried by one electron.

26.1 Mass of an Electron

Observations and Data

Table 1

Trial	Coil current, I (A)	Magnetic induction, B (T, N/A · m)	Potential difference, V (V)	Radius, r (m)
1				
2				
3				

Table 2

Trial	B^2 (N/A · m)^2	r^2 (m^2)	Charge on one electron, q (C)	mass/charge (kg/C)	Mass of electron (kg)
1					
2					
3					

Analysis

1. Calculate B^2, r^2, m/q, and the mass of an electron. Enter the results in Table 2.
2. Determine the average mass for one electron.

3. Compare the average value of the mass of an electron with the accepted value and find the relative error.

4. Despite the error in your values, what is the significance of these experimental results?

Application

The magnetic field at the surface of Earth is about 5×10^{-5} T. Instead of the air-core solenoid, could Earth's magnetic field be used to deflect the beam of electrons? If so, propose a design for an experiment to accomplish this and describe the required components and procedure.

EXPERIMENT
27.1 Planck's Constant

Purpose
Determine the value of Planck's constant.

Concept and Skill Check

While studying radiation emitted from glowing, hot material, Max Planck assumed that the energy of vibration, E, of the atoms in a solid, could have only specific frequencies, f. He proposed that vibrating atoms emit radiation only when their vibrational energy is changed and that energy is quantized, changing only in multiples of hf. This relationship is given by $E = nhf$, where n is an integer and h is a constant. A light-emitting diode, or LED, is a modern application of this phenomenon.

An LED is a device made of a semiconductor wafer, which has been "doped" with two different types of impurities. A semiconductor doped with impurities that have loosely bound electrons donates those electrons and is designated an n-type material, while a semiconductor doped with acceptor impurities has "holes" that collect electrons and is designated a p-type material. The combination of n-type and p-type impurities in a semiconductor forms a pn junction that acts like a vacuum tube diode, permitting current to flow in only one direction. If a DC is applied in the circuit when the pn junction is reverse biased, the diode has a very high resistance and does not conduct current. When the pn junction is forward biased, there is a very low resistance, and a large current can flow through the diode. An LED is a specially doped diode that emits light when current moves across a forward-biased pn junction. LEDs can produce light in a wide variety of wavelengths, from the far-infrared to the near-ultraviolet region. The different wavelengths of visible light in LEDs are produced by varying the type and amount of impurity added to the semiconductor crystal structure.

When current moves across a forward-biased pn junction, free electrons from the n-type material are injected into the p-type material, as shown in Figure 1. When these carriers recombine, energy is released. The energy released can be in the form of light or of heat from vibrations in the crystal lattice. The proportions of heat and light produced are determined by the recombination process taking place. As Planck proposed, the energy produced is given by $E = hf = hc/\lambda$, where E is the energy in joules, h is Planck's constant, c is the speed of light ($c = 3.0 \times 10^8$ m/s), f is the frequency of the emitted light, and λ is the wavelength of the emitted light. In an LED, energy is supplied from a battery or DC power supply. Electrical energy supplied to the charge is given by $E = qV$, where E is the energy in joules, q is an elementary charge ($q = 1.6 \times 10^{-19}$ C), and V is the energy per charge in volts. Equating these two relationships for E yields

$$qV = \frac{hc}{\lambda}.$$

Figure 1. A forward-biased, light-emitting diode pn junction.

Rearranging terms and solving for h gives

$$h = \frac{qV\lambda}{c}.$$

A typical curve for a graph of current versus voltage in a forward-biased diode is shown in Figure 2. The point at which recombination begins producing a significant amount of light, compared to that of heat, is at the knee. At the knee, the resistance drops sharply and the current increases rapidly within the diode. In this experiment, you will measure the current and various voltages across a forward-biased LED to find the voltage, V, where recombination begins to cause a large amount of emitted light. With this information, the value for Planck's constant can be determined.

Figure 2. A typical curve of a forward-biased LED.

Materials

green, red, and yellow light-
emitting diodes (LEDs)
2 1.5-V batteries or 3-V
power supply

battery holder
22-Ω resistor
1000-Ω potentiometer
connecting wires

ammeter, 0–50 mA DC
voltmeter, 0–5 VDC
knife switch

Procedure

1. Wire the circuit, as shown in Figure 3. CAUTION: *Handle the LEDs carefully; their wire leads are fragile and will not tolerate much bending.* Be sure to observe the correct polarity for the meters. Have your teacher inspect your wired circuit before you continue with this activity.

Figure 3. Schematic diagram of a circuit to measure voltage and forward current across a light-emitting diode.

2. Record in Table 1 the colors and the wavelengths of the LEDs supplied by your teacher.
3. CAUTION: *At no time during the experiment should the current to the LED exceed 25 mA.* Rotate the potentiometer control to its center position. Close the switch and observe the voltage on the voltmeter. Slowly adjust the voltage to approximately 2.0 V. If the LED is not glowing, open the switch and reverse the LED leads. The rotatable potentiometer forms a voltage divider network across the power supply to supply voltages from 0–3 V. Beginning at 1.50 V, and increasing in increments of 0.05–0.10 V until the current is less than or equal to 25 mA, collect current readings for the various voltage settings. Record your data in Table 2. When you have taken the last reading near, but less than, or equal to 25 mA, turn off the current to the circuit.
4. Replace the LED with one of another color and repeat Step 3. Collect data for all of the LEDs.

EXPERIMENT 27.1 Planck's Constant

Observations and Data

Table 1

LED	LED color	Wavelength (nm)
1		
2		
3		

Table 2

LED 1		LED 2		LED 3	
Voltage (V)	Current (mA)	Voltage (V)	Current (mA)	Voltage (V)	Current (mA)

Planck's Constant

NAME ————————————————————————

Analysis

1. Make a single graph that plots voltage on the horizontal axis and current on the vertical axis. Plot each set of LED data separately and label each curve. As the curve moves from zero current through the knee to a linear relationship, determine the point where the graph becomes linear. Hint: The current will be approximately 5–10 mA. For each LED curve, find the corresponding voltage for this point. This is the voltage at which recombination is producing a significant amount of light. List below the voltages for each LED.

   a. red voltage:

   b. yellow voltage:

   c. green voltage:

2. Calculate the value of Planck's constant for each LED. Show your work.

3. Compute the relative error for Planck's constant for each trial, using $h = 6.626 \times 10^{-34}$ J·s as the accepted value.

4. What approximate value for V might be expected for an LED that produces blue light and for one that produces infrared light?

Application

What advantages are there to using light-emitting diodes rather than a regular, incandescent light bulb?

EXPERIMENT
27.2
The Photoelectric Effect

Purpose

Investigate the photoelectric effect to determine the relationship between the frequency of incident light falling on a phototube and the kinetic energy of ejected photoelectrons.

Concept and Skill Check

Electrons, called photoelectrons, are ejected from the cathode of a phototube only if the frequency of the incident electromagnetic radiation is above a certain minimum value, called the threshold frequency. The phototube is a round, evacuated glass tube containing a semicircular-shaped cathode and a small, centrally located anode wire. Light shining on the cathode causes emission of photoelectrons, which travel through the tube and strike the anode. As shown in the figure, the anode is connected by an external wire to an associated amplifier circuit. A current flow through this wire, detected by the microammeter, indicates when a photoelectron current is present. A potentiometer located on the photoelectric-effect module allows adjustment of the applied voltage. The voltage is adjusted until it balances the kinetic energy of the photoelectrons. This balance is indicated by the absence of a photoelectron current, and the voltage required to stop the current is the stopping voltage. The energy associated with a potential difference is given by $E = qV$, where E is the energy in joules, q is an elementary charge with $q = 1.6 \times 10^{-19}$ C, and V is the voltage in volts.

Figure 1. Circuit diagram of phototube, amplifier, and stopping voltage potentiometer.

Albert Einstein further explained the photoelectric effect in terms of the photoelectric equation, $KE = hf - hf_o$, where h is Planck's constant, f is the frequency of incident light, f_o is the threshold frequency, and KE is the kinetic energy of the emitted photoelectrons. In this experiment, you will shine light through colored filters onto a phototube and measure the voltage needed to stop a photoelectron current flowing through the tube.

Materials

photoelectric-effect
  module with amplifier
voltmeter, 0–5 VDC

microammeter, 0–100μA
colored filters: red, green,
  blue, and yellow

light source: 40-W
  incandescent light bulb
  in socket

Procedure

1. Set up the photoelectric-effect module, voltmeter, microammeter, and associated current amplifier, according to the instructions supplied with the equipment. Make any necessary calibration adjustments that are specified in the manufacturer's instructions.

The Photoelectric Effect

NAME —————————————————————

2. Place the light source in front of the window opening to the photoelectric tube. Place one of the colored filters over the window. Check that the filter completely covers the opening and prevents stray light from entering the window.
3. Slowly adjust the stopping voltage until the photocurrent drops to zero. Record in Table 1 the filter color and its associated stopping voltage.
4. Replace the filter with one of another color. Repeat Step 3 with this filter and then with all the other filters.
5. Determine the energy associated with each stopping voltage by multiplying the stopping voltage by 1.6×10^{-19} C. Record the values in Table 1.

Observations and Data

Table 1

Filter color	Stopping voltage (V)	Energy (J)

Table 2

Filter color	Wavelength (m)	Frequency (Hz)

Analysis

1. Record in Table 2 the filter colors from Table 1 and the wavelength for each color. Use the wavelengths provided by your teacher, or find the wavelengths in a reference book. Calculate the frequency associated with each wavelength, using $c = f\lambda$, where $c = 3.0 \times 10^8$ m/s.
2. The energy equivalent to the stopping voltage is the energy needed to match the kinetic energy of the photoelectrons. Plot a graph with kinetic energy of photoelectrons, in joules, on the vertical axis and the frequency of incident light on the horizontal axis. Draw a straight line that best fits your data.
3. What is the value and significance of the line that intersects the x-axis at other than 0,0?

4. Determine the slope of the line. What is its significance?

Application

In photographic dark rooms, red "safe lights" are used while pictures are processed. The safe lights can be used because they do not further expose the film or paper. Why are safe lights red?

EXPERIMENT

28.1 : Spectra

Purpose

Observe and record the emission spectra of several gases.

Concept and Skill Check

When solids are heated until they glow, their atoms produce a continuous spectrum. But those substances that are vaporized by heating in a flame can emit light characteristic of the elements in the substance. For example, a solution of sodium chloride placed on a platinum wire and held in a flame emits a bright, yellow light. Another method of spectrum analysis involves the application of high voltage across a gas-filled glass tube. Gas atoms that are under low pressure and excited by an electrical discharge give off light in characteristic wavelengths. The emitted light is passed through a spectroscope, which breaks light into its constituent components for analysis. A gas viewed through a spectroscope, such as the one shown in Figure 1, forms a series of bright lines known as a bright-line or emission spectrum. Since each element produces a unique bright-line spectrum or pattern, spectroscopy is a valuable branch of science for detecting the presence of elements. Sodium, for example, gives off bright, yellow light that appears as two adjacent bright lines of yellow when its gas is viewed through the spectroscope. A gas is identified by comparing the wavelengths of its emission spectrum to the spectrum produced by a known gas. In this experiment, you will use a spectroscope to determine the bright-line spectra characteristic of different elements.

Spectrum tube

Spectroscope

Figure 1. Look through the spectroscope at the emitted light of the spectrum tubes.

EXPERIMENT

28.1 Spectra

NAME —————————————————————

Materials

spectroscope
spectrum-tube
  power supply

spectrum tubes: argon, bromine,
  chlorine, hydrogen, helium, krypton,
  mercury vapor, neon, nitrogen, xenon,
  oxygen, and carbon dioxide

40-W incandescent light
  bulb and socket
thermal mitt

Procedure

CAUTION: *Voltage of several thousand volts exists at the power supply and spectrum tubes. Do not touch the spectrum-tube power supply or spectrum tubes when power is applied. Use thermal mitts to handle the tubes.*

1. Obtain a spectroscope and look through it at an incandescent light bulb. The spectrum should appear when the slit in the spectroscope is pointed just off center of the glowing filament. Practice moving the spectroscope until you see a bright, clear image.
2. Verify that the power to the spectrum-tube power supply is turned off. Insert one of the spectrum tubes into the sockets. Helium or hydrogen is a good first choice.
3. Turn on the power supply. Darken the room but leave enough background lighting to illuminate the spectroscope scales. If an exposed window is the background lighting source, point the spectroscope away from the window, since daylight will affect the observed gas spectrum. Adjust the spectroscope until the brightest image is oriented on your scale. Some of the spectrum tubes produce light so dim that you must be very close to them to get good observations of the spectral lines. Record in Table 1 the bright lines of the observed spectrum. Turn off the power supply and, using a thermal mitt, carefully remove the hot spectrum tube. Your teacher will tell you where these hot tubes should be placed to prevent other students from accidentally touching them and getting burned.
4. Repeat Steps 2 and 3 using all the other spectrum tubes. Record your observations in Table 1.

Observations and Data
Table 1

Figure 2. Draw in lines at the proper locations on the scale and of the correct width and intensity to reflect what you have observed. On the answer line at the right of each scale, write the name of the element you are observing and analyzing.

Table 1 (continued)

λ(x10⁻⁷m) 4   5   6   7   ——————————

λ(x10⁻⁷m) 4   5   6   7   ——————————

λ(x10⁻⁷m) 4   5   6   7   ——————————

λ(x10⁻⁷m) 4   5   6   7   ——————————

λ(x10⁻⁷m) 4   5   6   7   ——————————

λ(x10⁻⁷m) 4   5   6   7   ——————————

λ(x10⁻⁷m) 4   5   6   7   ——————————

λ(x10⁻⁷m) 4   5   6   7   ——————————

λ(x10⁻⁷m) 4   5   6   7   ——————————

28.1 Spectra

Analysis

1. Compare the color of light emitted by the spectrum tube to that observed through the spectroscope. Explain any differences.

2. Compare the intensities of the observed spectral lines for each element.

3. Observe a fluorescent light bulb with the spectroscope. While a continuous spectrum will be visible, you will also see a bright-line spectrum. Compare this spectrum with those of the gases observed in this activity and identify the gas in a fluorescent light bulb.

Applications

1. Describe the uses of a spectroscope in the science of astronomy.

2. Suggest a practical use for a spectroscope in the laboratory.

EXPERIMENT
29.1
Semiconductor Properties

Purpose

Investigate the voltage-current relationship in a semiconductor diode.

Concept and Skill Check

The diode is the simplest type of semiconductor device. It is made of a semiconductor material, such as germanium or silicon, that is specially doped with two types of impurity. The *n*-type end of the diode is doped with a donor impurity, such as arsenic, that has loosely bound electrons. The *p*-type end is doped with an acceptor impurity, such as gallium, that has "holes" for electrons. Figure 1 shows a schematic representation of the diode.

Diode   Diode symbol

Figure 1.

When a direct current is applied in one direction, called reverse bias, the diode has a very high resistance and does not conduct current. However, when current is applied in the other direction, called forward bias, there is a very low resistance, and a large current flows through the diode. In this experiment, you will forward- and reverse-bias a diode and measure the current as a function of the applied voltage. Silicon diodes begin to conduct current in the forward-biased direction when the voltage reaches about 0.6 V. A germanium diode begins to conduct at about 0.2 V.

Materials

1N4004 diode (rectifier) or
   equivalent; milliammeter,
   0–100 mA or 0–500 mA
voltmeter, 0–5 VDC
1.5–3-V battery or DC
   power supply, 0–6 V

10-Ω resistor
1000-Ω resistor
1000-Ω potentiometer
power supply, 6 VAC, or AC adapter,
   such as that used for a tape recorder

connecting
   wires
switch
oscilloscope

Procedure

1. Connect the circuit as shown on the schematic diagram in Figure 2. The voltage is applied to the *pn* junction such that the *p*-type end is positive with respect to the *n*-type end. Note that a band or ring around one end of the diode corresponds to the *n*-type end.

Figure 2. Schematic diagram of a forward-biased circuit.

2. Close the switch and slowly increase the voltage from 0.00 V to 0.80 V in 0.1-V increments, measuring the circuit current at each step. Record the current readings in Table 1. When you have taken the last reading, open the switch to turn off the current to the circuit.

Semiconductor Properties

NAME

3. Reverse the diode so that the positive end of the diode, the *p*-type end, is attached to the ammeter. Close the switch and slowly increase the voltage from 0.00 V to 0.80 V in 0.1-V increments, measuring the circuit current at each step. Record the current readings in Table 2. When you have taken the last reading, open the switch to turn off the current to the circuit.
4. Connect an alternating-current source—from a power supply or from a small adapter for a tape recorder—and a diode, as shown in Figure 3. CAUTION: *Under no circumstances should the diode be connected to the 120-V alternating current of a standard electrical outlet.* Attach an oscilloscope across the AC input. Close the switch to apply the AC power and observe the wave shape on the oscilloscope screen. In Table 3, draw the wave shape. Turn off the AC power. Connect the oscilloscope leads across the 1000-Ω resistor. Close the switch to apply current to the diode. Observe the wave shape on the oscilloscope screen. In Table 3, draw this other wave shape. Open the switch.

Figure 3. Schematic diagram of an alternating current (AC) source and a diode.

Observations and Data
Table 1

Forward-Biased Diode								
Voltage (V)	0.00	0.10	0.20	0.30	0.40	0.50	0.60	0.70	0.80
Current (mA)									

Table 2

Reverse-Biased Diode								
Voltage (V)	0.00	0.10	0.20	0.30	0.40	0.50	0.60	0.70	0.80
Current (mA)									

Table 3

Diode with AC Power	
AC wave shape	
AC wave shape through a diode	

Semiconductor
Properties

NAME ———————————————————————

Analysis

1. Plot a graph of current versus voltage, with current on the vertical axis. Set up the horizontal axis with both negative and positive voltages and center the vertical axis. The negative voltage values represent the reverse-biased diode, while the positive voltage values represent the forward-biased diode.

2. Compare the graph of current versus voltage with a diode in the circuit to a similar graph with a resistor in the circuit.

3. What is unique about the current flow through a diode?

4. Is the diode you used a germanium or a silicon diode? What data support your answer?

5. Compare the two current wave shapes you observed. Explain any differences.

6. Describe the wave shape of the AC input across the 1000-Ω resistor if the diode is reversed.

Semiconductor Properties

Application

The circuit that you constructed with the single diode and an alternating current input is called a half-wave rectifier. Conventional current flow is in the direction of the arrow on the diode symbol. A full-wave rectifier circuit, shown in Figure 4, is used in electronic equipment, such as computers, televisions, stereo receivers, and amplifiers, to provide a clean source of power. Draw the wave shape that you predict would appear across the output load resistor, R_L, for the circuit shown in Figure 4.

Figure 4. Full-wave rectifier circuit.

Extension

Build the circuit shown in Figure 4 and attach the oscilloscope to the output load resistor. Compare your predicted wave shape to the one you observe.

EXPERIMENT 29.2 : Integrated Circuit Logic Devices

Purpose

Become familiar with, assemble, and test simple integrated circuit logic devices.

Concept and Skill Check

An integrated circuit, IC, consists of from dozens to millions of elements, such as transistors, resistors, diodes, and conductors, that together form one or more electronic circuits. The various individual components are manufactured on an appropriately doped piece of semiconductor substrate, usually silicon. These components are built up layer by layer on the substrate material and integrated electrically to perform a specific function. After construction, small wires are attached to connecting pads on the integrated circuit and run to external metal leads or terminals. The integrated circuit is then packaged in a plastic or ceramic container to protect it from moisture and environmental pollutants.

Data entered into a microcomputer or a calculator are usually manipulated with binary mathematics. In the binary system, all numbers are represented by combinations of 0's and 1's. This system can be interpreted by transistor circuitry in integrated circuits. A transistor switch that is turned on represents a 1, and a switch that is turned off represents a 0. An integrated circuit has one or more gates, the basic building block of electronic logic systems. A gate is a type of electronic switch that controls the current flowing between the terminals. The output of an IC can be monitored by using an LED as a logic probe. When a transistor circuit is turned on, the LED probe lights to indicate a logical 1 (a true condition). When the transistor circuit is turned off, the LED does not light to indicate a logical 0 (a false condition).

The binary operations are sometimes referred to as logical operations or are called Boolean logic: if *a* and *b* then *c*. In order to add large numbers or to handle more complicated operations, such as multiplication or division, many logical operations must be performed. In this experiment, you will set up several simple integrated circuit logic devices and determine experimentally the truth tables for each integrated circuit.

Materials

breadboard	connecting wires, # 22 gauge	CMOS integrated circuits:
9-V battery	light-emitting diode (LED)	4081, 4071, 4001, 4011
9-V battery clip	330-Ω resistor	

Procedure

1. Study your breadboard. There is a center channel running lengthwise across the middle of the board. An integrated circuit is placed on the board such that pins from one side of the IC fit into holes on one side of the channel, and pins from the other side of the IC fit into holes on the opposite side of the channel. Along each outer edge of the breadboard are two rows, or buses, of electrically connected holes that run parallel to the center channel. Insert a lead from each side of the battery to a hole in each row, as shown in Figure 1 on the next page. This procedure creates a row of positive and a row of negative connecting points. Between the center channel and each outer bus are columns of electrical connecting points. All columns between the center channel and the positive or negative bus are electrically connected. Electrical connections to the board are made by carefully inserting exposed wires into the holes of the breadboard.

Figure 1. Layout of the breadboard.

2. Place the light-emitting diode in the lower right corner of the breadboard with one lead in one of the holes of the negative bus. Place the other lead in one of the column holes. Connect a 330-Ω resistor between a hole in the column where the LED is located and an adjacent column. Attach a long wire to the column where the 330-Ω resistor terminates. This wire is your test probe. To determine if the LED is correctly wired, touch the test probe to a hole along the positive bus. If the LED does not light, unplug it and reverse the holes into which the two wires are inserted. The LED should now light. If it does not, ask your teacher for help.

3. Disconnect the 9-V battery. Use caution while handling the integrated circuits since they can be damaged by static electricity. You can discharge any excess static electricity by touching a water faucet before handling an IC. Select the 4081 integrated circuit. In a 4081 integrated circuit, there are four AND gates. An AND gate symbol is shown in Figure 2(a) and is represented mathematically by $Z = A \cdot B$, which means Z equals A and B. The schematic representation of the four gates in the 4081 (quad 2-In AND gate) is shown in Figure 2(b).

(a)   (b)

Figure 2. (a) AND gate symbol and (b) diagram of 4081 integrated circuit.

Notice that it is a 14-pin IC. Pin 14 is the positive-voltage input and pin 7 is the negative-voltage input to power the integrated circuit. Look on the top of the IC. The orientation of the IC is usually identified by a semicircular notch located at the end by pins 1 and 14 and an index mark, such as a hole or dot, by pin 1. Carefully place the 4081 IC into your breadboard with pin 1 located toward the negative bus. Reversing the IC usually destroys it. One power lead of an IC must be connected to a positive bus and the other to a negative bus. Connect a wire to one of the holes in the column associated with pin 7 and attach the other end to the negative bus. Likewise, connect a wire from a hole associated with pin 14 to the positive bus. One of the

Integrated Circuit Logic Devices

AND gates is connected to pins 1, 2, and 3. Place the free end of the test probe wire to the AND gate output pin 3. Connect one long wire to a hole in the column that corresponds to pin 1 and another long wire to a hole in the column that corresponds to pin 2. These two wires will be connected to the negative or positive bus to provide the input logical 0's and 1's.

4. Connect the 9-V battery. Let the wire connected to pin 1 be input *A* and the wire connected to pin 2 be input *B*. Record your observations in Table 1 under the output column *Z*. Connect both inputs to the negative bus producing a 0,0 input to the AND gate. Observe the test probe LED. Move input *B* to the positive bus producing a 0,1 input to the AND gate. Observe the test probe LED. Move input *A* to the positive bus and input *B* to the negative bus producing a 1,0 input to the AND gate. Observe the test probe LED. Finally connect input *B* to the positive bus producing a 1,1 input to the AND gate. Observe the test probe LED. Demonstrate the AND gate logic to your teacher before proceeding.

(a)   **(b)**

Figure 3. (a) OR gate symbol and (b) diagram of 4071 integrated circuit.

5. Figure 3(a) shows an OR gate symbol and is mathematically represented by $Z = A+B$, which means *Z* equals *A* or *B*. Figure 3(b) shows a schematic representation of a 4071 IC containing four OR gates (quad 2-In OR gate). The electrical connections are the same as those of the 4081. Without removing the wire connections, replace the 4081 IC with the 4071. Repeat the steps to test the four possible input combinations and record your output observations in Table 2. Demonstrate the OR gate to your teacher before proceeding.

(a)   **(b)**

Figure 4. (a) NOR gate symbol and (b) diagram of 4001 integrated circuit.

6. Figure 4(a) shows a NOR gate symbol, while Figure 4(b) shows a schematic representation of a 4001 IC containing four NOR gates (quad 2-In NOR gate). The NOR is mathematically represented by $Z = \overline{A+B}$, which means *Z* equals not *A* or not *B*. The electrical connections are the same as those of the 4071. Without removing the wire connections, replace the 4071 IC with the 4001 IC. Repeat the steps to test the four possible input combinations and record your output observations in Table 3. Demonstrate the NOR gate to your teacher before proceeding.

Integrated Circuit
Logic Devices

NAME —————————————————

(a)

(b)

Figure 5. (a) NAND gate symbol and (b) diagram of 4011 integrated circuit.

7. Figure 5(a) shows a NAND gate symbol while Figure 5(b) shows a schematic representation of a 4011 IC containing four NAND gates (quad 2-In NAND gate). The NAND is mathematically represented by $Z = \overline{A \cdot B}$, which means Z equals not A and not B. The electrical connections are the same as those of the 4001. Without removing the wire connections, replace the 4001 IC with the 4011 IC. Repeat the steps to test the four possible input combinations and record your output observations in Table 4. Demonstrate the NAND gate to your teacher before proceeding.

8. Gates can be and usually are combined to produce other logic combinations or to produce a simple logic output when the desired logic gate is unavailable. Use your 4011 quad NAND gate IC and wire the circuit shown in Figure 6. Remember to wire the power to the IC through pins 7 and 14 as before. Test the possible combinations for inputs A and B. Record your results in Table 5 for the combination of NAND gates. Demonstrate the NAND gate combination to your teacher.

Figure 6. Combination of three NAND gates.

Observations and Data

Table 1

AND Gate Truth Table		
Inputs		Output
A	B	Z
0	0	
0	1	
1	0	
1	1	

Teacher's signature

Table 2

OR Gate Truth Table		
Inputs		Output
A	B	Z
0	0	
0	1	
1	0	
1	1	

Teacher's signature

Table 3

NOR Gate Truth Table		
Inputs		Output
A	B	Z
0	0	
0	1	
1	0	
1	1	

Teacher's signature

Integrated Circuit Logic Devices

Table 4

NAND Gate Truth Table		
Inputs		Output
A	B	Z
0	0	
0	1	
1	0	
1	1	

Teacher's signature

Table 5

NAND Gate Combination Truth Table		
Inputs		Output
A	B	Z
0	0	
0	1	
1	0	
1	1	

Teacher's signature

Analysis

1. Compare the truth table (Table 5) results for the combination of NAND gates with the other circuits and determine the type of logic it performs.

2. Compare the OR and NOR functions.

3. Compare the AND and NAND functions.

4. Predict the result of hooking together the inputs on a NAND gate.

5. Predict the result of hooking together the inputs on a NOR gate.

EXPERIMENT
29.2 Integrated Circuit Logic Devices

NAME ———————————————————

Application

Digital integrated circuits are found in common electronic equipment, such as automobiles, cellular phones, dishwashers, stoves, security systems, and telephones. Simple logic gates can be used to implement functions, such as turning on an alarm. In a car, for example, if the ignition is turned on and the gearshift is engaged, and if either of the seats is occupied and the corresponding seat belt is not fastened, an alarm will sound. Use the following symbols with the information given above to write an appropriate logic statement using a "+" for an OR and a "·" for an AND.

Symbol	Information
A	alarm on
I	ignition on
L	left front seat occupied
B_L	left front seat belt not fastened
R	right front seat occupied
B_R	right front seat belt not fastened
G	gearshift engaged

Extension

Use the 4011 quad 2 NAND gate IC to wire the circuit shown in Figure 7. This circuit is useful in many applications and is called an Exclusive-OR (XOR). Set up and complete a truth table for the various input combinations.

Figure 7. Combination of four NAND gates to produce an XOR.

EXPERIMENT
30.1
Radiation Properties

Purpose

Determine how the intensity of radiation varies with distance from the radioactive source.

Concept and Skill Check

Three types of radiation emitted by a radioactive substance are alpha, beta, and gamma radiation. An alpha particle is a helium nucleus, a beta particle is an electron, and a gamma ray is a high-energy photon. Radiation can be detected by a Geiger-Mueller tube. Gamma rays or charged particles pass through a thin window at one end of the Geiger-Mueller tube. When the radioactive particle passes into the tube, it ionizes a gas atom. As the resulting charged particles are accelerated toward the electrodes in the tube, they collide with other gas atoms. The avalanche of charged particles creates a current pulse that causes a potential difference in the Geiger-Mueller tube circuit. The voltage is amplified and produces an audible signal or advances a counter. In this experiment, you will use a Geiger-Mueller tube to determine the relationship between the intensity of radiation of a radioactive source and the distance from that source.

Materials

Geiger counter or scaler	tweezers or tongs	meter stick
beta source	gloves	masking tape
gamma source	stopwatch or watch with second hand	

Procedure

CAUTION: *Handle the radioactive materials with tweezers, tongs, or gloves. Do not bring any food, drink, or make-up into the laboratory. Wash your hands with soap and water before you leave the laboratory.*

Arrangement of Geiger-Mueller tube and meter stick.

1. Set up the Geiger-Mueller equipment according to your teacher's instructions. Handle the Geiger-Mueller tube carefully, as it is fragile and expensive. Carefully lay the tube on the lab table and secure it with a piece of masking tape, as shown in the figure. Place the meter stick with one end next to the Geiger-Mueller tube window.

2. Set the radioactive samples about 1–2 m from the Geiger-Mueller tube so that their influence on the detector is minimal. Turn on the counter and measure the background radiation for one minute. On the line provided above Table 1, record the value of the background radiation in counts per minute (c/min).

3. Place the beta source 2 cm from the window of the Geiger-Mueller tube. The sensitivity of Geiger counters varies, as do the activities of the radioactive samples, which depend on age and type. If the sample appears to be too active, move it several centimeters farther away from the tube. Turn on the counter and measure the activity for one minute. Record in Table 1 the measured activity value and the corresponding distance of the source from the tube.

4. Move the beta source 1 cm farther from the tube and repeat the measurement. Record in Table 1 the measured value of activity at that distance. Move the radioactive source and take measurements for one-minute periods of time until the activity drops to a value equal to or lower than the background radiation level. Record the measured activity in Table 1.

30.1 Radiation Properties

NAME —————————————————————————

Observations and Data

Background radiation = ———————————— c/min

Table 1

Distance (cm)	Measured activity (c/min)	Adjusted activity (c/min)	Distance^2 (cm^2)	1/Distance^2 (cm^{-2})
2				
3				
4				
5				
6				
7				
8				
9				
10				
11				
12				
13				
14				
15				
16				
17				
18				
19				
20				

EXPERIMENT 30.1 Radiation Properties

Analysis

1. Calculate the adjusted activity for each reading by subtracting the background activity from each of the measured values; record the adjusted values in Table 1. Find the squares of the distances and record these values in Table 1. Calculate the reciprocals of the distances squared and record these values in Table 1.

2. Plot a graph of activity versus distance, with adjusted beta activity on the y-axis and distance on the x-axis.

3. Plot a graph of measured activity versus the reciprocal of distance squared, with the activity on the y-axis and the reciprocal of distance squared on the x-axis.

4. What is the source of background radiation that you measured in Step 2?

5. What do your two graphs reveal about the nature of radiation and the relationship of radioactive intensity with distance?

6. Was it necessary to subtract the background radiation?

Application

A radioactive source has a measured activity of 10 000 c/min at a distance of 5 cm. What activity would be expected at three times this distance?

Extension

Repeat the experiment with the gamma source. Set up a data table to record the measured activity for each distance from the source. Do the necessary calculations and plot the two graphs, as described in Questions 1 through 3.

EXPERIMENT

31.1 : Radioactive Shielding

Purpose

Distinguish between alpha, beta, and gamma radiation by comparing the ability of these radioactive sources to penetrate different materials.

Concept and Skill Check

Alpha, beta, or gamma radiation is released when changes take place in the nucleus of an atom. Recall that an alpha particle is a helium nucleus, a beta particle is an electron, and a gamma ray is a high-energy photon. The mechanics of radiation absorption vary with the type of radioactive source, the initial energy of the radioactive particle or ray, and the type of absorbing material. There is a close relationship between the initial energy of the alpha particle and its penetration of a particular absorbing material. However, because the alpha particle is a helium nucleus with a double-positive charge, its state of ionization makes it extremely interactive. Thus, despite its relative heaviness, an alpha particle is quickly absorbed. Since beta particles have the same mass as the electrons in the absorber, the beta particle is deflected in collisions with other electrons; it does not follow a well-defined path through the material. For beta particles, penetration is inversely proportional to the density of the absorbing material.

While charged particles gradually lose their energy in many collisions, photons lose all their energy in a single collision. Therefore, absorption of gamma rays is defined in terms of the absorption coefficient, the reciprocal of which yields the thickness of the absorber that reduces the number of photons in a beam by a certain percentage. Thus, the intensity of a gamma ray is reduced exponentially as it penetrates a given material. In this experiment, you will measure and compare the penetrating ability of alpha, beta, and gamma radiation through cardboard, aluminum, and lead absorbers.

Materials

Geiger counter or scaler
stand for Geiger-Mueller tube
alpha, beta, and gamma
   sources

5-cm × 5-cm pieces of
   cardboard, aluminum,
   and lead (10 of each)

tweezers, tongs, or gloves
stopwatch or electronic
   counter

Procedure

CAUTION: *Handle the radioactive materials with tweezers, tongs, or gloves. Do not bring any food, drink, or make-up into the laboratory. Wash your hands with soap and water before you leave the laboratory.*

1. Set up the Geiger counter according to the teacher's instructions. Handle the Geiger-Mueller tube carefully, as it is fragile and expensive. Place the Geiger-Mueller tube into a stand so that it is oriented vertically, as shown in the figure.

Geiger-Mueller
tube

Radioactive
source

Arrangement of Geiger-Mueller tube and radioactive source in stand.

31.1 Radioactive Shielding

NAME _____

2. In order to obtain the many required readings in the short period of time available, you will make counts for only ten seconds. Since radioactive decay is spontaneous and does not always occur at a constant rate, it is possible that some of the measured activities may be a little larger or smaller than expected. Several types of Geiger counters have electronic timers that turn on the counter for specific periods of time. If your Geiger counter has an electronic timer, the teacher will describe how to use it. Otherwise, use a stopwatch to time the counting. Turn on the counter and measure the background radiation for ten seconds. Record this value on the line above Table 1.

3. Place the alpha sample under the Geiger-Mueller tube. Measure the activity for ten seconds and record the value in Table 1. For best results, place the alpha source close to the window of the Geiger tube. Most alpha sources have small half-lives, and the activity drops quickly, even over a period of just one year. Place two sheets of cardboard on top of the alpha source and measure the activity for ten seconds. Record the value in Table 1. Continue adding layers of cardboard in pairs until the activity drops to that of the background radiation level. Record all values of activity in Table 1.

4. Remove the cardboard and repeat the process with aluminum sheets. Record the values of activity in Table 1. Once the measured activity drops to that of the background radiation level, stop measuring.

5. Remove the alpha source and repeat the procedure with the beta source, testing the shielding capacity of cardboard, aluminum, and lead. Record the values of activity in Table 1. Once the measured activity drops to that of the background radiation level, stop measuring.

6. Replace the beta source with the gamma source. Repeat the procedure with layers of cardboard, aluminum, and lead and record the values of activity in Table 1.

7. Return the radioactive sources to their appropriate storage containers, as instructed by the teacher.

Observations and Data

Background radiation = _____ c/10 s

Table 1

Number of sheets	Measured Activity (c/10 s)							
	Cardboard			Aluminum			Lead	
	alpha	beta	gamma	alpha	beta	gamma	beta	gamma
0								
2								
4								
6								
8								
10								

31.1 Radioactive Shielding

Analysis

1. Which type of radiation is most easily absorbed? Which type of radiation is least easily absorbed?

2. How much and what type of material is required to reduce the various radiation sources to one-half of their activity?

3. Explain how to identify an unknown radiation source.

4. Was it possible in this experiment to eliminate all of the gamma radiation? Explain.

Application

How much lead would be required to reduce to one-fourth the intensity of radiation from a gamma source?

Extension

How thick must an absorber be to reduce to zero the intensity of a photon beam?

APPENDIX A

Natural Trigonometric Functions

Angle (°)	sin	cos	tan	Angle (°)	sin	cos	tan
0	.0000	1.0000	.0000	46	.7193	.6947	1.0355
1	.0175	.9998	.0175	47	.7314	.6820	1.0724
2	.0349	.9994	.0349	48	.7431	.6691	1.1106
3	.0523	.9986	.0524	49	.7547	.6561	1.1504
4	.0698	.9976	.0699	50	.7660	.6428	1.1918
5	.0872	.9962	.0875	51	.7771	.6293	1.2349
6	.1045	.9945	.1051	52	.7880	.6157	1.2799
7	.1219	.9925	.1228	53	.7986	.6018	1.3270
8	.1392	.9903	.1405	54	.8090	.5878	1.3764
9	.1564	.9877	.1584	55	.8192	.5736	1.4281
10	.1736	.9848	.1763	56	.8290	.5592	1.4826
11	.1908	.9816	.1944	57	.8387	.5446	1.5399
12	.2079	.9781	.2126	58	.8480	.5299	1.6003
13	.2250	.9744	.2309	59	.8572	.5150	1.6643
14	.2419	.9703	.2493	60	.8660	.5000	1.7321
15	.2588	.9659	.2679	61	.8746	.4848	1.8040
16	.2756	.9613	.2867	62	.8829	.4695	1.8807
17	.2924	.9563	.3057	63	.8910	.4540	1.9626
18	.3090	.9511	.3249	64	.8988	.4384	2.0503
19	.3526	.9455	.3443	65	.9063	.4226	2.1445
20	.3420	.9397	.3640	66	.9135	.4067	2.2460
21	.3584	.9336	.3839	67	.9205	.3907	2.3559
22	.3746	.9272	.4040	68	.9272	.3746	2.4751
23	.3907	.9205	.4245	69	.9336	.3584	2.6051
24	.4067	.9135	.4452	70	.9397	.3420	2.7475
25	.4226	.9063	.4663	71	.9455	.3256	2.9042
26	.4384	.8988	.4877	72	.9511	.3090	3.0777
27	.4540	.8910	.5095	73	.9563	.2924	3.2709
28	.4695	.8829	.5317	74	.9613	.2756	3.4874
29	.4848	.8746	.5543	75	.9659	.2588	3.7321
30	.5000	.8660	.5774	76	.9703	.2419	4.0108
31	.5150	.8572	.6009	77	.9744	.2250	4.3315
32	.5299	.8480	.6249	78	.9781	.2079	4.7046
33	.5446	.8387	.6494	79	.9816	.1908	5.1446
34	.5592	.8290	.6745	80	.9848	.1736	5.6713
35	.5736	.8192	.7002	81	.9877	.1564	6.3138
36	.5878	.8090	.7265	82	.9903	.1392	7.1154
37	.6018	.7986	.7536	83	.9925	.1219	8.1443
38	.6157	.7880	.7813	84	.9945	.1045	9.5144
39	.6293	.7771	.8098	85	.9962	.0872	11.4301
40	.6248	.7660	.8391	86	.9976	.0698	14.3007
41	.6561	.7547	.8693	87	.9986	.0523	19.0811
42	.6691	.7431	.9004	88	.9994	.0349	28.6363
43	.6820	.7314	.9325	89	.9998	.0175	57.2900
44	.6947	.7193	.9657	90	1.0000	.0000	
45	.7071	.7071	1.0000				

APPENDIX B

B:1. Common Physical Constants

Absolute zero = $-273.15°C = 0$ K
Acceleration due to gravity at sea level, (Washington, D.C.): $g = 9.80$ m/s^2
Atmospheric pressure (standard): 1 atm = 1.013×10^5 Pa = 760 mm Hg
Avogadro's number: $N_A = 6.02 \times 10^{23}$ mol^{-1}
Charge of one electron (elementary charge): $e = -1.602 \times 10^{-19}$ C
Coulomb's law constant: $K = 9.0 \times 10^9$ N $\cdot$ m^2/C^2
Gas constant: $R = 8.31$ J/mol $\cdot$ K
Gravitational constant: $G = 6.67 \times 10^{-11}$ N $\cdot$ m^2/kg^2
Heat of fusion of ice: 3.34×10^5 J/kg
Heat of vaporization of water: 2.26×10^6 J/kg
Mass of electron: $m_e = 9.1 \times 10^{-31}$ kg = 5.5×10^{-4} u
Mass of neutron: $m_n = 1.675 \times 10^{-27}$ kg = 1.00867 u
Mass of proton: $m_p = 1.673 \times 10^{-27}$ kg = 1.00728 u
Planck's constant: $h = 6.625 \times 10^{-34}$ J/Hz (J $\cdot$ s)
Velocity of light in a vacuum: $c = 2.99792458 \times 10^8$ m/s

B:2. Conversion Factors

Mass: 1000 g   = 1 kg
          1000 mg   = 1 g

Volume: 1000 mL   = 1 L
            1 mL   = 1 cm^3

Length: 1000 mm   = 1 m
           100 cm   = 1 m
          1000 m   = 1 km

1 atomic mass unit (u) = 1.66×10^{-27} kg = 931 MeV/c^2
1 electron volt (eV) = 1.602×10^{-19} J
1 joule (J) = 1 N $\cdot$ m = 1 V-C
1 coulomb = 6.242×10^{18} elementary charge units

B:3. Color Response of Eye to Various Wavelengths of Light

Color	Wavelength in nm	Wavelength in m
Ultraviolet	less than 380	less than 3.8×10^{-7}
Violet	400–420	4.0–4.2×10^{-7}
Blue	440–480	4.4–4.8×10^{-7}
Green	500–560	5.0–5.6×10^{-7}
Yellow	580–600	5.8–6.0×10^{-7}
Red	620–700	6.2–7.0×10^{-7}
Infrared	above 760	above 7.6×10^{-7}

B:4. Prefixes Used with SI Units

Prefix	Symbol	Fraction	Prefix	Symbol	Multiplier
Pico	p	10^{-12}	Tera	T	10^{12}
Nano	n	10^{-9}	Giga	G	10^{9}
Micro	μ	10^{-6}	Mega	M	10^{6}
Milli	m	10^{-5}	Kilo	k	10^{3}
Centi	c	10^{-2}	Hecto	h	10^{2}
Deci	d	10^{-1}	Deka	da	10^{1}

APPENDIX C

Properties of Common Substances

C:1. Specific Heat and Density

Substance	Specific heat (J/kg · K)	Density
Alcohol	2450	0.8
Aluminum	903	2.7
Brass	376	8.5 varies by content
Carbon	710	1.7–3.5
Copper	385	8.9
Glass	664	2.2–2.6
Gold	129	19.3
Ice	2060	0.92
Iron (steel)	450	7.1–7.8
Lead	130	11.3
Mercury	138	13.6
Nickel	444	8.8
Platinum	133	21.4
Silver	235	10.5
Steam	2020	—
Tungsten	133	19.3
Water	4180	1.0 at 4°C, 0.99 at 0°C
Zinc	388	7.1

C:2. Index of Refraction

Substance	Index of refraction
Air	1.00029
Alcohol	1.36
Benzene	1.50
Beryl	1.58
Carbon dioxide	1.00045
Cinnamon oil	1.6026
Clove oil	1.544
Diamond	2.42
Garnet	1.75
Glass, crown	1.52
Glass, flint	1.61
Mineral oil	1.48
Oil of wintergreen	1.48
Olive oil	1.47
Quartz, fused	1.46
Quartz, mineral	1.54
Topaz	1.62
Tourmaline	1.63
Turpentine	1.4721
Water	1.33
Water vapor	1.00025
Zircon	1.87

C:3. Spectral Lines of Elements

Element	Wavelength (nanometers)	Color
Argon	many close lines	
	706.7	red (strong)
	696.5	red (strong)
	603.2	orange
	591.2	orange
	588.8	orange
	550.6	yellow
	545.1	green
	525.2	green
	522.1	green
	518.7	green
	451.0	purple
	433.3	purple
	430.0	purple
	427.2	purple
	420.0	purple
Barium	659.5	red
	614.1	orange
	585.4	yellow
	577.7	yellow
	553.5	green (strong)
	455.4	blue (strong)
Bromine	many green lines	
	481.7	green
	478.6	blue
	470.5	blue
	many purple lines	
Calcium	445.4	blue
	443.4	blue-violet
	442.6	violet (strong)
	396.8	violet (strong)
	393.3	violet (strong)
Chromium	520.8	green
	520.6	green
	520.4	green
	428.9	violet (strong)
	427.4	violet (strong)
	425.4	violet (strong)
Copper	521.8	green
	515.3	green
	510.5	green
Hydrogen	656.2	red
	486.1	green
	434.0	blue-violet
	410.1	violet
Helium	706.5	red
	667.8	red
	587.5	orange (strong)
	501.5	green
	471.3	blue
	388.8	violet (strong)

Element	Wavelength (nanometers)	Color
Iodine	many lines	
	546.4	green (strong)
	516.1	green (strong)
Krypton	many faint close lines	
	587.0	orange (strong)
	557.0	yellow (strong)
	455.0	blue
	442.5	blue
	441.0	blue
	430.2	blue-violet
Mercury	623.4	red
	579.0	yellow (strong)
	576.9	yellow (strong)
	546.0	green (strong)
	435.8	blue-violet
	many lines in the violet and ultra violet	
Nitrogen	567.6	green (strong)
	566.6	green
	410.9	violet (strong)
	409.9	violet
Potassium	404.7	violet (strong)
	404.4	violet (strong)
Lithium	670.7	red (strong)
	610.3	orange
	460.3	violet
Sodium	589.5	yellow (strong)
	588.9	yellow (strong)
	568.8	green
	568.2	green
Neon	many lines in the red	
	640.2	orange (strong)
	585.2	yellow (strong)
	583.2	yellow (strong)
	540.0	green (strong)
Strontium	496.2	blue-green
	487.2	blue
	483.2	blue
	460.7	blue (strong)
	430.5	blue-violet
	421.5	violet
	407.7	violet
Xenon	492.3	blue-green
	484.4	blue
	482.9	blue
	480.7	blue
	469.7	blue
	467.1	blue (strong)
	462.4	blue (strong)
	460.3	blue
	458.3	blue
	452.4	blue
	450.0	blue (strong)

APPENDIX D
Rules for the Use of Meters
Introduction
Electric meters are precision instruments and must be handled with great care. They are easily damaged physically or electrically and are expensive to replace or repair. Meters are damaged physically by bumping or dropping and electrically by allowing excessive current to flow through the meter. The heating effect in a circuit increases with the square of the current. The wires inside the meter actually burn through if too much current flows through the meter. When possible, use a switch in the circuit to prevent having the circuit closed for extended periods of time. Note that meters are generally designed for use in either AC or DC circuits and are not interchangeable. In DC circuits, the polarity of the meter with respect to the power source in the circuit is critical. Be sure to use the proper meter for the type of circuit you are investigating. Always have your teacher check the circuit to be sure you have assembled it correctly.

The Voltmeter
A voltmeter is used to determine the potential difference between two points in a circuit. It is always connected in parallel, never in series, with the element to be measured. If you can remove the voltmeter from the circuit without interrupting the circuit, you have connected it correctly.

On a DC voltmeter, the terminals are marked $+$ or $-$. The positive terminal should be connected either directly or through components to the positive side of the power supply. The negative terminal must be connected either directly or through circuit components to the negative side of the power supply. After you have connected the voltmeter, close the switch for a moment to see if the polarity is correct.

Some meters have several ranges from which to choose. You may have a meter with ranges from 0–3 V, 0–15 V, and 0–300 V. If you do not know the potential difference across the circuit on which the voltmeter is to be used, choose the highest range initially, and then adjust to a range that gives readings in the middle of the scale (when possible).

The Ammeter
An ammeter is used to measure the current in a circuit and must always be connected in series. Since the internal resistance of an ammeter is very small, the meter will be destroyed if it is connected in parallel. When you connect or disconnect the ammeter, the circuit must be interrupted. If the ammeter can be included or removed without breaking the circuit, the ammeter is incorrectly connected.

Like a voltmeter, an ammeter may have different ranges. Always protect the instrument by connecting it first to the highest range and then proceeding to a smaller scale until you obtain a reading in the middle of the scale (when possible).

On a DC ammeter, the polarity of the terminals is marked $+$ or $-$. The positive terminal should be connected either directly or through components to the positive side of the power supply. The negative terminal must be connected either directly or through circuit components to the negative side of the power supply. After you have connected the ammeter, close the switch for a moment to see if the polarity is correct.

The Galvanometer

A galvanometer is a very low resistance instrument used to measure very small currents in microamperes. Thus, it must be connected in series in a circuit. The zero point on some galvanometers is in the center of the scale, and the divisions are not calibrated. This type of galvanometer measures the presence of a very small current, its direction, and its relative magnitude. A low resistance wire, called a shunt, may be connected across the terminals of the galvanometer to protect it. If the meter does not register a current, the shunt is then removed.

Potentiometer (variable resistors)

A potentiometer is a precision instrument that contains an adjustable resistance element. When placed in a circuit, a potentiometer allows gradual changing of the resistance which, in turn, causes the current and voltage to vary. Some power resistors are called rheostats.

APPENDIX E

Resistor Color Code

Suppose that a resistor has the following four color bands:

1st band	2nd band	3rd band	4th band
brown	black	yellow	gold
1	0	4	± 5%

The value of this resistor is $10 \times 10\,000 \pm 5\% = 100\,000 \pm 5\%$, or it has a range of 80 000 Ω to 120 000 Ω.

Resistance Color Codes (resistance given in ohms)

Color	Digit	Multiplier	Tolerance (%)
Black	0	1	
Brown	1	10	
Red	2	100	
Orange	3	1000	
Yellow	4	10 000	
Green	5	100 000	
Blue	6	1 000 000	
Violet	7	10 000 000	
Gray	8		
White	9		
Gold		0.1	5
Silver		0.0 1	10
No color			20

APPENDIX F

Preparation of Formal Laboratory Reports

Ordinarily, the reports you write for the experiments in this manual will be simple summaries of your work. Laboratory data sheets are provided in the manual for this purpose. In the future, you may be called upon to write more formal reports for other science courses. There is an accepted procedure for writing these reports. The procedure is outlined below. Your teacher may require that you write a number of reports in accordance with this outline so that you learn how to prepare reports properly.

Sections to be included in a formal laboratory report include the following: Introduction, Data, Results/Analysis, Graphs, Sample Calculations, Discussion, Conclusions.

I. Introduction

    A. Heading

       This includes the experiment number and title, date, name, and your partner's name if you do a joint experiment. When two students work together using the same apparatus, they are partners for data collection purposes, yet each must write a separate report.

    B. Diagrams

       1. Make sketches of mechanical apparatus (if called for).

       2. Draw complete electric circuit diagrams showing all electrical components. Label the polarity of all DC meters and power sources.

    C. Provide a brief explanation or title for each diagram.

    D. Include an elaboration or summary of the concept, purpose, procedure, theory, or the history of the experiment.

II. Data

    A. Use only the original record of the measurements made during the experiment. Never jot the data down on scrap paper for future use. Prepare a data sheet and use it.

III. Results/Analysis

    A. The results section consists of a tabulation of all intermediate calculated values and final results.

    B. Whenever there are several results, the numerical values should be recorded in a table.

    C. Tables must have titles. Headings and extra notes may be required to make the analysis or significance of the results clear to the reader.

IV. Graphs

    A. Use adequate labels (title, legend, names of quantities and units).

    B. Draw the best, smooth curve possible; do not draw curves dot-to-dot.

V. Sample Calculations

A. Each sample calculation should include the following items:
1. an equation in a familiar form
2. an algebraic solution of the equation for the desired quantity
3. substitution of known values with units
4. numerical answer with units

For example, if $d = 10$ m and $t = 2$ s, to solve for a:

using $d = v_i t + \frac{1}{2}at^2$, where $v_i = 0$,

$$a = 2d/t^2 = (2)(10 \text{ m})/(2 \text{ s})^2 = 5 \text{ m/s}^2.$$

VI. Discussion

In some cases, the conclusions of an experiment are so obvious that the discussion section may be omitted. However, in these instances a short statement is appropriately included. More often, some discussion of the results will be required to make their significance clear. You may also wish to comment upon possible sources of error and to suggest improvements in the procedure or apparatus.

VII. Conclusions

The conclusion is an important part of every report. The conclusions must be the individual work of the student who writes the report and should be completed without the assistance of anyone, unless it is the teacher.

The conclusion consists of one or more well-written paragraphs summarizing and drawing together only the main results and indicating their significance in relationship to the observed data.

A. Conclusions must cover each point of the subject.
B. Conclusions must be based upon the results of the experiment and the data.
C. If conclusions are based upon graphs, reference must be made to the graph by its full title.
D. Clarity and conciseness are particularly important in conclusions. The personal form should be avoided except, perhaps, in the discussion. Therefore, do not use the words *I* or *we* unless there is a special reason for doing so.